Foundations of Education

Foundations of Education helps aspiring teachers interpret the craft of teaching within the historical, philosophical, cultural, and social contexts of education inside and outside of schools. This volume contains substantial selections from those works widely regarded as central to the development of the field. These are the "essential texts" that lay the basis of further study for any serious student of education. The text is organized around the separate foundations disciplines—history, politics, sociology, philosophy—and includes extended selections from the works of John Dewey and W.E.B. DuBois to contemporary thinkers such as Maxine Greene and Diane Ravitch. Noted scholar Susan F. Semel provides an introductory essay as well as questions for further discussion that contextualize the readings and highlight the selections' continued importance and application to today's most pressing educational issues.

Exhibiting both breadth and depth, this text is ideal as a reader for courses in foundations and history of education courses.

Susan F. Semel is Professor of Education at The City College of New York as well as The Graduate Center of CUNY.

The Essential Texts

Philosophy of Education: The Essential Texts, Edited by Steven M. Cahn
Foundations of Education: The Essential Texts, Edited by Susan F. Semel

Foundations of Education

The Essential Texts

Edited by Susan F. Semel

Routledge
Taylor & Francis Group

NEW YORK AND LONDON

First published 2010
by Routledge
711 Third Avenue, New York, NY 10017

Simultaneously published in the UK
by Routledge
2 Park Square, Milton Park, Abingdon, Oxon OX14 4RN

Routledge is an imprint of the Taylor & Francis Group, an informa business

© 2010 Taylor and Francis

Typeset in Minion by Swales & Willis Ltd, Exeter, Devon

Library of Congress Cataloging-in-Publication Data
Semel, Susan F.
Foundations of education : the essential texts / edited by Susan F. Semel.
p. cm. — (The essential texts)
Includes bibliographical references and index.
1. Education—United States—History. 2. Education—United States—Philosophy.
3. Education—Study and teaching—United States. 4. Education—Aims and objectives—United States.
I. Title.
LA212.S46 2010
370.973—dc22
2010003912

ISBN10: (hbk) 0–415–80624–0
ISBN10: (pbk) 0–415–80625–9

ISBN13: (hbk) 978–0–415–80624–4
ISBN13: (pbk) 978–0–415–80625–1

Contents

Part III
The Sociology of Education

Part IV
The Philosophy of Education

Acknowledgments

I would like to thank the following individuals who have contributed to the publication of this reader. At Routledge, my editor, Catherine Bernard, worked with me from the very beginning, helping me to refine my selections. Her editorial assistant, Georgette Enriquez, supervised the final phase of production, seeing it through to publication. At City College, my assistant, Kathy Vargas, provided important clerical support.

I would also like to thank my family members for their support. My son, John W. Semel, who does not always get my undivided attention, has provided me with an important example of fortitude in the face of adversity; my daughter, Margaret D. Semel, who is developmentally disabled and cannot always comprehend what I do, nevertheless tries to understand why I cannot be present all the time for her because of my work. Finally, I would like to thank my husband and partner in life, Alan R. Sadovnik for providing both the intellectual and emotional support necessary for me to see this project through to completion.

Introduction

Susan F. Semel

Issues connected to schooling are daily features in the media. Although the public schools have been critiqued almost from their inception in the nineteenth century, they have been subject to particularly intense criticism in the past three decades, culminating in the passage of the federal No Child Left Behind law in 2001. This law aimed at reducing the achievement gap among racial, ethnic, social class and gender groups in American public schools affects schooling on a daily basis; thus, students, teachers, parents and policy makers must understand the complex issues related to school improvement. The foundations of education: history, sociology, politics and philosophy of education help us to view the schools analytically and together they provide us with an understanding of the connections between teacher, student, school, and society. Additionally they relate educational organization and processes to educational theories and practices. Finally, they connect these relationships to meaningful activity, such as the improvement of our schools and help practitioners understand and navigate the educational system. Thus, the foundations of education are an important lens for understanding the complexities of No Child Left Behind (NCLB) as well as myriad other complex issues and questions related to schooling in America.

Over the past decade policymakers have increasingly pointed to teacher and principal quality as the single most important problem in schools, especially with primarily low income students and students of color in underserved urban and rural areas (Darling-Hammond, 2007, 2009; Levine, 2005, 2006). Educational policymakers have stressed the necessity of training and retaining high quality teachers and have argued that profound changes in teacher education, especially in college and university teacher education programs are essential. In a recent lecture at Teachers College, Columbia University, Secretary of Education Arne Duncan called for systemic improvements in these programs and a national commitment to improving the quality of teachers and principals, without which educational reforms would fail (Duncan, 2009). Within this context, like many others making this critique of teacher education, he called for an increase in rigor and that programs ensure that their graduates know the subjects they will teach.

Although there is little to disagree with in such calls for teacher and principal quality, as with most educational reforms over the past three decades, my response is often "Yes, but" (Semel, 1996). Whereas these types of school-level reforms are necessary to reduce the achievement gaps, they are nonetheless insufficient, as they fail to address myriad problems outside schools, such as poverty, which are associated with social class and racial differences in achievement (Rothstein, 2004).

Moreover, they ignore a different criticism of teacher education programs: that they have ignored the foundations of education within their curricula, a key to understanding the complexities of educational problems and their solutions. Over the past three decades, state education departments and national accreditation agencies, such as the National Council for the Accreditation of Teacher Education (NCATE) and the Teacher Education Accreditation Council (TEAC) have emphasized the mechanics of teaching (the *how*) and the content of teaching (the *what*), but for all intents and purposes have ignored the social and philosophical contexts of teaching (the *why*). One of the reasons that educational problems have been so difficult to solve is because such a narrow minded preoccupation with this technocratic model of teaching and learning results in these reforms never getting to the heart of the matter, their underlying causes. The core principle of this reader is that the foundations of education must reemerge as a central building block of teacher and principal education, rather than as an afterthought as has been the case in the recent past.

An important tool that drives the selection of the subsequent readings is the foundations perspective (Sadovnik, Cookson and Semel, 2006). This consists of four interrelated approaches or disciplinary lenses: historical, political, sociological and philosophical. The history, politics, sociology and philosophy, of education or what are commonly referred to as the foundations of education are by no means separate and distinct perspectives. On one hand, they represent the unique vantage points of the separate disciplines of history, political science, sociology and philosophy. On the other hand, taken together they are four disciplinary approaches (and often interdisciplinary) that look at the relationships between their central areas of concern.

The History of Education

History of education is concerned with "what was." It provides us with an understanding of the past, the complexities of the present and the possibilities of what the future holds in store for us. You are about to enter or are a current participant in an educational system that looks the way it does today because of past events that shaped the educational world that you, as educators, will inherit. Likewise, you in turn will be the next generation to influence the shape of schools of tomorrow. Our schools look and work the way they do because of complex historical events and processes. To understand the educational problems of today, you must first have a perspective from which to comprehend these historical processes. This is an important value and purpose of the history of education.

Some people believe that those ignorant of the past are doomed to repeat it. Although it is highly unlikely that history of education is a tool for eliminating mistakes altogether, for the study of history of education reveals numerous repeated errors of judgment; nevertheless, ignorance of the past is a major barrier to educational improvement. Thus, the insights readings in history of education may provide you with are crucial to a foundations perspective. For example, the reading included from historian of education David Tyack's *The One Best System* examines the rise of the administrative progressives in the march towards bureaucratization of the schools and the ascendancy of the testing and measurements movement. W.E.B. DuBois, a sociologist, in his piece from *The Souls of Black Folk*, provides a historical account of the barriers African-Americans encountered from reconstruction onward in their quest for equality.

Understanding the History of U.S. Education: Different Historical Interpretations

The history of education in the United States has been one of conflict, struggle, and disagreement. However, historians of education have developed differing theories for explaining these.

The different interpretations of U.S. educational history revolve around the tensions between equity and excellence, between the social and intellectual functions of schooling, and over differing responses to the questions: Education in whose interests? Education for whom? The U.S. school system has expanded to serve more students for longer periods of time than any other system in the modern world. This occurred, first, by extending primary school to all through compulsory education laws during the Common School Era; second, by extending high school education to the majority of adolescents by the end of the Progressive Era; and third, by extending postsecondary education to the largest number of high school graduates in the world by the 1990s. However, historians and sociologists of education disagree about whether this pattern of increased access means a pattern of educational success.

The Democratic-Liberal School

Democratic-liberals believe that the history of U.S. education involves the progressive evolution, albeit flawed, of a school system committed to providing equality of opportunity for all. Democratic-liberal historians suggest that each period of educational expansion involved the attempts of liberal reformers to expand educational opportunities to larger segments of the population and to reject the conservative view of schools as elite institutions for the meritorious (which usually meant the privileged). These historians have portrayed the Common School Era as a victory for democratic movements and the first step in opening U.S education to all. Furthermore, they portray the early school reformers such as Horace Mann and Henry Barnard as reformers dedicated to egalitarian principles. Lawrence A. Cremin, in his three-volume history of U.S. education (1972, 1980, 1988) and in a study of the Progressive Era (1961), portrays the evolution of U.S. education in terms of two related processes: popularization and multitudinousness (Cremin, 1988). For Cremin, educational history in the United States involved both the expansion of opportunity and purpose. That is, as more students from diverse backgrounds went to school for longer periods of time, the goals of education became more diverse, with social goals often becoming as or more important than intellectual ones. Cremin did not deny the educational problems and conflicts; he noted the discrepancies between opportunity and results, particularly for the economically disadvantaged. Moreover, he never relinquished his vision that the genius of U.S. education is in its commitment to popularization and multitudinousness. Cremin's focus on diversity in American education can be clearly seen in the article included in this reader: in it he begins to explore the many strands and complex nature of American progressive education, the longest lasting educational reform in our history.

Although democratic-liberals tend to interpret U.S. educational history optimistically, the evolution of the nation's schools has been a flawed, often conflictual march toward increased opportunities. Thus, historians such as Cremin do not see equity and excellence as inevitably irreconcilable as much as the tensions between the two resulting in necessary compromises. The ideals of equality and excellence are just that: ideals. Democratic-liberals believe that the U.S. educational system must continue to move closer to each, without sacrificing one or the other too dramatically.

The Radical-Revisionist School

Beginning in the 1960s, the optimistic vision of the democratic-liberal historians began to be challenged by radical historians of education. These radical-revisionist historians of education revised provided a more critical, less optimistic analysis. These historians, including Michael Katz (1968), Joel Spring (1972), and Clarence Karier (1976), argued that U.S. education expanded to meet the needs of the elites in society for the control of the working class and immigrants, and for economic efficiency and productivity. In addition, radicals suggested that expanded opportunity did not translate into more egalitarian results. Rather, they point out that each period of educational reform (the Common School Era, the Progressive Era, the post-World War II) led to increasing stratification within the educational system, with working class, poor, and minority students getting the short end of the stick.

One of the problems with this view, pointed out by other radicals who generally agreed with this interpretation, is that it views the expansion of education as imposed on the poor and working class from above and often against their will. An alternative radical view is that the explanation of educational expansion is a more conflictual one rather than a simplistic tale of elite domination.

Overall, radical historians agree that the results of educational expansion rarely met their stated democratic aspirations. They suggest that each new expansion increased stratification of working-class and disadvantaged students within the system, with these students less likely to succeed educationally. For example, political economists Samuel Bowles and Herbert Gintis (1976) noted that the expansion of the high school resulted in a comprehensive secondary system that tracked students into vocational and academic curriculums with placement, more often than not, determined by social class background and race. Furthermore, the expansion of higher education in the post-World War II period often resulted in the stratification between community colleges that stressed vocational education and four-year colleges and universities that stressed the liberal arts and sciences. Once again, radicals argue that placement in the higher education system is based on social class and race. Thus, the radical interpretation of U.S. educational history is a more pessimistic one. While acknowledging educational expansion, they suggest that this process benefited the elites more than the masses and failed to produce either equality of opportunity or results. Further, they underscore the ironic nature of the debates about equity and excellence: those who bemoan the decline of standards seeking to reimpose excellence with little regard for equality.

Conservative Perspectives

In the 1980s, a rising tide of conservative criticism swept education circles. Arguing that U.S. students knew very little and that U.S. schools were mediocre, conservative critics such as William Bennett, Chester Finn, Jr., Diane Ravitch, E.D. Hirsch, Jr., and Allan Bloom all pointed to the failure of liberal-progressive education to fulfill its lofty social goals without sacrificing academic quality. Although critics such as Ravitch and Hirsch supported the democratic-liberal goal of equality of opportunity and mobility through education, they believed that the historical pursuit of social and political objectives resulted in significant harm to the traditional academic goals of schooling.

Diane Ravitch (1977) provided a passionate critique of the radical-revisionist perspective and a defense of the democratic-liberal position. Yet, in the 1980s, Ravitch moved from this centrist position to a more conservative stance. In a series of essays and books, including *The Troubled Crusade* (1983) and *Left Back* (2000), Ravitch argued that the preoccupation with using education to solve social problems has not solved these problems and, simultaneously, has led to the erosion of educational excellence. Although Ravitch remained faithful to the democratic-liberal belief that schools have expanded opportunities to countless numbers of the disadvantaged and immigrants, she has argued that the adjustment of the traditional curriculum to meet the needs of all of these groups has been a violation of the fundamental function of schooling, which is to develop the intellect.

As you will see in her chapter in the politics section of this reader, Ravitch's political position is far more complex than that of other conservative critics who bemoan the decline of standards. Ravitch understands the conflictual nature of U.S. educational history and simultaneously praises the schools for being a part of large-scale social improvement while damning them for losing their academic standards in the process. Recently, Ravitch has moved back to a more liberal perspective, arguing that the No Child Left Behind Law has resulted in an over-emphasis on testing and a narrowing of the curriculum.

Finally, the history of U.S. education has involved five related patterns. First, it has been defined by the expansion of schooling to increasingly larger numbers of children for longer periods of time. Second, with this expansion has come the demand for equality of opportunity and ways to decrease inequality of results. Both of these patterns have helped lead to the third, the polarization over goals, curriculum, and method, and fourth, conflict between the goals of education: education for a common culture, and education for the diversity of a pluralistic society. And fifth are the tensions between popularization and educational excellence. All of these processes speak to the fact that Americans have always asked a great deal, perhaps too much, from their schools, and that conflict and controversy are the definitive features of the evolution of the school.

The Politics of Education

The politics of education is concerned with "who controls the schools." As stated above, in this discussion schools have been the subject of considerable conflict about goals, methods, curriculum, and other important issues. Policy decisions are rarely made in a smooth consensual manner; rather there are often compromises based on the resolutions of battles between various interest groups. Schools in the United States are contested terrains in which various interest groups attempt to use political strategies to shape the educational system to best represent their interests and needs.

The lens of political science helps us understand power relations and the way interest groups use the political process to maximize their advantages within organizations. A political science perspective focuses on the politics of education—on power relations; on the relationship between the local, state, and federal governments and education; on school financing and law; and on the question of who controls the schools.

Political scientists often ask how democratic are our schools? Are educational policies shaped by the pluralistic input of many groups or are they shaped by political elites? The political science approach to education will allow you to examine the complexities of questions such as these, while also providing important insights into education policy and change.

Of particular interest and import to life in schools is the issue of organizational politics within schools. How does an interest group within a school, such as administrators, teachers, students, and parents arrive at policy? Who decides which tests to use and why? Which reading program, which textbook? The politics of education are important both on the micro and macro levels and color the way we teach and learn. Which groups have the power to shape educational decisions for their own benefit? What are the patterns of political conflict and consensus? How do the relationships between these groups help define the educational debates of today? Through a close look at the politics of education, you will become aware of how these group interactions are essential for understanding schools and, more importantly, the ability of teachers to shape and change the educational system.

Political Perspectives

Debates about educational issues often focus on different views concerning the goals of schools and their place within society. From the inception of the U.S. republic through the present, there have been significantly different visions of U.S. education and the role of schools in society. Although many of the views are complex, it is helpful to simplify them through the use of a political typology. In its most simple form, the different visions of U.S. education can be discussed in terms of conservative, liberal, and radical perspectives. Although the nature of these approaches has changed over time, what follows is a contemporary model of how each perspective views a number of related educational issues.

The conservative, liberal, and radical perspectives all look at educational issues and problems from distinctly different, although at times overlapping, vantage points. Although there are areas of agreement, they each have distinctly different views on education and its role in U.S. society. Moreover, they each have fundamentally different viewpoints on social problems and their solution in general, and their analysis of education is a particular application of this more general world view. This will become evident as you read the selections in the history and politics of education sections of the reader by Ravitch, who encompasses both the conservative and liberal vantage points; Cremin, the consummate liberal, and Bowles and Gintis and Anyon, exemplars of the radical position.

Discussions of education often refer to traditional and progressive visions. Although these terms have a great deal in common with the conservative, liberal, and radical perspectives they are sometimes used interchangeably or without clear definitions, and therefore there is often confusion concerning terminology. For the purpose of clarification, traditional visions tend to view the schools as necessary to the transmission of the traditional values of U.S. society, such as hard work, family unity, individual initiative, and so on. Progressive visions tend to view the schools as central to solving social problems, as a vehicle for upward mobility, as essential to the development of individual potential, and as an integral part of a democratic society. Traditionalism tends to be on a continuum from conservative to the liberal perspectives.

Progressivism tends to be on a continuum from the liberal to the radical perspectives. Nevertheless, the role of the school is a central focus of each of the perspectives and is at the heart of their differing analyses. The school's role in the broadest sense is directly concerned with the aims, purposes, and functions of education in a society.

Conservatives see the role of the school as providing the necessary educational training to ensure that the most talented and hard-working individuals receive the tools necessary to maximize economic and social productivity. In addition, conservatives believe that schools socialize children into the adult roles necessary to the maintenance of the social order. Finally, they see the school's function as one of transmitting the cultural traditions through what is taught (the curriculum). Therefore, the conservative perspective views the role of the school as essential to both economic productivity and social stability.

The liberal perspective, while also stressing the training and socializing function of the school, sees these aims a little differently. In line with the liberal belief in equality of opportunity, it stresses the school's role in providing the necessary education to ensure that all students have an equal opportunity to succeed in society. Whereas liberals also point to the school's role in socializing children into societal roles, they stress the pluralistic nature of U.S. society and the school's role in teaching children to respect cultural diversity so that they understand and fit into a diverse society. On the political level, liberals stress the importance of citizenship and an educated citizenry for participation in a democratic society. Finally, the liberal perspective stresses individual as well as societal needs and thus sees the school's role as enabling the individual to develop his or her talents, creativity, and sense of self. For liberals the role of education is to balance the needs of society and the individual in a manner that is consistent with a democratic and meritocratic society. Liberals envision a society in which citizens participate in decision making, in which adult status is based on merit and achievement, and in which all citizens receive a fair and equal opportunity for economic wealth, political power, and social status.

The radical perspective, given its vastly differing view on U.S. society, likewise has a significantly different view of what the school's role is. Although radicals believe schools ought to eliminate inequalities, they argue that the school's role is to reproduce the unequal economic conditions of the capitalist economy and to socialize individuals to accept the legitimacy of the society. Through what radicals term social and cultural reproduction, the school's role is to perpetuate the society and to serve the interests of those with economic wealth and political power. Most important, through a vastly unequal educational system, radicals believe that schools prepare children from different social backgrounds for different roles within the economic division of labor. The radical perspective, unlike the liberal, views equality of opportunity as an illusion and as no more than an ideology used to convince individuals that they have been given a fair chance, when in fact they have not. Therefore, the radical perspective argues that schools reproduce economic, social, and political inequality within U.S. society.

Conservatives, liberals, and radicals have differing views on the role of the school in meeting the goals of equality of opportunity and providing for social mobility.

Conservatives believe that schools should ensure that all students have the opportunity to compete individually in the educational marketplace and that schools should be meritocratic to the extent that individual effort is rewarded. Based on the belief that individuals succeed largely on their own accord, conservatives argue that the role of the school is to provide a place for individual merit to be encouraged and rewarded.

Liberals believe that schools should ensure that equality of opportunity exists and that inequality of results be minimized. Based on the historical record, the liberal perspective indicates that although schools have made a significant difference in the lives of countless Americans and have provided upward mobility for many individuals, there remain significant differences in the educational opportunities and achievement levels for rich and poor.

Radicals believe that schools should reduce inequality of educational results and provide upward social mobility, but that historically the schools have been ineffective in attaining these noble goals. Moreover, the radical perspective argues that under capitalism schools will remain limited, if not wholly unsuccessful, vehicles for addressing problems of inequality—problems that radicals suggest are structurally characteristic of capitalism.

If, as radicals and many liberals suggest, schooling has not sufficiently provided a reduction in inequality of results, and as educational achievement is closely related to student socioeconomic backgrounds, then the explanation of why certain groups, particularly from lower socioeconomic backgrounds, perform less well in school is a crucial one. Conservatives argue that individuals or groups of students rise and fall on their own intelligence, hard work, and initiative, and that achievement is based on hard work and sacrifice. The school system, from this vantage point, is designed to allow individuals the opportunity to succeed. If they do not, it may be because they are, as individuals, deficient in some manner or because they are members of a group that is deficient.

The liberal perspective argues that individual students or groups of students begin school with different life chances and therefore some groups have significantly more advantages than others. Therefore, society must attempt through policies and programs to equalize the playing field so that students from disadvantaged backgrounds have a better chance.

Radicals, like liberals, believe that students from lower socioeconomic backgrounds begin schools with unequal opportunities. Unlike liberals, however, radicals believe that the conditions that result in educational failure are caused by the economic system, not the educational system, and can only be ameliorated by changes in the political-economic structure.

The Sociology of Education

Sociology of education is concerned with "what is." With the growth of schooling questions arose about the relationship between school and society. A number of thinkers believed that schools would help usher in a modern era in which merit and effort would replace privilege and inheritance as the criteria for social and occupational success.

Sociologists of education generally shared in this optimism and as a result they began to explore the ways in which students were socialized for adult status, they examined the school as a social system, and they analyzed the effects of education on students' life chances. They believed that they could improve education through the application of social scientific theory and research. However, beginning in the 1960s, sociologists of education became more skeptical and critical about the role of education in the United States as studies indicated that schooling often reproduced rather than ameliorated inequalities.

Because of their scientific orientation, sociologists of education in general want to know what really goes on in schools and what the measurable effects of education are on individuals and on society. The hallmark of the sociological approach to education is empiricism, or the collection and analysis of social facts or data within a theoretical context that allows researchers to build a coherent set of findings. Thus, sociologists of education are interested in collecting data and they try to assertion without evidence.

The sociological method is particularly useful when educational practices are related to educational outcomes. Thus, those of us interested in school improvement can have some confidence that these results are valid and generalizable, and not simply opinion or wishful thinking. Nevertheless, results are always subject to interpretation because all knowledge is, in a sense, the result of competing interpretations of events and ideas.

The methods of sociology are useful tools for understanding how schools actually interact with society. Although social science has no monopoly on wisdom or knowledge, it is based on an honest attempt to be objective, scientific, and empirical. Like history, sociology grounds us in the social context and tempers our educational inquiries by contrasting the real with the ideal. The sociological approach is fundamental to the foundations perspective because it keeps one's observations focused and testable. Without knowing what is (to the best of our abilities), one cannot make the "ought" to be a reality.

Theoretical Perspectives

The sociology of education is a contentious field and the questions sociologists ask about the relation between school and society are fundamental and complex. Because the scope of these questions is so large, sociologists usually begin their studies with an overall picture of how society looks in its most basic form. This is where theory comes in. Theory is like an x-ray machine; it allows one to see past the visible and obvious and examine the hidden structure. Unlike x-ray pictures, however, theoretical pictures of society are seldom crystal clear or easy to interpret. Theory is a conceptual guide to understanding the relation between school and society because it gives one the intellectual scaffolding from which to hang empirical findings. Essentially, there are three major theories about the relation between school and society: functional, conflictual, and interactional.

Functional sociologists begin with a picture of society that stresses the interdependence of the social system; these researchers often examine how well the parts are integrated with each other. Functionalists view society as a kind of machine, where one part articulates with another to produce the dynamic energy required to make society work. Perhaps the earliest sociologist to embrace a functional point of view about the relation of school and society was Emile Durkheim (1858–1917), who virtually invented the sociology of education in the late nineteenth and early twentieth centuries. While Durkheim recognized that education had taken different forms at different times and places, he believed that education, in virtually all societies, was of critical importance in creating the moral unity necessary for social cohesion and harmony. For Durkheim, moral values were the foundation of society. Durkheim's emphasis on values and cohesion set the tone for how present-day functionalists approach the study of education. Functionalists tend to assume that consensus is the normal state in society and that conflict represents a breakdown of shared values. In a highly integrated, well-functioning society, schools socialize students into the appropriate values and sort and select students according to their abilities. Educational reform, then, from a functional point of view, is supposed to create structures, programs, and curricula that are technically advanced, rational, and encourage social unity. It should be evident that most U.S. educators and educational reformers implicitly base their reform suggestions on functional theories of schooling. When, for example, *A Nation at Risk* was released in 1983, the argument was made by the authors of the report that schools were responsible for a whole host of social and economic problems. There was no suggestion that perhaps education might not have the power to overcome deep, social, and economic problems without changing other aspects of U.S. society.

Not all sociologists of education believe that society is held together by shared values alone. Some sociologists argue that the social order is not based on some collective agreement, but on the ability of dominant groups to impose their will on subordinate groups through force, cooptation, and manipulation. In this view, the glue of society is economic, political, cultural, and military power. Ideologies or intellectual justifications created by the powerful are designed to enhance their position by legitimizing inequality and the unequal distribution of material and cultural goods as an inevitable outcome of biology, or history. Clearly, conflict sociologists do not see the relation between school and society as unproblematic or straightforward. Whereas functionalists emphasize cohesion in explaining social order, conflict sociologists emphasize struggle. From a conflict point of view, schools are similar to social battlefields, where students struggle against teachers, teachers against administrators, and so on. These antagonisms, however, are most often muted for two reasons: the authority and power of the school and the achievement ideology. In effect, the achievement ideology convinces students and teachers that schools promote learning and sort and select students according to their abilities and not according to their social status. In this view, the achievement ideology disguises the real power relations within the school, which, in turn, reflect and correspond to the power relations within the larger society (Bowles and Gintis, 1976).

Although Karl Marx (1818–1883) did not address education specifically, he is the intellectual founder of the conflict school in the sociology of education. Marx's powerful and often compelling critique of early capitalism has provided the intellectual energy for subsequent generations of liberal and leftist thinkers who believe that the only way to a more just and productive society is the abolition or modification of capitalism and the introduction of socialism. Political economists Bowles and Gintis, in their book *Schooling in Capitalist America* (1976), used a Marxist perspective for examining the growth of the U.S. public school. To their minds, there was a direct correspondence between the organization of schools and the organization of society, and, until society is fundamentally changed, there is little hope of real school reform. It has been argued by other conflict sociologists of education, however, that traditional Marxism is too deterministic and overlooks the power of culture and individuals in promoting change.

An early conflict sociologist who took a slightly different theoretical orientation when viewing society was Max Weber (1864–1920). Like Marx, Weber was convinced that power relations between dominant and subordinate groups structured societies, but unlike Marx, Weber believed that class differences alone could not capture the complex ways human beings form hierarchies and belief systems that make these hierarchies seem just and inevitable. Thus, Weber examined status cultures as well as class position as an important sociological concept, because it alerts one to the fact that people identify their group by what they consume and with whom they socialize. The Weberian approach to studying the relation between school and society has developed into a compelling and informative tradition of sociological research. Researchers in this tradition tend to analyze school organizations and processes from the point of view of status competition and organizational constraints.

A major research tradition that has emerged from the Weberian school of thought is represented by Randall Collins (1971, 1979), who has maintained that educational expansion is best explained by status group struggle. He argued that educational credentials, such as college diplomas, are primarily status symbols rather than indicators of actual achievement. The rise of credentialism does not indicate that society is becoming more expert, but that education is increasingly used by dominant groups to secure more advantageous places for themselves and their children within the occupation and social structure. Collins' piece included in this reader, provides a comparative analysis of functionalist and conflict theories and helps to explain why practitioners are required to obtain more and more "credentials"; first to become teachers and then, to solidify their positions and advance on the salary scale.

A recent variation of conflict theory that has captured the imagination of some U.S. sociologists began in France and England during the 1960s. Unlike most Marxists who tend to emphasize the economic structure of society, cultural reproduction theorists, such as Bourdieu and Passeron (1977), examined how "cultural capital" knowledge and experiences related to art, music, and literature and "social capital" social networks and connections are passed on by families and schools. The concepts of cultural and social capital are important because they suggest that, in understanding the transmission of inequalities, one ought to recognize that the cultural and social characteristics of individuals and groups are significant indicators of status and class position.

A growing body of literature suggests that schools pass on specific social identities that either enhance or hinder the life chances of their graduates. For example, a graduate from an elite prep school has educational and social advantages over many public school graduates in terms of college attendance and occupational mobility. This advantage has very little to do with what prep school students learn in school, and a great deal to do with the power of their schools' reputations for educating members of the upper class.

The conflict perspective, then, offers important insights about the relation between school and society. As you think about schools and education, try to utilize functional and conflict theoretical perspectives as a way of organizing your readings and perceptions.

A third theory, interactional theory about the relation of school and society, is a critique and elaboration of the functional and conflict perspectives. The critique arises from the observation that functional and conflict theories are very abstract and emphasize structure and process at a very general level of analysis. Although this level of analysis helps in understanding education in the "big picture," these theories do not provide a snapshot of what schools are like on an everyday level. What do students and teachers actually do in school? Interactional theories attempt to make the commonplace strange by turning on their heads everyday taken-for-granted behaviors and interactions between students and students, and between students and teachers. It is exactly what one does not question that is most problematic at a deep level. For example, the processes by which students are labeled gifted or learning disabled are, from an interactional point of view, important to analyze, because such processes carry with them many implicit assumptions about learning and children. By examining the interactional aspects of school life, we are better able to understand why particular educational outcomes occur. The reading by Lortie illustrates the power of interactionist theory in helping educators understand the everyday processes in schools and how they affect teachers.

Some of the sociology of education's most brilliant theorists have attempted to synthesize these three approaches. Basil Bernstein (1977, 1990), for instance, has argued that the structural aspects of the educational system and the interactional aspects of the system reflect each other and must be viewed wholistically. He has examined how speech patterns reflect students' social-class backgrounds and how students from working-class backgrounds are at a disadvantage in the school setting because schools are essentially middle-class organizations. Bernstein has combined a class analysis with an interactional analysis, which links language with educational processes and outcomes.

The Philosophy of Education

Philosophy of education is concerned with "what ought to be." It helps practitioners to interrogate the "how" and the "why" of life in classrooms, the choices that they make in their daily contexts of schools and beyond in the larger world of schooling. In order to comprehend fully the world of schooling, educators must possess a social and intellectual context (the foundations perspective). An understanding of the philosophy of education is essential in building this perspective.

Because philosophy is often not seen as practical, it is often considered unimportant in the world of practice. Yet every choice that we make as practitioners is governed by personal beliefs and experiences both in the classroom and in the world.

Classroom practice is inextricably linked to theory and/or belief systems whether or not we wish to acknowledge this phenomenon. We can see the relationship between educational practices and philosophy by posing questions and offering answers, which in turn usually lead to more questions; somewhat unsettling for those of us who are more concerned with what we will teach tomorrow than thinking about why we teach what we teach or how we teach it. Nevertheless, by asking educators to reflect on the "what" and "how" as we go about teaching in our classrooms, we may begin to realize that our decisions and actions are shaped by a host of human experiences firmly rooted in both our broader notion of culture and our particular cultural contexts. For example, why do some practitioners prefer informal classroom settings to formal ones? Why might some lean toward the adoption of cooperative learning, scaffolding curriculum, culturally relevant pedagogy? The preferences we have may best be clarified and expressed through the study of the philosophy of education.

Finally, philosophy of education is distinct from philosophy because it links ideas to the reality of classrooms and schools and because it requires an interdisciplinary approach to understand the theoretical building blocks of practice. Often, as students of the philosophy of education you will read selections from literature, psychology, sociology, and history, as well as philosophy to be able to effect a personal synthesis of the human experience, reflect on world views, and make intensely personal choices as to what sort of practitioners you will be. Thus philosophy of education empowers you to examine what ought to be and enables you to envision the type of teachers you want to be and the types of schools that ought to exist.

The study of philosophy of education as an integral part of the foundations perspective allows practitioners to reflect on educational issues from a particular philosophical perspective. This perspective encourages logical, systematic thinking. It stresses the importance of ideas and encourages the act of reflection on every aspect of practice. Thus, philosophy acts as the building block for the reflective practitioner.

Practitioners often argue that although philosophy of education may add another dimension to the way in which they view schools, nevertheless, they haven't the time for a discipline that does not offer tangible results. Rather, they wish to learn what to do, not why to do it. Therefore, for many practitioners, the practice of teaching is reduced to action devoid of a rationale or justification.

I believe that the practice of teaching cannot be separated from a philosophical foundation. Philosophy, as applied to education, allows practitioners to apply systematic approaches to problem solving in schools and illuminates larger issues of the complex relationship of schools to the social order.

Philosophy of education differs from philosophy. Philosophy of education is firmly rooted in practice, whereas philosophy, as a discipline, stands on its own with no specific end in mind. Given this difference, it is necessary to consider for a moment how a particular philosophy might affect practice. John Dewey, the most important philosopher of education and the founder of progressive education in the late nineteenth and early twentieth centuries, exemplified this form of philosophy, termed pragmatism.

All practitioners, regardless of their action orientation, have a personal philosophy of life that colors the way in which they select knowledge; order their classrooms; interact with students, peers, parents, and administrators; and select values to emphasize within their classrooms. Engaging in philosophy helps practitioners to clarify what they do or intend to do and, as they act or propose to act, to justify or explain why they do what they do in a logical, systematic manner. Thus, the activity of doing philosophy aids them in understanding two very important notions: (1) who they are or intend to be and (2) why they do or propose to do what they do. Furthermore, through the action of clarification and justification of practice, they think about practice and acquire specific information, which lends authority to their decision making.

Although people exist as individuals, they also exist within the greater context of their culture. Through interactions with the norms common to the culture, people form attitudes, beliefs, and values, which are then transmitted to others. As people go about this process of acquiring cultural norms, they may accept norms wholeheartedly, accept norms partially, or, in certain instances, totally reject them. Whatever people choose to embrace, if their choices are made in a logical, rational manner, they are engaged in the process of "doing philosophy." To proceed in doing philosophy, certain key questions are posed that can be divided into three specific areas of philosophical inquiry. The first is called metaphysics, a branch of philosophy that concerns itself with questions about the nature of reality. The second is called epistemology, a branch of philosophy that concerns itself with questions about the nature of knowledge. Last is axiology, a branch of philosophy that concerns itself with the nature of values. These distinctions in philosophy are important for practitioners, since ideas generated by philosophers about education usually fall under a particular branch of philosophy, such as epistemology. Furthermore, the ideas generated by philosophers interested in particular questions help people to clarify their own notions of existence, knowledge, and values; in sum, one's personal philosophy of life. Moreover, this philosophy of life, as one comes to understand it, becomes the foundation upon which people construct pedagogic practice. Both the pieces by Maxine Greene and Jane Roland Martin encourage practitioners to "do philosophy" but in different ways. Greene exhorts teachers to move to action: to come together and question rules that they know from their practice do not make sense. Martin provides practioners with another way of thinking about what they do from a feminist perspective—a perspective that has been missing from the conversation, historically dominated by men.

The Foundations Perspective: Educational Literacy and Empowerment

The history, philosophy, politics, and sociology of education are separate disciplines; they are rarely used in isolation and are most often combined to ask the type of questions I have discussed. Although the selections in this book are often written from one of the perspectives, they generally use more than one of the disciplinary approaches. In fact, they are usually multidisciplinary and/or interdisciplinary (i.e., integrating more than one discipline). Moreover, the foundations perspective is a way of viewing schools that uses each of the approaches—the historical, the political, the sociological and the philosophical—in an integrative manner.

Practitioner voices have long been silent in discussions of educational reform. On one hand, college professors, politicians, policy makers and other educational experts all write about what is wrong with schools, but often without the practical experiential foundation of what it is like in the classroom. On the other hand, practitioners often criticize these writings because the experts lack an understanding of what is termed "life in the trenches." However, many practitioners show the same kind of oversight when they criticize the experts—they sometimes believe that the voice of experience is sufficient to describe, understand, and change schools. What is needed is a perspective that relates theory and practice so that practitioners can combine their experiential knowledge with a broader, more multidimensional analysis of the context in which their experiences occur. The foundations perspective provides a theoretical and empirical base, but it alone is similarly insufficient as a tool for optimal understanding and effective change. When combined with the experiential voice of practitioners, however, the foundations perspective becomes a powerful tool in the development of their active voice about educational matters.

Sociologists argue that the individual does not always have the ability to understand the complex social forces that affect him or her and make up a society simply by virtue of living in the society. Likewise, practitioners, solely by virtue of their classroom experiences, do not always have the tools to make sense of the world of education. In fact, some teachers are too close and subjectively involved to have the emotional distance that is required for critical analysis. I am not suggesting that a practitioner's experience is unimportant; but rather that the theoretical and empirical insights of the foundations of education must comprise a crucial part of a practitioner's perspective on education and thereby contribute to foundational literacy. Foundational literacy is the ability to connect knowledge, theory, and research evidence to the everyday experiences of educational practice. Through the use of a foundations perspective, amplified by the readings in this text as will become apparent in the next section, teachers can develop this essential ability and become what is termed "reflective practitioners."

Students and practitioners often ask whether foundational literacy will help them solve problems. Am I suggesting that a foundational understanding of the educational system result in its improvement? Of course not! Understanding the schools and improving them are two different matters. Without changes in the factors that affect the schools, as well as changes in the structure and processes within the schools, it is highly unlikely that large-scale change or even significant improvement will take place. What I am saying, however, is that practitioners must be part of the ongoing dialogue focused on improving schools, and in order to contribute meaningfully to this dialogue they need more than their own experiences. They need the knowledge, confidence, and authority that are products of foundational literacy.

Developing foundational literacy is a first and necessary step toward bringing the active voice of practitioners into the educational debates so that, together with other professionals, they will become intimately involved in the development of a better educational world. It will not be easy. As a historian of education, I do not pretend that the record suggests that we should be overly optimistic; neither does it suggest, however, that we should lose hope. It is my hope that the readings in this book will give you the tools to become part of this ongoing effort—the quest for improved schools, more qualified practitioners, and a just society.

The Readings

The selections in *Foundations of Education: The Essential Texts* have been selected to reflect and illuminate the foundations disciplines and help you to develop your own foundational literacy. Taken from hundreds of essential readings, they provide examples of the power of each discipline individually and combined for understanding educational problems. Although others might have been selected, the twelve that follow typify the value of the foundations perspective for educators.

Part I, The History of Education, examines a number of critical issues in the history of education, including the role of race, the progressive movement in education in the twentieth century and the development of urban schools during the first part of that century.

In Chapter 1, sociologist and historian W.E.B. DuBois in "Of Mr. Booker T. Washington and Others," challenges the notion held by Booker T. Washington of accommodation and gradualism as the strategy for blacks in America to achieve equality in American society. Whereas Washington represented the moderate position in the African Americans' struggle for equality, DuBois argued for a more proactive position. He included as his agenda, voting rights, equality before the law, and an educational meritocracy for black youth. He urged African-Americans to "strive for the rights which the world accords to men" and reminds them of the words that "the sons of the Fathers would fain forget: 'We hold these truths to be self-evident: That all men are created equal; that they are endowed by their Creator with certain unalienable rights; that among these are life, liberty, and the pursuit of happiness.'" The Washington-DuBois debate exemplified their different views of the importance of education for "freedmen" or the freed slaves. For Washington practical, agricultural and vocational education represented the most rapid path to upward mobility; for DuBois, an elite liberal arts education equal to that of the white "aristocracy" was essential for African-American leadership and ascendency. These differing paths mirror tracking students into vocational or academic tracks, often based on race, which began during the Progressive Era and persists today.

In Chapter 2, historian Lawrence A. Cremin, in "The Progressive Movement in American Education: A Perspective," writes of the longest lasting educational reform in our history, Progressive Education. He locates the movement in education within the larger historical movement of the Progressive Era, which began as a social and political reform movement, particularly in the cities across America which were experiencing unprecedented rapid industrialization and immigration. Important for us, he locates the different themes present in progressive education and presents the reform itself as ongoing, taking on different manifestations of core beliefs and practices at different historical moments. This article was a prelude to his classic book, *The Transformation of the School* (1961), which traced the different types of progressives, scientists (administrative progressives), sentimentalists (child-centered), and radicals (social reconstructionists) and their role in the development and evolution of this multifaceted movement.

In Chapter 3, historian David B. Tyack, in "Inside the System: The Character of Urban Schools, 1890–1940," from his classic, *The One Best System,* traces the history of bureaucratization of urban public schooling and much, much more. Particularly, he discusses the emerging system and examines the battles between two emergent camps: the administrative progressives, wedded to the application of social science to management, and the pedagogic progressives, who represent the child-centered approach to education. This chapter represents the discussion of the administrative progressives who ultimately "won" although both strains continue to exist in our educational system.

Part II, The Politics of Education, examines the differences between radical and liberal approaches to education. Through an examination of their differing views on the purposes of schooling and the limits and possibilities of school reform the following readings demonstrate how authors with different political perspectives view the history of schooling in the United States.

In Chapter 4, "Broken Promises: School Reform in Retrospect," from their classic book *Schooling in Capitalist America* (1976), political economists Samuel Bowles and Herbert Gintis apply their neo-Marxist correspondence theory to the history and politics of school reform in the United States. They examine the contradictions between liberal educational reform and the operation of the capitalist political economy to argue that despite the best intentions of these reforms they are insufficient to accomplish their goals of democracy, equity and meritocracy.

In Chapter 5, "What 'Counts' as Educational Policy? Notes toward a New Paradigm," educational theorist Jean Anyon argues that reforms aimed at the school level are doomed to failure. Rather, she indicates that systemic societal reform aimed at the political, social, and economic levels of society are necessary to reduce educational inequalities. Through an analysis of the relationship between labor market conditions and educational credentials, she indicates that unless more high paying jobs consistent with higher levels of education are created, then schools that succeed in producing more highly educated graduates will result in their being overeducated for the increasing number of low paying service positions. Furthermore, Anyon argues that educational failure by low-income children is a result of factors outside of schools, especially those related to the pernicious effects of poverty.

In Chapter 6, "The Democratic-Liberal Tradition Under Attack," historian Diane Ravitch provides a critique of radical historians of education arguing that the democratic-liberal reforms have increased equality of opportunity and that the U.S. educational system, while not perfect, has helped to promote democratic values of equity and meritocracy. In this selection, she argues that U.S. education has served the interests of low-income, minority and immigrant students in their pursuit of the American Dream.

Part III, The Sociology of Education, examines theories in the sociology of education, as well as their application to a number of important issues, in particular issues of educational inequality, teacher roles and professionalism, and the use of ability grouping and tracking as a vehicle for meritocratic selection or to reproduce existing social inequalities.

In Chapter 7, "Functional and Conflict Theories of Educational Stratification," sociologist Randall Collins provides a comparison of functionalist and conflict theories in the sociology of education and the foundation of his status-competition theory of educational expansion.

Through the use of empirical data, Collins rejects the functionalist argument that the expansion of schooling in the twentieth century was due to the expansion of knowledge and the subsequent increase in job requirements. Rather, he argues that competition among groups competing for pieces of the occupational and economic pie have resulted in advantaged groups raising the stakes in order to maintain their advantages over less advantaged groups.

In Chapter 8, "The Logic of Teacher Sentiments," from his classic book, *Schoolteacher* (1975), sociologist Dan Lortie examines the organizational role, beliefs and values of teachers. Through an examination of the structural and organizational features of schools, the recruitment, retention and socialization processes for teachers, and how teacher sentiments are related to these, Lortie demonstrates the power of sociological analysis for understanding teaching as an occupation rather than as a calling or profession.

In Chapter 9, "The Tracking Wars" from her classic book, *Keeping Track* (1985, 2005), sociologist Jeannie Oakes examines the effects of ability grouping (separating students based on different abilities) and its related process, tracking, separating students into separate and distinctive curricula. In the first edition of the book, Oakes investigated whether or not tracking provided a meritocratic selection process based on ability in order to ensure that students received an appropriate curriculum and pace of instruction, or whether it placed students based on race, social class, gender or ethnicity for different educational and occupational destinations, often independent of ability. Oakes concluded it was the latter, with tracking serving to reproduce existing inequalities. In this selection from the second edition, Oakes reviews the battles over tracking and detracking and the empirical evidence from sociological studies over the past three decades

Part IV, The Philosophy of Education, illustrates the importance of philosophy of education on pedagogical practice. Through three classic readings, the "what ought to be" is examined.

In Chapter 10, "Experience and Education," from his classic book, *Experience and Education* (1938), philosopher John Dewey provides probably his most accessible work on his theories of education. Because of the perceived ambiguity of his writings on education, and because few educators actually read his most important work for them, *Democracy and Education*, myriad manifestations of progressive schooling emerged based on child-centered experiential education, supposedly influenced by Dewey. Often, more like Rablais than Dewey the practice amounted to "do as you wish" or abdication of responsibility on the part of the teacher. Here Dewey sets the record straight particularly regarding "experience" noting that experiences are an integral part of education but they must be carefully planned in an experience continuum within the child's education.

In Chapter 11, "Wide-Awakeness and the Moral Life," educational philosopher Maxine Greene raises the issues of passivity and acceptance on the part of teachers as they go about their daily work. She asks why they accept practices that are mandated when they know that they are detrimental to their classroom work. Further, she urges teachers to come together and protest what they instinctively know is wrong: to adopt a state of what she calls "wide-awakeness." In the current period of educational reform, driven by the quest for accountability and measurable results, her words are particularly timely.

In Chapter 12, "The Ideal of the Educated Person," philosopher Jane Roland Martin challenges the traditional notion of what constitutes an educated person by examining the gendered nature of its definition. She urges us to take into account the "lives, experiences and actions" of women, the way they "think, learn, and view the world" in creating a "gender-sensitive ideal" of an educated person. Through her piece we are left with the importance of attending to gender differences in education in general, as well as the need to redefine the traditionally taught subject matter within the discipline of philosophy of education and in all educational curricula.

References

Bernstein, B. (1977). *Class, Codes and Control* (Vol. 3). London: Routledge, Kegan and Paul.

Bernstein, B. (1990). *The Structuring of Pedagogic Discourse* (Vol. 4 of Class, Codes and Control). London: Routledge.

Bourdieu, P. and Passeron, J.C. (1977). *Reproduction in Education, Society and Culture.* Beverly Hills: Sage.

Bowles, S. and Gintis, H. (1976). *Schooling in Capitalist America.* New York: Basic Books.

Collins, R. (1971). "Functional and conflict theories of educational stratification." *American Sociological Review,* 36(6): 1002–1019.

Collins, R. (1979). *The Credential Society.* New York: Academic Press.

Cremin, L.A. (1961). *The Transformation of the School.* New York: Vintage Books.

Cremin, L.A. (1972). *American Education: The Colonial Experience, 1607–1783.* New York: Harper and Row.

Cremin, L.A. (1980). *American Education: The National Experience, 1783–1876.* New York: Harper and Row.

Cremin, L.A. (1988). *American Education: The Metropolitan Experience, 1876–1990.* New York: Harper and Row.

Darling-Hammond, L. and Bransford, J.(2007). *Preparing Teachers for a Changing World: What Teachers Should Learn and Be Able to Do.* Hoboken, NJ: Jossey Bass, 2007

Darling-Hammond, L., Meyerson, D., LaPointer, M., and Orr, M.T. (2009). *Preparing Principals for a Changing World: Lessons from Effective School Leadership Programs.* Hoboken, NJ: Jossey Bass, 2009.

Duncan, A. (2009). U.S. secretary of education Arne Duncan says colleges of education must improve for reforms to succeed. Washington, D.C.: U.S. Department of Education, October 22, 2009, http://www.ed.gov/news/pressreleases/2009/10/10222009a.html.

Karier, C. (ed.) (1976). *The Shaping of the American Educational State.* New York: Free Press.

Katz, M. (1968). *The Irony of Early School Reform.* Cambridge, MA.: Harvard University Press.

Levine, A. (2005). *Educating School Leaders.* Washington, D.C. The Education Schools Project.

Levine, A. (2006). *Educating School Teachers.* Washington, D.C. The Education Schools Project.

Ravitch, D. (1977). *The Revisionists Revised.* New York: Basic Books.

Ravitch, D. (1983). *The Troubled Crusade.* New York: Basic Books.

Ravitch, D. (2000). *Left Back: A Century of Failed School Reforms.* New York: Simon and Schuster.

Rothstein, R. (2004). *Class and Schools: Using Social, Economic and Educational Reform to Close the Black-White Achievement Gap.* New York: Teachers College Press.

Sadovnik, A.R., Cookson, P.W. and Semel, S.F. (2006). *Exploring Education: An Introduction to the Foundations of Education* (Third edition). Needham Heights, MA: Allyn and Bacon.

Semel, S.F. (1996). "'Yes, But . . .': Multicultural Education and the Reduction of Educational Inequality." Review Essay of *Handbook of Research on Multicultural Education.* Edited by James A. Banks and Cherry McGee Banks. (Macmillan, 1995). *Teachers College Record,* 98(1): 153–177.

Spring, J. (1972). *Education and the Rise of the Corporate State.* Boston: Beacon Press.

Part I
The History of Education

1

Of Mr. Booker T. Washington and Others

W.E.B. DuBois

From birth till death enslaved; in word, in deed, unmanned!
Hereditary bondsmen! Know ye not
Who would be free themselves must strike the blow?

Byron[1]

Easily the most striking thing in the history of the American Negro since 1876 is the ascendancy of Mr. Booker T. Washington. It began at the time when war memories and ideals were rapidly passing; a day of astonishing commercial development was dawning; a sense of doubt and hesitation overtook the freedmen's sons,—then it was that his leading began. Mr. Washington came, with a simple definite programme, at the psychological moment when the nation was a little ashamed of having bestowed so much sentiment on Negroes, and was concentrating its energies on Dollars. His programme of industrial education, conciliation of the South, and submission and silence as to civil and political rights, was not wholly original; the Free Negroes from 1830 up to wartime had striven to build industrial schools, and the American Missionary Association had from the first taught various trades; and Price and others had sought a way of honorable alliance with the best of the Southerners. But Mr. Washington first indissolubly linked these things; he put enthusiasm, unlimited energy, and perfect faith into this programme, and changed it from a by-path into a veritable Way of Life. And the tale of the methods by which he did this is a fascinating study of human life.

It startled the nation to hear a Negro advocating such a programme after many decades of bitter complaint; it startled and won the applause of the South, it interested and won the admiration of the North; and after a confused murmur of protest, it silenced if it did not convert the Negroes themselves.

To gain the sympathy and cooperation of the various elements comprising the white South was Mr. Washington's first task; and this, at the time Tuskegee was founded, seemed, for a black man, well-nigh impossible. And yet ten years later it was done in the word spoken at Atlanta: "In all things purely social we can be as separate as the five fingers, and yet one as the hand in all things essential to mutual progress." This "Atlanta Compromise" is by all odds the most notable thing in Mr. Washington's career. The South interpreted it in different ways: the radicals received it as a complete surrender of the demand for civil and political equality; the conservatives, as a generously conceived working basis for mutual understanding. So both approved it, and to-day its author is certainly the most distinguished Southerner since Jefferson Davis, and the one with the largest personal following.

Next to this achievement comes Mr. Washington's work in gaining place and consideration in the North. Others less shrewd and tactful had formerly essayed to sit on these two stools and had fallen between them; but as Mr. Washington knew the heart of the South from birth and training, so by singular insight he intuitively grasped the spirit of the age which was dominating the North. And so thoroughly did he learn the speech and thought of triumphant commercialism, and the ideals of material prosperity, that the picture of a lone black boy poring over a French grammar amid the weeds and dirt of a neglected home soon seemed to him the acme of absurdities. One wonders what Socrates and St. Francis of Assisi would say to this.

And yet this very singleness of vision and thorough oneness with his age is a mark of the successful man. It is as though Nature must needs make men narrow in order to give them force. So Mr. Washington's cult has gained unquestioning followers, his work has wonderfully prospered, his friends are legion, and his enemies are confounded. To-day he stands as the one recognized spokesman of his ten million fellows, and one of the most notable figures in a nation of seventy millions. One hesitates, therefore, to criticise a life which, beginning with so little, has done so much. And yet the time is come when one may speak in all sincerity and utter courtesy of the mistakes and shortcomings of Mr. Washington's career, as well as of his triumphs, without being thought captious or envious, and without forgetting that it is easier to do ill than well in the world.

The criticism that has hitherto met Mr. Washington has not always been of this broad character. In the South especially has he had to walk warily to avoid the harshest judgments,—and naturally so, for he is dealing with the one subject of deepest sensitiveness to that section. Twice—once when at the Chicago celebration of the Spanish-American War he alluded to the color-prejudice that is "eating away the vitals of the South," and once when he dined with President Roosevelt—has the resulting Southern criticism been violent enough to threaten seriously his popularity. In the North the feeling has several times forced itself into words, that Mr. Washington's counsels of submission overlooked certain elements of true manhood, and that his educational programme was unnecessarily narrow. Usually, however, such criticism has not found open expression, although, too, the spiritual sons of the Abolitionists have not been prepared to acknowledge that the schools founded before Tuskegee, by men of broad ideals and self-sacrificing spirit, were wholly failures or worthy of ridicule. While, then, criticism has not failed to follow Mr. Washington, yet the prevailing public opinion of the land has been but too willing to deliver the solution of a wearisome problem into his hands, and say, "If that is all you and your race ask, take it."

Among his own people, however, Mr. Washington has encountered the strongest and most lasting opposition, amounting at times to bitterness, and even to-day continuing strong and insistent even though largely silenced in outward expression by the public opinion of the nation. Some of this opposition is, of course, mere envy; the disappointment of displaced demagogues and the spite of narrow minds. But aside from this, there is among educated and thoughtful colored men in all parts of the land a feeling of deep regret, sorrow, and apprehension at the wide currency and ascendancy which some of Mr. Washington's theories have gained. These same men admire his sincerity of purpose, and are willing to forgive much to honest endeavor which is doing something worth the doing. They cooperate with Mr. Washington as far as they conscientiously can; and, indeed, it is no ordinary tribute to this man's tact and power that, steering as he must between so many diverse interests and opinions, he so largely retains the respect of all.

But the hushing of the criticism of honest opponents is a dangerous thing. It leads some of the best of the critics to unfortunate silence and paralysis of effort, and others to burst into speech so passionately and intemperately as to lose listeners. Honest and earnest criticism from those whose interests are most nearly touched,—criticism of writers by readers, of government by those governed, of leaders by those led,—this is the soul of democracy and the safeguard of modern society. If the best of the American Negroes receive by outer pressure a leader whom they had not recognized before, manifestly there is here a certain palpable gain. Yet there is also irreparable loss,—a loss of that peculiarly valuable education which a group receives when by search and criticism it finds and commissions its own leaders. The way in which this is done is at once the most elementary and the nicest problem of social growth. History is but the record of such group-leadership; and yet how infinitely changeful is its type and character! And of all types and kinds, what can be more instructive than the leadership of a group within a group?—that curious double movement where real progress may be negative and actual advance be relative retrogression. All this is the social student's inspiration and despair.

Now in the past the American Negro has had instructive experience in the choosing of group leaders, founding thus a peculiar dynasty which in the light of present conditions is worth while studying. When sticks and stones and beasts form the sole environment of a people, their attitude is largely one of determined opposition to and conquest of natural forces. But when to earth and brute is added an environment of men and ideas, then the attitude of the imprisoned group may take three main forms,—a feeling of revolt and revenge; an attempt to adjust all thought and action to the will of the greater group; or, finally, a determined effort at self-realization and self-development despite environing opinion. The influence of all of these attitudes at various times can be traced in the history of the American Negro, and in the evolution of his successive leaders.

Before 1750, while the fire of African freedom still burned in the veins of the slaves, there was in all leadership or attempted leadership but the one motive of revolt and revenge,—typified in the terrible Maroons, the Danish blacks, and Cato of Stono, and veiling all the Americas in fear of insurrection. The liberalizing tendencies of the latter half of the eighteenth century brought, along with kindlier relations between black and white, thoughts of ultimate adjustment and assimilation. Such aspiration was especially voiced in the earnest songs of

Phyllis, in the martyrdom of Attucks, the fighting of Salem and Poor, the intellectual accomplishments of Banneker and Derham, and the political demands of the Cuffes.

Stern financial and social stress after the war cooled much of the previous humanitarian ardor. The disappointment and impatience of the Negroes at the persistence of slavery and serfdom voiced itself in two movements. The slaves in the South, aroused undoubtedly by vague rumors of the Haytian revolt, made three fierce attempts at insurrection,—in 1800 under Gabriel in Virginia, in 1822 under Vesey in Carolina, and in 1831 again in Virginia under the terrible Nat Turner. In the Free States, on the other hand, a new and curious attempt at self-development was made. In Philadelphia and New York color-prescription led to a withdrawal of Negro communicants from white churches and the formation of a peculiar socio-religious institution among the Negroes known as the African Church,—an organization still living and controlling in its various branches over a million of men.

Walker's wild appeal against the trend of the times showed how the world was changing after the coming of the cotton-gin. By 1830 slavery seemed hopelessly fastened on the South, and the slaves thoroughly cowed into submission. The free Negroes of the North, inspired by the mulatto immigrants from the West Indies, began to change the basis of their demands; they recognized the slavery of slaves, but insisted that they themselves were freemen, and sought assimilation and amalgamation with the nation on the same terms with other men. Thus, Forten and Purvis of Philadelphia, Shad of Wilmington, Du Bois of New Haven, Barbadoes of Boston, and others, strove singly and together as men, they said, not as slaves; as "people of color," not as "Negroes." The trend of the times, however, refused them recognition save in individual and exceptional cases, considered them as one with all the despised blacks, and they soon found themselves striving to keep even the rights they formerly had of voting and working and moving as freemen. Schemes of migration and colonization arose among them; but these they refused to entertain, and they eventually turned to the Abolition movement as a final refuge.

Here, led by Remond, Nell, Wells-Brown, and Douglass, a new period of self-assertion and self-development dawned. To be sure, ultimate freedom and assimilation was the ideal before the leaders, but the assertion of the manhood rights of the Negro by himself was the main reliance, and John Brown's raid was the extreme of its logic. After the war and emancipation, the great form of Frederick Douglass, the greatest of American Negro leaders, still led the host. Self-assertion, especially in political lines, was the main programme, and behind Douglass came Elliot, Bruce, and Langston, and the Reconstruction politicians, and, less conspicuous but of greater social significance Alexander Crummell and Bishop Daniel Payne.

Then came the Revolution of 1876, the suppression of the Negro votes, the changing and shifting of ideals, and the seeking of new lights in the great night. Douglass, in his old age, still bravely stood for the ideals of his early manhood,—ultimate assimilation *through* self-assertion, and on no other terms. For a time Price arose as a new leader, destined, it seemed, not to give up, but to re-state the old ideals in a form less repugnant to the white South. But he passed away in his prime. Then came the new leader. Nearly all the former ones had become leaders by the silent suffrage of their fellows, had sought to lead their own people alone, and were usually, save Douglass, little known outside their race. But Booker T. Washington arose as essentially the leader not of one race but of two,—a compromiser between the South, the North, and the Negro. Naturally the Negroes resented, at first bitterly, signs of compromise which surrendered their civil and political rights, even though this was to be exchanged for larger chances of economic development. The rich and dominating North, however, was not only weary of the race problem, but was investing largely in Southern enterprises, and welcomed any method of peaceful cooperation. Thus, by national opinion, the Negroes began to recognize Mr. Washington's leadership; and the voice of criticism was hushed.

Mr. Washington represents in Negro thought the old attitude of adjustment and submission; but adjustment at such a peculiar time as to make his programme unique. This is an age of unusual economic development, and Mr. Washington's programme naturally takes an economic cast, becoming a gospel of Work and Money to such an extent as apparently almost completely to overshadow the higher aims of life. Moreover, this is an age when the more advanced races are coming in closer contact with the less developed races, and the race-feeling is therefore intensified; and Mr. Washington's programme practically accepts the alleged inferiority of the Negro races. Again, in our own land, the reaction from the sentiment of war time has given impetus to race-prejudice against Negroes, and Mr. Washington withdraws many of the high demands of Negroes as men and American citizens. In other periods of intensified prejudice all the Negro's tendency to self-assertion has been called forth; at this period a policy of submission is advocated. In the history of nearly all other races and peoples the doctrine preached at such crises has been that manly self-respect is worth more than lands and houses, and that a people who voluntarily surrender such respect, or cease striving for it, are not worth civilizing.

In answer to this, it has been claimed that the Negro can survive only through submission. Mr. Washington distinctly asks that black people give up, at least for the present, three things,—

First, political power,

Second, insistence on civil rights,

Third, higher education of Negro youth,—

and concentrate all their energies on industrial education, the accumulation of wealth, and the conciliation of the South. This policy has been courageously and insistently advocated for over fifteen years, and has been triumphant for perhaps ten years. As a result of this tender of the palm-branch, what has been the return? In these years there have occurred:

1. The disfranchisement of the Negro.
2. The legal creation of a distinct status of civil inferiority for the Negro.
3. The steady withdrawal of aid from institutions for the higher training of the Negro.

These movements are not, to be sure, direct results of Mr. Washington's teachings; but his propaganda has, without a shadow of doubt, helped their speedier accomplishment. The question then comes: Is it possible, and probable, that nine millions of men can make effective progress in economic lines if they are deprived of political rights, made a servile caste, and allowed only the most meagre chance for developing their exceptional men? If history and reason give any distinct answer to these questions, it is an emphatic *No*. And Mr. Washington thus faces the triple paradox of his career:

1. He is striving nobly to make Negro artisans business men and property-owners; but it is utterly impossible, under modern competitive methods, for workingmen and property-owners to defend their rights and exist without the right of suffrage.

2. He insists on thrift and self-respect, but at the same time counsels a silent submission to civic inferiority such as is bound to sap the manhood of any race in the long run.
3. He advocates common-school and industrial training, and depreciates institutions of higher learning; but neither the Negro common-schools, nor Tuskegee itself, could remain open a day were it not for teachers trained in Negro colleges, or trained by their graduates.

This triple paradox in Mr. Washington's position is the object of criticism by two classes of colored Americans. One class is spiritually descended from Toussaint the Savior, through Gabriel, Vesey, and Turner, and they represent the attitude of revolt and revenge; they hate the white South blindly and distrust the white race generally, and so far as they agree on definite action, think that the Negro's only hope lies in emigration beyond the borders of the United States. And yet, by the irony of fate, nothing has more effectually made this programme seem hopeless than the recent course of the United States toward weaker and darker peoples in the West Indies, Hawaii, and the Philippines,—for where in the world may we go and be safe from lying and brute force?

The other class of Negroes who cannot agree with Mr. Washington has hitherto said little aloud. They deprecate the sight of scattered counsels, of internal disagreement; and especially they dislike making their just criticism of a useful and earnest man an excuse for a general discharge of venom from small-minded opponents. Nevertheless, the questions involved are so fundamental and serious that it is difficult to see how men like the Grimkes, Kelly Miller, J.W.E. Bowen, and other representatives of this group, can much longer be silent. Such men feel in conscience bound to ask of this nation three things:

1. The right to vote.
2. Civic equality.
3. The education of youth according to ability.

They acknowledge Mr. Washington's invaluable service in counselling patience and courtesy in such demands; they do not ask that ignorant black men vote when ignorant whites are debarred, or that any reasonable restrictions in the suffrage should not be applied; they know that the low social level of the mass of the race is responsible for much discrimination against it, but they also know, and the nation knows, that relentless color-prejudice is more often a cause than a result of the Negro's degradation; they seek the abatement of this relic of barbarism, and not its systematic encouragement and pampering by all agencies of social power from the Associated Press to the Church of Christ. They advocate, with Mr. Washington, a broad system of Negro common schools supplemented by thorough industrial training; but they are surprised that a man of Mr. Washington's insight cannot see that no such educational system ever has rested or can rest on any other basis than that of the well-equipped college and university, and they insist that there is a demand for a few such institutions throughout the South to train the best of the Negro youth as teachers, professional men, and leaders.

This group of men honor Mr. Washington for his attitude of conciliation toward the white South; they accept the "Atlanta Compromise" in its broadest interpretation; they recognize, with him, many signs of promise, many men of high purpose and fair judgment, in this section; they know that no easy task has been laid upon a region already tottering under heavy burdens. But, nevertheless, they insist that the way to truth and right lies in straightforward honesty, not in indiscriminate flattery; in praising those of the South who do well and criticising uncompromisingly those who do ill; in taking advantage of the opportunities at hand and urging their fellows to do the same, but at the same time in remembering that only a firm adherence to their higher ideals and aspirations will ever keep those ideals within the realm of possibility. They do not expect that the free right to vote, to enjoy civic rights, and to be educated, will come in a moment; they do not expect to see the bias and prejudices of years disappear at the blast of a trumpet; but they are absolutely certain that the way for a people to gain their reasonable rights is not by voluntarily throwing them away and insisting that they do not want them; that the way for a people to gain respect is not by continually belittling and ridiculing themselves; that, on the contrary, Negroes must insist continually, in season and out of season, that voting is necessary to modern manhood, that color discrimination is barbarism, and that black boys need education as well as white boys.

In failing thus to state plainly and unequivocally the legitimate demands of their people, even at the cost of opposing an honored leader, the thinking classes of American Negroes would shirk a heavy responsibility,—a responsibility to themselves, a responsibility to the struggling masses, a responsibility to the darker races of men whose future depends so largely on this American experiment, but especially a responsibility to this nation,—this common Fatherland. It is wrong to encourage a man or a people in evil-doing; it is wrong to aid and abet a national crime simply because it is unpopular not to do so. The growing spirit of kindliness and reconciliation between the North and South after the frightful differences of a generation ago ought to be a source of deep congratulation to all, and especially to those whose mistreatment caused the war; but if that reconciliation is to be marked by the industrial slavery and civic death of those same black men, with permanent legislation into a position of inferiority, then those black men, if they are really men, are called upon by every consideration of patriotism and loyalty to oppose such a course by all civilized methods, even though such opposition involves disagreement with Mr. Booker T. Washington. We have no right to sit silently by while the inevitable seeds are sown for a harvest of disaster to our children, black and white.

First, it is the duty of black men to judge the South discriminatingly. The present generation of Southerners are not responsible for the past, and they should not be blindly hated or blamed for it. Furthermore, to no class is the indiscriminate endorsement of the recent course of the South toward Negroes more nauseating than to the best thought of the South. The South is not "solid"; it is a land in the ferment of social change, wherein forces of all kinds are fighting for supremacy; and to praise the ill the South is to-day perpetrating is just as wrong as to condemn the good. Discriminating and broad-minded criticism is what the South needs,—needs it for the sake of her own white sons and daughters, and for the insurance of robust, healthy mental and moral development.

To-day even the attitude of the Southern whites toward the blacks is not, as so many assume, in all cases the same; the ignorant Southerner hates the Negro, the workingmen fear his competition, the money-makers wish to use him as a laborer, some of the educated see a menace in his upward development, while others—usually the sons of the masters—wish to help him to rise. National opinion has enabled this last class to maintain the Negro common schools, and to protect the Negro partially in property, life, and limb. Through the pressure of the money-makers, the Negro is in danger of being reduced to semi-slavery, especially in the country districts; the workingmen, and those of the educated who fear the Negro, have united to disfranchise him, and some have urged his deportation; while the passions of the ignorant are easily aroused to lynch and abuse any black man. To praise this intricate whirl of thought and prejudice is nonsense; to inveigh indiscriminately against "the South" is unjust; but to use the same breath in praising Governor Aycock, exposing Senator Morgan, arguing with Mr. Thomas Nelson Page, and denouncing Senator Ben Tillman, is not only sane, but the imperative duty of thinking black men.

It would be unjust to Mr. Washington not to acknowledge that in several instances he has opposed movements in the South which were unjust to the Negro; he sent memorials to the Louisiana and Alabama constitutional conventions, he has spoken against lynching, and in other ways has openly or silently set his influence against sinister schemes and unfortunate happenings. Notwithstanding this, it is equally true to assert that on the whole the distinct impression left by Mr. Washington's propaganda is, first, that the South is justified in its present attitude toward the Negro because of the Negro's degradation; secondly, that the prime cause of the Negro's failure to rise more quickly is his wrong education in the past; and, thirdly, that his future rise depends primarily on his own efforts. Each of these propositions is a dangerous half-truth. The supplementary truths must never be lost sight of: first, slavery and race-prejudice are potent if not sufficient causes of the Negro's position; second, industrial and common-school training were necessarily slow in planting because they had to await the black teachers trained by higher institutions,—it being extremely doubtful if any essentially different development was possible, and certainly a Tuskegee was unthinkable before 1880; and, third, while it is a great truth to say that the Negro must strive and strive mightily to help himself, it is equally true that unless his striving be not simply seconded, but rather aroused and encouraged, by the initiative of the richer and wiser environing group, he cannot hope for great success.

In his failure to realize and impress this last point, Mr. Washington is especially to be criticised. His doctrine has tended to make the whites, North and South, shift the burden of the Negro problem to the Negro's shoulders and stand aside as critical and rather pessimistic spectators; when in fact the burden belongs to the nation, and the hands of none of us are clean if we bend not our energies to righting these great wrongs.

The South ought to be led, by candid and honest criticism, to assert her better self and do her full duty to the race she has cruelly wronged and is still wronging. The North—her co-partner in guilt—cannot salve her conscience by plastering it with gold. We cannot settle this problem by diplomacy and suaveness, by "policy" alone. If worse come to worst, can the moral fibre of this country survive the slow throttling and murder of nine millions of men?

The black men of America have a duty to perform, a duty stern and delicate,—a forward movement to oppose a part of the work of their greatest leader. So far as Mr. Washington preaches Thrift, Patience, and Industrial Training for the masses, we must hold up his hands and strive with him, rejoicing in his honors and glorying in the strength of this Joshua called of God and of man to lead the headless host. But so far as Mr. Washington apologizes for injustice, North or South, does not rightly value the privilege and duty of voting, belittles the emasculating effects of caste distinctions, and opposes the higher training and ambition of our brighter minds,—so far as he, the South, or the Nation, does this,—we must unceasingly and firmly oppose them. By every civilized and peaceful method we must strive for the rights which the world accords to men, clinging unwaveringly to those great words which the sons of the Fathers would fain forget: "We hold these truths to be self-evident: 'That all men are created equal; that they are endowed by their Creator with certain unalienable rights; that among these are life, liberty, and the pursuit of happiness.'"

Notes

1. From *Childe Harold's Pilgrimage* (1812), by George Gordon, Lord Byron.
2. From "A Great Camp-Meeting in the Promised Land."

2

The Progressive Movement in American Education: A Perspective

Lawrence A. Cremin

In this historical study Mr. Cremin examines the sources of the progressive movement in education and places the movement of educational protest within the context of the social and political
reform of the Progressive Era. John Dewey is seen both as a synthesizer and an originator of
progressive thought in education, and the Progressive Education Association is viewed in a new
perspective.

   Mr. Cremin is Professor of Education at Teachers College, Columbia University. This article is
a section of his forthcoming book dealing with the history of the progressive movement in
American education.

I

The circulation of *The Forum* was climbing in 1892—and no wonder. The stuffy, moribund
New York monthly had seemingly sprung to life under the imaginative editorship of Walter
Hines Page.[1] Energetic, knowledgeable, uncompromising in his journalistic standards, the
progressive young Southerner was running article after article that the would-be conversa-
tionalist simply could not afford to miss: Henry Cabot Lodge and Jacob Schiff on politics; Jane
Addams and Jacob Riis on social reform; and William James on psychical research. Well-nigh
anything *The Forum* printed was likely to be discussed; but Page himself never anticipated the
controversy destined to arise over Joseph Mayer Rice's series on the schools.

   1892 was much like any other year, and Dr. Johnson's injunction about the fatal dullness of
education was as pertinent then as now. Yet Page had been intrigued by Rice's pedagogical
criticism. Apparently all was not right with the nation's much-vaunted schools, and Page, ever
the journalist, sensed news. Moreover, if anyone could come up with some first-rate articles,
it was Rice. Astute, opinionated, and sharp in his judgments, Rice was a young New York pedi-
atrician whose interest in prophylaxis had led him to some searching questions about the city's
schools—questions so pressing that he spent the period between 1888 and 1890 studying

pedagogy at Jena and Leipzig.[2] He returned bearing some fairly definite ideas about a "science of education"—dangerous luggage for a young man of thirty-three—and spent 1891 looking for a means of publicizing them. A series of columns in *Epoch*,[3] a small New York weekly, and a piece in the December *Forum*[4] provided his first opportunities. His pungent writing inevitably attracted comment, and near the end of 1891, Page made him a novel proposal.

On behalf of *The Forum* Rice was to prepare a firsthand appraisal of American public education. From Boston to Washington, from New York to St. Louis, he was to visit classrooms, talk with teachers, attend school board meetings, and interview parents. He was to place "no reliance whatever" on reports by school officials; his goal was to render an objective assessment for the public. The proposal could not have been more welcome. Rice left on January 7, 1892. His tour took him to thirty-six cities; he talked with some 1200 teachers; he returned late in June, his notes crammed with statistics, illustrations, and judgments.[5] The summer was given to writing; and the first article appeared in October. Within a month, he and Page both knew they had taken an angry bull by the horns. By the time the final essay had been published the following June, Rice's name had become a byword—frequently an epithet—to schoolmen across the nation.[6]

Rice's story bore all the earmarks of the journalism destined to make "muckraking" a household word in America. In city after city public apathy, political interference, corruption, and incompetence were conspiring to ruin the schools. A teacher in Baltimore told him: "I formerly taught in the higher grades, but I had an attack of nervous prostration some time ago, and the doctor recommended rest. So I now teach in the primary, because teaching primary children does not tax the mind." A principal in New York, asked whether students were allowed to move their heads, answered: "Why should they look behind when the teacher is in front of them?" A Chicago teacher, rehearsing her pupils in a "concert drill," harangued them with the command: "Don't stop to think, tell me what you know!" In Philadelphia, the "ward bosses" controlled the appointment of teachers and principals; in Buffalo, the city superintendent was the single supervising officer for seven hundred teachers. With alarming frequency the story was the same: political hacks hiring untrained teachers who blindly led their innocent charges in sing-song drill, rote repetition, and meaningless verbiage.

But the picture was not uniformly black; here and there Rice found encouraging departures from the depressing rule. In Minneapolis, "a very earnest and progressive corps of teachers" was broadening the school program around the three R's and dealing sympathetically with children from "even the poorest immigrant homes." In Indianapolis, where politics had been firmly excluded from the management of schools, competent "progressive" teachers were attempting to introduce "the idea of unification" into the curriculum, combining the several subjects "so they may acquire more meaning by being seen in their relations to one another." At LaPorte, Indiana, Rice saw exciting progress in drawing, painting, and clay modelling, as well as encouraging efforts to teach pupils "to be helpful to each other." And finally at Francis Parker's world-famous Cook County Normal School, "one of the most progressive as well as one of the most suggestive schools" he had seen, Rice found examples par excellence of the "all-side" education of children; nature study, art, social activities, and the three R's all taught by an inspired, enthusiastic staff.

The final article in the June *Forum* was a call to action. All citizens could have the life and warmth of the "progressive school" for their children. The way was simple and clear: led by an aroused public, the school system would have to be "absolutely divorced from politics in every sense of the word"; direct, thorough, and scientific supervision would have to be introduced; and teachers would have to endeavor constantly to improve their professional and intellectual competence. "The general educational spirit of the country is progressive," Rice concluded; it remained only for the public in local communities throughout the nation to do the job.

The response to Rice's series could itself be the subject of a fascinating essay. Newspaper reaction was about what one would expect—a rather general sympathy typified, perhaps, by a January editorial in the *Boston Daily Advertiser*: ". . . it must be admitted that the examples which he has cited do show a regrettable condition of affairs, and one that decidedly demands improvement. There is far too much of the mechanical in the existing system, especially in the 'busy work,' which here, as almost everywhere else, means a hindrance rather than a help to child education."[7] The Chicago *Dispatch* thought it "a shame and a disgrace that Chicago's public schools cannot be kept above the level of ward politics," while the Detroit *Free Press* believed Rice's criticisms "so full of sound sense and of suggestion for improvement that they must commend themselves even to those who have been hit the hardest, and result sooner or later in correction of the defects and abuses pointed out."[8]

Much more intriguing, however, was the reaction of the professional press—a reaction which ranged from chilling disdain to near-hysteria. Boston's *Journal of Education* characterized Rice as a young man who had "demonstrated beyond cavil that he is merely a sensational critic. . . ."[9] *Education*, widely read by classroom teachers in New England, ran a searing editorial in December, picturing Rice as a carping journalist who had "recently abandoned the work of physicking his patients for a course in pedagogy in Germany."[10] Comments in succeeding months only elaborated this theme, pillorying the *Forum* series as radical, high-university, expert-type criticism by an intellectual snob who had completely missed the point of American public education.[11]

In New York the editor of *The School Journal* early adopted a characteristically sensible wait-and-see attitude, writing in a November issue: "Dr. Rice has entered a new field. We have said repeatedly that at some time the schools would have the electric light turned on them, and have asked if they were ready. We ask it again."[12] Two months later, after Rice's article on New York had appeared, *The School Journal* was less concerned with illumination. Rice's criticisms were "weak and inconsequential"; if the schools produced results, that was all that could be asked of them.[13] Not to be outdone by its older and more respected competitor, the magazine *School* excoriated the series from the beginning. It interspersed barbed editorials with letters from self-appointed defenders of the schools who contended that Rice's foreign training, lack of classroom experience, inadequate evidence, and anti-public-school bias had rendered him unfit to judge American education.[14] By March the editor of *School* had vowed he would provide the self-styled "expert" no more free advertising by commenting on his errors[15]—a pledge he broke only once (in April) to castigate *The School Journal* for giving "timid, half-hearted support to the cheap criticisms and the charlatanism of an alleged expert in *The Forum*. . . ."[16]

And so the criticism mounted—along with the circulation of *The Forum*. Several months later, after Rice's articles had been published in book form, Nicholas Murray Butler took the opportunity to ponder their total impact—or lack of it—in a perceptive review:[17]

The purpose of this book is excellent. Its results have been meager. Two reasons explain this. The first is that the author's judgments carry no personal weight. He is unknown to

the educationists and school men of this country. The second is that school superintendents, principals, and teachers are to the last degree impatient of criticism and suggestion.
They resent them as a reflection on their personal character. As one man they rush to the
defense. The better among them excuse the worse, and the worse grow abusive. This attitude is sustained by the agents of the more unscrupulous among the schoolbook publishing houses, who are selling hundreds of thousands of worthless old text-books each
year and do not wish to have to replace them with better ones, adapted to new educational methods, until the plates absolutely fall to pieces. They are satisfied with the
schools as they are. The so-called educational journal is another factor. It enthusiastically
belabors any chance critic who comes along, for the happy teacher who absorbs and
applies its patent methods, at a dollar or two a year, must not be disturbed in his happiness. Else he might not want the patent methods any longer—at a dollar or two a year.

After sketching the gist of Rice's findings, Butler concluded: "It is unfair to decry this book
because Dr. Rice is unknown or because he has said and done some foolish things. His criticisms are honestly offered and must be considered on their merits. They are worth having if
they do nothing more than check the national vice of vaingloriousness and the schoolmaster's
habit of exultant boasting."

Rice himself remained undaunted. He continued to write for *The Forum*, and some of his
later articles such as "The Futility of the Spelling Grind" (providing evidence from tests on
33,000 schoolchildren that there is no significant correlation between amount of time devoted
to spelling homework and competence in the high art itself) were widely read and quoted.[18] In
1897 he became editor of *The Forum*—with disheartening results in the business office. Two
more books flowed from his pen—one on *Scientific Management in Education* (1913), the
other on municipal government.[19] He even founded a society for educational research. But
when he died, in 1934, he was virtually unknown, remembered only—when at all—as one of
the founders of the American testing movement. An unfortunate fate for this erstwhile progressive, but an occupational hazard of those who would father reform. For reform movements are notoriously ahistorical in outlook. They look forward rather than back; and when
they do need a history, they frequently prefer the fashioning of ideal ancestors to the acknowledgment of mortals.

II

In one sense, the progressive movement in American education begins with Rice. Why so? He
was certainly not the first to protest the dull, routinized character of the post-Civil-War
schools. Francis W. Parker, called by Dewey the father of progressive education, had undertaken the reform of the Quincy schools as early as the seventies, and while he himself had made
little effort to publicize his work, the "Quincy System" had excited national—indeed, world-
wide—interest. In 1882 Joseph Rodes Buchanan, physician, lecturer, and sometime professor
of medicine, had published a lengthy critique of American schools and colleges called *The New
Education*,[20] a book which the redoubtable old reformer Benjamin O. Flower later called a pioneer work of educational protest in America.[21] Wherein, then, did Rice's ill-fated *Forum* series
constitute a beginning? Largely in three aspects: in their synthetic character—that is, in the
many separate strands of contemporary protest they were able to weave together into a single

reform program; in their perception of the educational problem as national in scope; and in the political sophistication exhibited by their plea for broad public support as the antidote to political corruption and professional incompetence. The progressive movement begins with Rice *precisely because he saw it as a movement.* It is this growing self-consciousness more than anything else which sets the progressivism of the nineties apart from its sources in preceding decades.

There is currently afoot a simple story of the rise of progressivism in American education—one that has fed mercilessly on the fears of anxious parents and the hostilities of suspicious conservatives. In it John Dewey—somewhat like Abou ben Adhem—figuratively awakes one morning with a new vision of the American school; the vision is progressive education. Over the years, with the aid of a dedicated group of crafty professional lieutenants at Teachers College, Columbia University, he is able to foist the vision off on the unsuspecting American people. The story usually ends with a plea for the exorcising of this devil from our midst and a return to the ways of the fathers.[22] The morality play has always been an important brand of American political rhetoric—used well by reformers and reactionaries alike. The point is never to confuse it with history.

Actually, one of the most pervasive characteristics of the progressive movement in American education, from its very beginning, has been its completely pluralistic, frequently contradictory character. Consider for a moment merely a few of the many themes of educational protest vigorously sounded during the years around the turn of the century. There was the demand for manual training and vocational education, one which combined in a characteristic American way the political claims of an expanding industrial economy with an older Pestalozzian idea that worthy education deals with "whole children"—hands and hearts as well as heads. Hence the curious joining during the 1880s of Calvin Woodward's contentious rhetoric[23] about manual training being economically useless but educationally important, to the more mundane demands of urban workingmen for "practical preparation for life."

There was the continuing pressure from settlement workers, sensitive to the pedagogical vacuums created by broken homes and working parents, compellingly aware of the education of the streets, and deeply convinced of the need for school programs in domestic science, manual arts, and child care. It was all well and good for beleaguered boards of education to protest that schools could not do everything, that teachers had not been trained, that money was not available. Somehow the settlement workers kept talking in high-flown phrases about popular need, public welfare and social reform.[24]

Then there were the immigrants—the millions who crowded the teeming ghettos that were "the breeding places of social, moral, and ideological disease." They would have to be "Americanized"—a process which appeared simpler to nativist orators than to the slum teachers who found themselves giving hundreds of baths each week.[25] Being an American was more than a matter of mouthing McGuffey, they found; and although the syllabi said nothing about baths, there were the children and there were the lice. Little wonder that protests about the irrelevancy of education multiplied and pedagogical tracts began to discuss health, citizenship, and family living along with reading, writing, and arithmetic.[26]

There were voices, too, from the universities. As Charles Donovan has pointed out in a penetrating study of the social sciences and education before 1900,[27] there was growing agreement among liberal sociologists and economists that universal popular education was the key to rational social progress. But it could never be routinized mass education; it would have to be schooling "in contact with reality"—critical, unified, and charged with social meaning. "The teacher who realizes his social function," wrote sociologist Albion Small of Chicago in 1897, "will not be satisfied with passing children to the next grade. He will read his success only in the record of men and women who go from the school eager to explore wider and deeper these social relations, and zealous to do their part in making a better future. We are dupes of faulty ideas if we imagine that schools can do much for social progress until they are motivated by this insight and this temper."[28]

From university lecture halls and laboratories there also flowed radical new views of the child and the ways in which he learns. Psychologist G. Stanley Hall and his colleagues at Clark University were publishing mountains of data in the columns of *Pedagogical Seminary* about the nature and growth of children. Applying the exciting new theory of evolution to child study, Hall concluded that the development of the child follows laws of its own—laws with which teachers had best not interfere. And then in a series of biting attacks on traditional schooling, he stood pedagogy on its head with a romantic Rousseauan notion of a *pedocentric* (Hall loved to invent words!) school. "The guardians of the young," he proclaimed, "should strive first of all to keep out of nature's way, and to prevent harm, and should merit the proud title of defenders of the happiness and rights of children."[29] His injunction was both stirring and vague—the first requisites of any successful slogan.

At Chicago, Dewey, Mead, and Angell were laying the groundwork of a functionalist theory of behavior destined to play a substantial part in breaking the hold of Titchener's structuralism on American psychology. Borrowing James's notion of habit, they viewed learning as the active enterprise of a total organism in a "genuine social situation"—an enterprise in which the modification of behavior and attitudes was the abiding outcome. The implications for singsong drill and heads which did not move "because teacher was in front" were rather obvious, as Dewey pointed out in a number of popular pamphlets[30] as well as in the more systematic *How We Think* (1910).

At Columbia James's ideas were wrought into an even more activist and empirical psychology by his student Edward L. Thorndike. Beginning his investigations into animal learning with chickens in Mrs. James's basement, Thorndike soon progressed to cats, dogs, mice, and monkeys out at Western Reserve University. There, the imaginative young James Earl Russell found him, and "satisfied that he was worth trying out with humans," brought him to Teachers College.[31] In a brilliant career spanning forty years Thorndike instructed a whole generation of American educators in the now-familiar doctrines of connectionism. Once again, the clash with older theories of learning was head-on, as Thorndike himself pointed out in his continuing concern for individual differences and his classic destruction of faculty psychology.

Thorndike's total influence on American education has yet to be assessed; we know it is both prodigious and various.[32] One associates him with the testing movement, with the education of the intellectually gifted, and with the early study of adult learning. Less widely recognized, perhaps, is his influence on school administration. George D. Strayer recounts that it was in Thorndike's classes that he first grasped the vision of a "scientific school administration" which would combine the best of sociology, education, and government. Although Strayer's school surveys were by no means the first in America—the 1898 survey of the Chicago schools was for years used as a textbook in school administration courses[33]—they were among the first to be rooted in an explicit administrative theory. This theory, which came increasingly into vogue around 1900,[34] held that the schools belong to the people, that the people should enjoy a high degree of autonomy in managing them; that the primary problem of good school management is its divorce from ordinary politics; that this can best be accomplished by centralizing educational authority in a strong, expert superintendent of schools, reserving business and financial matters to a small, public-spirited responsible board of education. The curse of traditional school management had been corruption, incompetence, irresponsibility, and—worst of all—inefficiency. The expert survey was to be the prime device for building the efficient school system.

We have seen something like the main propositions of this theory at the heart of Rice's recommendations as early as 1893. Even more intriguing, perhaps—and a subject which needs much more careful study—is their close resemblance to the more general ideas of political progressivism. Thus, in his classic study of *The Progressive Movement* (1915), Benjamin Parke DeWitt mentions the removal of corrupt or special influence, home rule by small boards readily answerable to citizens, and efficiency as three of the main planks in the platform of progressive municipal reform. While few of the calls for municipal reform between 1895 and 1910 included lengthy discussions of education, the omission is probably due more to widespread progressive agreement on the advisability of separating education and politics than it is to lack of concern.[35] In reality, school reform and municipal reform were frequently if not always facets of the same progressive movement; to understand them as such is to expand significantly our comprehension of progressivism both in politics and in education.

Finally, mention should be made of the various currents of protest stirring within the teaching profession itself. To begin, here more than elsewhere the influence of European pedagogy made its strongest mark. Thus, many who had never seen Hall's *Pedagogical Seminary* regularly drank at the fountain of *The Kindergarten Magazine*, imbibing pure Froebel under the label of "progressivism" or more frequently, "the new education." Hence the currency of such Idealist ideas as the inborn divinity of the child, the centrality of his growth, and the importance of play, art, music, expression, and manual training in his proper educational development. Others studied Francis W. Parker's *Talks on Pedagogics* (1894)—one of the earliest native efforts to state a full-blown philosophy of progressive education and a fascinating potpourri of Froebel, Herbart, and American transcendentalism. Here they found not only the pedagogical methods Parker had introduced at Quincy—with their dramatic attention to the "individual needs" of children—but a stirring defense of these methods as the only proper bulwarks of a free, democratic America.[36] Still others, unsung and unremembered, heard the hundreds of reformist speeches delivered each year to teachers' institutes, professional meetings, and citizen groups, speeches which talked of a hoped-for better school just over the pedagogical horizon.

In the colleges, too, there was talk of a "new education," with Charles W. Eliot and George Herbert Palmer using the phrase repeatedly in describing Harvard's experiments with scientific studies and the elective system.[37] At Chicago, Thorstein Veblen was less sanguine about any genuine freedom in the American university until its deliverance from the hands of the businessman—the theme of his pungent treatise *The Higher Learning in America* (1918). And at Wisconsin, President Charles Van Hise, in whose appointment LaFollette had played such a significant part, was vigorously extending the University's role in the Progressive state administration by taking knowledge to the people for use in solving their economic, social, and political problems. "I shall never be content," he wrote, "until the beneficent influence of the University reaches every family in the State. This is my ideal of a State University."[38]

The themes of protest, then, were many and various. "Progressive education" meant different things to different progressives as each charted his course to the pedagogical promised land. Moreover, the diversity of the protest was paralleled at every point by the diversity of the people who sounded it. Once again, the relation between educational reform and the broader progressive movement of which it was a part needs far deeper study. For example, Eric Goldman's point in *Rendezvous with Destiny* about political protest coming "from the top down" as well as "from the bottom up" is compellingly pertinent in education. In Baltimore during the nineties, for example, the Federation of Labor and the Knights of Labor were frequently joined by the energetic ladies of the Arundell Good Government Club in their demands for curriculum revision, a compulsory education law, and a political housecleaning in the Board of Education.[39] Moreover, whenever more general municipal reform movements did appear, they frequently developed educational adjuncts. Thus in New York, the women's auxiliary of Club E of the Federation of Good Government Clubs in 1895 actually organized itself into the Public Education Association, a group which down to the present has militated for better programs and administration in the City's schools.[40] In 1898 eleven such organizations held the first Conference of Eastern Public Education Associations, devoting several days to discussions of overcrowding, bad lighting, and poor sanitary conditions in school buildings, the education of juvenile offenders, the reform of school board politics, and ways of arousing public interest in education. The meetings were filled with familiar figures in the municipal reform movements of the era.[41]

Those working with the Social Problem—what John Spargo called "that hideous phantasmagoria of hunger, disease, vice, crime, and despair"—were also inevitably thrust into the stream of educational protest. New York's Lillian Wald gave substantial attention to education in *The House on Henry Street* (1915); so did Jane Addams in *Twenty Years at Hull House* (1910). Indeed, when Miss Addams was appointed to the Chicago school board by a progressive mayor in 1905, she actually set out to convert the schools into miniature social settlements. "Our schools," she wrote, "must give the children better and truer standards for judging life. Life does not ask whether a man can read and write, so much as it asks whether he can use whatever facilities have been given him."[42] In New York, Jacob Riis did much to publicize the inadequacy and lifelessness of slum schools in *Children of the Poor* (1892), *A Ten Year War* (1900) and *The Battle with the Slum* (1902); while John Spargo wrote poignantly about "the tragedy and folly of attempting to educate the hungry, ill-fed school child" in *The Bitter Cry of the Children* (1906). In the South the same Walter Hines Page who had opened *The Forum's* columns to Joseph Mayer Rice called for educational reconstruction as the key remedy for the region's social and economic ills; and widely quoted addresses such as "The Forgotten Man" (1897) and "The School That Built a Town" (1901) paved the way for the dramatic work of the great philanthropic foundations during the early years of the present century.[43]

To point to the many different sorts of people who gave voice to early educational protest is in no way to deny the widespread quickening of reformist sentiment within the profession itself. By 1894, progressive teachers already had a native American hero from their own ranks: Francis W. Parker. Parker was not a "university expert"; himself a master teacher, he worked magnificently with children; and he had fought and won battles with "reactionary interests" in Ohio, in Quincy, and in the continuing guerrilla warfare at the Cook County Normal School.[44] Even the redoubtable Rice had acknowledged him to be the example par excellence of the progressive spirit in education.

From the hallowed halls of Harvard came a quite different call for reform: Charles W. Eliot's sharp attacks on the wastefulness of secondary and collegiate education. If Parker was the hero of those who loved children and saw them broken and bored in the elementary schools, Eliot was the hero of those who loved knowledge and saw it dehydrated, packaged, and monotonously parcelled out to generations of unwilling adolescents. His essays on *Educational Reform* (1898) ponder "the unity of educational reform," "the grammar school of the future," and "liberty in education"; they place him squarely in the ranks of those who over the centuries have cried out against schooling which provides everything but education.

Fully to grasp the sweep of the progressive spirit, however, we must acknowledge innumerable lesser figures who unassumingly—and frequently with little moral or financial support—undertook the work of reform. New York's Superintendent William Maxwell in 1909 wrote eloquently of a now-forgotten principal named Hugh O'Neill:[45]

> He was a constant visitor in the wretched homes of his pupils. He was a familiar figure in every street and alley. Careless, negligent parents he threatened or cajoled. He found means to clothe and feed cold and hungry children. He found employment after school hours for those who could continue in school no other way. He discovered that so-called athletic clubs were hiring the larger boys in his school to pummel each other into insensibility in the presence of hundreds of brutalized men; but it took only one visit from him to each club to break it up. He saw that there were children to whom books did not appeal, and for them he devised hand work. He was, I believe, the first man in the United States to introduce genuine manual training into an elementary school. His school became, as every public school ought to be, a social centre from which uplifting influences radiated.

Similarly forgotten schoolmen in Illinois and Iowa were celebrated in *The World's Work* for 1904.[46] O.J. Kern, Superintendent at Winnebago, had started an imaginative Farmer Boys' Experiment Club "to interest the children in common farm animals and plants" as well as a Home Culture Club to teach girls "home sanitation and decoration, the effects of bad air and poor light, and the hygienic furnishing of sleeping rooms." His school had become a veritable community center for the county. Superintendent W.N. Clifford of Council Bluffs had gone to the trouble of importing products from all over the world to enliven his geography program; he was taking his teachers on trips to cities near and far, making a genuine effort to give them firsthand experience as the basis for classroom instruction. The contrast with the sorry, boss-ridden schools of New York and Philadelphia was striking.

Thus did the "progressive spirit" manifest itself on all rungs of the academic ladder and in all segments of the teaching profession. Eliot campaigned in his way, Parker in his, and Hugh O'Neill in his. Still others, uncelebrated by their contemporaries and forgotten by history, pioneered in unnamed schools across the country, quietly building a patchwork of tiny oases to dot the pedagogical desert of the nineties. Diversity of protest and protestor was the theme; it was a diversity destined to leave its ineradicable mark on the progressive education movement.

Nowhere is the diversity more eloquently documented than in the now-famous *Schools of To-Morrow*, published in 1915 by John Dewey and his daughter, Evelyn. Over the years, Dewey's continuing sensitivity to the meaning of new pedagogical currents, his widely publicized work at the Laboratory School he and Mrs. Dewey had founded in 1896, his reputation as a tough-minded analyst of pedagogical schemes, and his unfailing support of progressive causes had combined to make him increasingly an acknowledged spokesman of the progressive movement. *Schools of To-Morrow* did much to secure this image of him in the public mind. Written neither as a textbook nor as a dogmatic exposition of "the new," it was designed "to show what actually happens when schools start out to put into practice, each in its own way, some of the theories that have been pointed to as the soundest and best ever since Plato, to be then laid politely away as precious portions of our 'intellectual heritage.'" The volume is a fascinating collection of glimpses—into Marietta Johnson's Organic School at Fairhope, Alabama, Junius L. Meriam's experimental school at the University of Missouri, the Francis Parker School at Chicago, Caroline Pratt's Play School in New York, the Kindergarten at Teachers College, Columbia University, and the public schools of Gary and Indianapolis. Within ten years it had gone through fourteen printings, unusual for any book, unheard-of for a book about education!

Even granting the disclaimers in his preface, it would have been too much to expect philosopher Dewey to refrain completely from injecting a general principle or two into his running commentary as tour guide through tomorrow's schools. And the perceptive reader might well have guessed that lengthy discourses on "education as natural development," "industrialism and educational readjustment," "freedom and individuality," and "the relation of school and community" presaged a somewhat more systematic theoretical venture. It was only a year until the appearance of *Democracy and Education*.[47] Dewey had spent his life as a philosopher seeking out and destroying dualism. What more characteristically Deweyan enterprise than a *magnum opus* which would weld the diverse strands of a quarter-century of educational protest into an integral, systematic theory. Such was the enterprise of *Democracy and Education*—a volume which by its very presence made 1916 a turning point in the progressive movement. For if the pluralism of prior years had made its indelible mark, the orchestration provided by Dewey could not help but lend new character. It would be only three years until the Progressive Education Association would come into being and take the orchestration as its theme song—even as Dewey himself refused to serve as conductor.

Dewey will never be famous as a stylist;[48] even so, *Schools of To-Morrow* and *Democracy and Education* would undoubtedly have made their mark on American pedagogical thought. Yet the process was undeniably hastened by the pen of the brilliant young critic, Randolph Silliman Bourne.[49] In the very first issue of Croly's *New Republic*, he had inveighed against the artificiality and dullness of the American schoolroom; his article only anticipated a steady flow of sparkling educational commentary. Whether he was excitedly reporting on Superintendent Wirt's imaginative innovations at Gary,[50] vigorously expounding Dewey's pedagogical ideas, or sharply attacking "wasted years" of "puzzle education" in the schools, Bourne was constantly performing a larger function; almost single-handed, he used the columns of *The New Republic* to popularize educational protest among progressive intellectuals. His articles, the most lucid nonprofessional expositions of educational reform between 1914 and 1917, command for him an enduring place in the progressive movement. While Max Lerner has perhaps exaggerated in arguing that Dewey's reputation derives in no small measure from Bourne's "ardent discipleship," Bourne's efforts were of singular value in putting progressives into touch with progressive education.[51]

The war intervened, and a society at war has little time for educational protest. The mathematics of ballistics, the horticulture of the victory garden, and the hygiene of civilian defense quickly overshadow talk about the integral development of head, heart, and hand; the quest for victory obscures prior but less pressing claims. For two years reform was in eclipse; among progressives attention veered sharply to the momentous issue of pacifism as the inevitable call for unity was sounded. The aftermath of war, however, brought hope; it would be different for the children in the better world ahead. Once again the spotlight was on reform, though reform, like America, had changed.

III

1919 brought progressive education an association.[52] A young man named Stanwood Cobb had become interested in the schools of tomorrow and had taken the lead, along with a number of like-minded Washington ladies, in forming an organization to advance the cause of educational reform. We are told they cast about for a name, rejecting "The Association for the Advancement of Experimental Schools" and "The Association for the Advancement of the New Schools" in favor of "The Association for the Advancement of Progressive Education." The winter of 1918–19 was given to drafting a statement of principles ("The aim of Progressive Education is the freest and fullest development of the individual, based upon the scientific study of his mental, physical, spiritual, and social characteristics and needs") and a plan of organization; and on April 4, 1919, in the hall of the Washington public library, "upward of a hundred people" launched the new association on its historic career. There were addresses by Cobb, Eugene Randolph Smith (Principal of the Park School in Baltimore), Anne E. George (Director of Washington's Montessori Schools), Marietta Johnson, and Otis Caldwell of the Lincoln School at Teachers College, Columbia University. Charles W. Eliot was elected honorary president, Dewey having declined. The participants left with the fires of reform burning brightly; and from that time forward—for better or for worse, as the preachers say—the fortunes of progressive education were inextricably wedded to the fortunes of the Progressive Education Association.[53]

This is not the place for a lengthy history of the PEA—much as one is needed. Suffice it to say that the Association quickly secured its place in the world of American education. Its membership climbed steadily, passing 5,000 in 1927 and reaching a peak of 10,500 in 1938. It inaugurated a quarterly, *Progressive Education*, which after 1924 quickly became both the voice of the organization and the American clearing house for educational experiments of every conceivable kind. It sought out and cemented ties with the New Education Fellowship, thus lending an international flavor to its work. As the twenties drew to a close there was little doubt that the PEA had done much in its own way to maintain a "progressive temper" in a decade when progressivism was so often in eclipse.

During the 1930s, aided by well over a million dollars in foundation money, the Association accelerated its efforts to reorganize secondary school programs, to promote intercultural education, to secure wiser use of human and physical resources, and to clarify and advance educational freedom on a wide front. An eight-year study involving thirty secondary schools and over two hundred colleges was undertaken to study empirically the educational effects of greater flexibility in high school programs; it typified the Association's widespread attempts to gain more general public acceptance of its viewpoint. There were conferences, summer institutes, and workshops for teachers; there were commissions and committees galore whose enthusiastic but frequently interminable deliberations could not help but leave their mark on a whole generation of American educational leaders. And slowly there were results as this or that segment of the Association's program was adopted in one or another of the nation's more important school systems. The late thirties saw the PEA in its prime; and though its membership never included more than an infinitesimal segment of the teaching profession, its influence on pedagogical thought and practice was profound. In the minds of many, the Association *was* progressive education.

But was it?[54] To raise the question is to suggest the significant differences which distinguish social movements from the organizations designed to advance them; it is to ponder what the church is to religion, what the party is to ideology. There is no doubt of the immeasurable service the PEA performed for the progressive movement in American education. It gave the movement unity, structure, voice, and visible form; it infused the movement with vitality and enthusiasm; and it provided the movement with leadership. What Bourne had done for the intellectuals in *The New Republic*, the PEA did for teachers at large in the columns of *Progressive Education*. In pamphlets, books, conferences, conventions, and committees the Association spread the word. And it measured its success in the slowly changing character of the American schoolroom.

But these services, however valuable, came at the almost inevitable price of parochialism and partisanship. The Association was committed to popularization, and popularization is rarely achieved by balanced, abstruse arguments. The popularizer seeks pungency and simplicity; the slogan soon replaces the extended discussion. Of course, the PEA was the first to contend that "progressive education" might be seen whole in Mr. Dewey's *Democracy and Education*. But *Democracy and Education*, however brilliant, is a long, involved, and frequently ambiguous book. Teachers were busy and parents were busier. Some shorter summing up, some statement of key ideas, was needed. And so, despite continuing protestations that progressive education was experimental and could not be defined, the inevitable definition occurred.

Even the sincerest leaders rarely see a movement whole, and as the work of defining went forward, certain strands of the larger movement were gradually overshadowed. During the twenties, as the intellectual *avant garde* became fascinated with the arts in general and Freud in particular, social reformism was virtually eclipsed by the rhetoric of child-centered pedagogy.[55] During the thirties, when influential groups within the profession sought to tie progressive education more closely to political progressivism,[56] the Association was literally racked by a paralyzing partisanship from which it never really recovered.[57] After World War II the added curse of inertness cast its pall over the enterprise.[58] By 1955 the enthusiasm, the money, and the members were gone; all that remained were the slogans.[59]

Even more significant, perhaps, was an inevitable concomitant of the effort to define: the continuing presence after 1919 of progressive currents which the Association refused to countenance. Upton Sinclair's *Goose-Step* (1922) and *Goslings* (1924) were ignored.[60] So was the Scopes trial (1925)—a veritable crisis of the soul in modern education. So was the much-publicized political attack on Superintendent McAndrew of Chicago (1927). So, too, were the reforms of Alexander Meiklejohn at Amherst and at the Experimental College of the University of Wisconsin.[61] By the thirties the CCC and the NYA could touch the lives of millions and yet draw only passing comment from the PEA.[62] They were progressivism to be sure; but they were not really "progressive education."

In sum, then, the PEA—for all its genuine accomplishment—was not the progressive movement. To advance this proposition is to rethink the whole recent history of American education, for it propels our interest beyond the excitement—but the relatively limited compass—of the work at Shady Hill, Beaver Country Day, Lincoln, and Winnetka to a concern with the diversity and fullness of the larger progressive movement. And even more important, perhaps, it recasts our perception of the present. For if the Association was not the progressive movement, the movement may yet be alive; the embers of a "new progressivism" may well be glowing in the ashes of the old.

Notes

1. The standard source on Page is Burton J. Hendrick, *The Life and Letters of Walter H Page.* Garden City: Doubleday, Page, 1925. 3 vols. Chapter II of the first volume deals with Page's career as a journalist.
2. A short biography of Rice appears in *The National Cyclopaedia of American Biography*, Vol. XII, pp. 203–4. The obituary in the *New York Times*, June 25, 1934 is also informative.
3. The series ran from October 23 through December 25, 1891. See *Epoch*, Vol. X (1891), pp. 179–82; 196–98; 212–15; 228–30; 244–46; 261–65; 282–85; 301–2; 320–22; 336–38.
4. "Need School Be a Blight to Child-Life?" *The Forum*, Vol. XII (1891–92); pp. 529–35.
5. *The Forum*, Vol. XIV (1892–93), pp. 145–46.
6. The articles ran in nine consecutive issues from October, 1892 through June, 1893. See *The Forum*, Vol. XIV (1892–93), pp. 145–58; 293–309; 429–44; 616–30; 753–67; Vol. XV (1893), pp. 31–42; 200–15; 362–76; 504–18. They were subsequently republished as *The Public-School System of the United States.* New York: Century, 1893.
7. *Boston Daily Advertiser*, January 27, 1893, p. 4.
8. Both quotations are taken from a series of extracts on "Dr. Rice's Visits" quoted in *The School Journal*, Vol. XLVI (1893), p. 450.
9. *Journal of Education*, Vol. XXXVII (1893), p. 72.
10. *Education*, Vol. XIII (1892–93), p. 245.
11. *Ibid.*, pp. 306–7; 354–57; 377–78; 501–3; 567.
12. *The School Journal*, Vol. XLV (1892), p. 444.
13. *Ibid.*, Vol. XLVI (1893), p. 153.
14. *School*, Vol. IV (1893), pp. 180; 193; 199; 210; 211; 250; 260. Typical of the defenders was Henry G. Schneider, a drawing teacher in New York's Grammar School 90. Several of his letters appeared both in *School* and in *Education* during the winter of 1892–93. As a rule they were sensible, forthright, and well-written. See *School*, Vol. IV (1893), pp. 193; 250; 260; *Education*, Vol. XIII (1892–93), pp. 354–57.
15. *School*, Vol. IV (1893), p. 260.
16. *Ibid.*, p. 322.
17. *Educational Review*, Vol. VI (1893), pp. 498–503.
18. *The Forum*, Vol. XXIII (1897), pp. 163–72.
19. The one on municipal government was a plea for scientific public administration called *The People's Government.* Philadelphia: Winston, 1915. Rice also published a *Rational Spelling Book* for the schools in 1898.
20. Boston: published by The Author, 1882.
21. B.O. Flower, *Progressive Men, Women, and Movements of the Past Twenty-Five Years.* Boston: New Arena, 1914, pp. 208–10.
22. The theme runs through Milo F. McDonald's *American Education: The Old, the Modern, and the "New."* New York: American Education Association, 1952. It is a view by no means confined to the lunatic fringe of reaction in American pedagogy.

23. Calvin Woodward, *Manual Training in Education*. London: Scott, 1890. Although published in England, the volume deals entirely with the American situation. Woodward also spoke and published widely in the United States.

24. Morris I. Berger's study of "The Immigrant, the Settlement, and the Public School," a 1956 Ph.D. Thesis at Columbia University, probes deeply into the influence of the settlements on educational thought and policy. For an excellent recent commentary on the place of the settlement in the larger progressive movement, see Arthur Mann, "British Social Thought and American Reformers of the Progressive Era," *Mississippi Valley Historical Review*, Vol. XLII (1955–56), pp. 672–92. It should also be pointed out that numerous other social movements, closely related to the settlement, pressed toward similar educational goals. Typical is the work of Joseph Lee, social worker, organizer of the Massachusetts Civic League, and father of the recreation movement in the United States, who advocated playgrounds, boys' clubs, baths, gymnasiums, and vacation schools as part of the regular educational program. See his *Constructive and Preventive Philanthropy*. New York: Macmillan, 1902 and *Play in Education*. New York: Macmillan, 1915.

25. Adele Marie Shaw, "The True Character of New York Public Schools," *The World's Work*, Vol. VII (1903–4), pp. 4207–8.

26. The problem is dealt with in a penetrating article by Alan M. Thomas, Jr., "American Education and the Immigrant," *Teachers College Record*, Vol. LV (1953–54), pp. 253–67. See also Isaac B. Berkson, *Theories of Americanization*. New York: Teachers College, Columbia University, 1920, and my own essay, "The Revolution in American Secondary Education: 1893–1918," *Teachers College Record*, Vol. LVI (1954–55), pp. 295–308.

27. Charles Francis Donovan, S.J., "Education in American Social Thought, 1865–1900." Unpublished Ph.D. Thesis, Yale University, 1948.

28. Albion Small, "The Demands of Sociology upon Pedagogy," *The American Journal of Sociology*, Vol. II (1897), p. 851.

29. G. Stanley Hall, "The Ideal School as Based on Child Study," *The Forum*, Vol. XXXII (1901–2), pp. 24–25. Hall's influence on progressive education is prodigious, but he is largely forgotten by contemporary educationists. Fred N. Kerlinger weakened an otherwise perceptive article on "The Origin of the Doctrine of Permissiveness in American Education" in the November, 1956 issue of *Progressive Education* by giving no attention whatever to Hall. In this connection it is also well to note the fascinating similarity between Hall's proposals and those later advanced by Freudians. There is no doubt that the child study movement helped pave the way for the enthusiastic reception given Freudian pedagogical ideas during the twenties. For a history of the child-study movement, see Wilbur Harvey Dutton, "The Child-Study Movement in America from Its Origin (1880) to the Organization of the Progressive Education Association (1920)." Unpublished Ed.D. Thesis Stanford University, 1945. The only extant study of the movement, it is unfortunately largely descriptive.

30. See, for example, *My Pedagogic Creed*. New York: Kellogg, 1897; *The School and Society*. Chicago: University of Chicago Press, 1899; and *The Child and the Curriculum*. Chicago: University of Chicago Press, 1902. *The School and Society* was probably one of the most widely read educational treatises of the period.

31. See James Earl Russell, *Founding Teachers College*. New York; Teachers College, Columbia University, 1937, p. 53.

32. A brief appraisal and a bibliography are given by Robert S. Woodworth in "Edward Lee Thorndike, 1874–1949," National Academy of Sciences, *Biographical Memoirs*, Vol. XXVII (1952), pp. 209–37. See also, H. Gordon Hullfish, *Aspects of Thorndike's Psychology in their Relation to Educational Theory and Practice*. Columbus: Ohio State University Press, 1926. Penetrating discussions of Hall, Dewey, and Thorndike are included in Merle Curti, *The Social Ideas of American Educators*. New York: Scribner's, 1935.

33. *Report of the Educational Commission of the City of Chicago.* Chicago: 1899.

34. See, for example, Truman A. DeWeese, "Better City School Administration," *Educational Review,* Vol. XX (1900), pp. 61–71.

35. The fact that different professors in different schools of the university taught the two subjects and independently wrote tracts on them might also be held accountable. An excellent example of a work which includes a discussion of education is Charles Zeublin, *American Municipal Progress.* New York: Macmillan, 1902. Zueblin was professor of sociology at the University of Chicago.

36. This argument became a strong one in the development of the early vocational guidance movement between 1900 and 1910. For contemporary sources, see Frank Parsons, *Choosing a Vocation.* Boston: Houghton Mifflin, 1909 and Meyer Bloomfield, *The Vocational Guidance of Youth.* Boston: Houghton Mifflin, 1911. Parsons, a pioneer in the guidance movement, is a significant figure in the history of American reform. He ran for the mayoralty of Boston in 1895 with Populist and Socialist support; he was active in the municipal reform movement; and in his later years he also interested himself in settlement work. For a history of the early guidance movement, see Ruth Beverly Wolf and Ruth Elizabeth Barry, "A History of the Guidance-Personnel Movement in Education." Unpublished Ed.D. Thesis, Teachers College, Columbia University, 1955.

37. Charles W. Eliot, "The New Education: Its Organization," *Atlantic Monthly,* Vol. XXIII (1869), pp. 203–20; 358–67; and George Herbert Palmer, *The New Education.* Cambridge: Houghton, Mifflin, 1885. For a general treatment of progressivism in higher education see R. Freeman Butts, *The College Charts Its Course.* New York: McGraw Hill, 1939.

38. Merle Curti and Vernon Carstensen, *The University of Wisconsin, 1848–1925.* Madison: University of Wisconsin Press, 1949. Vol. II, pp. 88–9. In connection with progressivism in the state universities mention should be made of Seaman Knapp's work, first at Iowa State Agricultural College and later with the United States Department of Agriculture. His idea of the demonstration farm literally revolutionized both American agriculture and American agricultural education. Knapp's influence has been too long ignored by historians of American education. See Joseph Cannon Bailey, *Seaman A. Knapp: Schoolmaster of American Agriculture.* New York: Columbia University Press, 1945.

39. See the excellent chapter on education in Charles Hirschfeld's *Baltimore, 1870–1890: Studies in Social History.* Baltimore: Johns Hopkins Press, 1941.

40. *First Annual Report of the Public Education Association.* New York: 1895.

41. *Fourth Annual Report of the Public Education Association,* New York; 1898. The societies developed into quite a movement in the East. See the extended discussion in *The School Journal,* Vol. LXXIV (1907), pp. 395–404 and in Howard W. Nudd, "Organized Citizen Effort in Behalf of Public Education," *Annals,* Vol. 105, pp. 58–63.

42. James Weber Linn, *Jane Addams: A Biography.* New York: Appleton-Century, 1935, p. 235.

43. The essays were recently reprinted under the title, *The School That Built a Town.* New York: Harper, 1952.

44. See Ida Heffron, *Francis Wayland Parker.* Los Angeles: Deach, 1934, and Edward Dangler, "The Educational Philosophy of Francis W. Parker," Unpublished Ph.D. Thesis, New York University, 1939.

45. W. H. Maxwell, "Stories from the Lives of Real Teachers," *The World's Work,* Vol. XVIII (1909), pp. 11877–78.

46. Walter Hines Page was then editing *The World's Work.* In 1903, apparently seeking circulation, he sent Adele Marie Shaw on a school-appraisal expedition similar to Rice's a decade before. Her series was much like the earlier one in *The Forum* except in its almost total failure to stimulate controversy. It testifies eloquently to the persistence of the conditions Rice had exposed in the early nineties. See *The World's Work,* Vol. VII (1903–4), pp. 4204–21; 4460–66; 4540–53; Vol. VIII (1904), pp. 4795–98; 4883–94; 4996–5004; 5244–54; 5405–14; Vol. IX (1904–5), pp. 5480–85.

Kern's work was not an isolated example, and it illustrates well the rural aspects of the progressive movement in education. See the far-reaching educational recommendations in the report of Theodore Roosevelt's Commission on Country Life (1909).

47. John Dewey, *Democracy and Education*. New York: Macmillan, 1916. Dewey himself sensed that some of his genius lay in his ability sensitively to orchestrate the progressive currents about him. See his gracious remarks on the occasion of his seventieth birthday celebration in *John Dewey: The Man and His Philosophy*. Cambridge: Harvard University Press, 1930, pp. 173–81.

48. Justice Holmes once said of *Experience and Nature*: "Although Dewey's book is incredibly ill written, it seemed to me after several rereadings to have a feeling of intimacy with the inside of the cosmos that I found unequaled. So me-thought God would have spoken had He been inarticulate but keenly desirous to tell you how it was." Mark DeWolfe Howe (Ed.), *Holmes-Pollock Letters*. Cambridge: Harvard University Press, 1941, Vol. II, p. 287.

49. For Bourne's important role see Louis Filler, *Randolph Bourne*. Washington: American Council on Public Affairs, 1943, as well as Bourne's own books, *The Gary Plan*. Boston: Houghton Mifflin, 1916 and *Education and Living*. New York: Century, 1917.

50. Bourne always thought of Gary as the embodiment of progressive education, interesting in view of the tendency during the twenties for the movement to become almost exclusively identified with upper-middle-class independent or suburban schools.

51. See Louis Filler, *op. cit.* p. 68.

52. My effort here is not to carry the history of the progressive movement down to the present; it is rather to suggest a new perspective for studying progressivism during the recent period.

53. The early history of the Association is given in Robert Holmes Beck, "American Progressive Education, 1875–1930." Unpublished Ph.D. Thesis, Yale University, 1942 and Berdine Jackman Bovard, "A History of the Progressive Education Association, 1919–1939." Unpublished Ph.D. Thesis, University of California at Berkeley, 1941. Of the two the Beck study is by far superior.

54. Neither Beck nor Bovard really raises the question. Both go to the nineteenth century and earlier for the roots of progressive education, but both accept rather uncritically the contention in Stanwood Cobb's manuscript history of the PEA's founding that the phrase "progressive education" was not used before 1919. Beck repeats the assertion in a recent volume entitled *The Three R's Plus*. Minneapolis: University of Minnesota Press, 1956, p. 4. The assertion is incorrect, but it reflects the almost universal belief that the PEA and the progressive movement in education were virtually identical.

55. William Heard Kilpatrick did devote his 1926 Kellogg Lectures at Rutgers University to *Education for a Changing Civilization*; and by 1929 George S. Counts had already published *School and Society in Chicago* and *Secondary Education and Industrialism*. Nevertheless, the characteristic work of the era was *The Child-Centered School* by Harold Rugg and Ann Shumaker. Yonkers: World Book, 1928.

56. Although the thirties saw the beginning of ideological fragmentation in the PEA once again, there is a characteristic work: William H. Kilpatrick *et. al.*, *The Educational Frontier*. New York: Appleton-Century, 1933. Much of the viewpoint in the volume had been stated earlier by George S. Counts in two essays which mark a turning point in the PEA's earlier commitment to child-centered pedagogy: "Dare Progressive Education Be Progressive?" *Progressive Education*, Vol. IX (1931–32), pp. 257–63 and *Dare the School Build a New Social Order?* New York: John Day, 1932. Both essays really accused the PEA of parochializing the progressive education movement; they represent a typically American Progressivism in a somewhat Marxian garb which marked many of the educational writings of the period.

57. The internal controversy had already been foreshadowed in an exchange of views by Boyd Bode, Joseph K. Hart, Francis Froelicher, Margaret Naumburg, Caroline Pratt, and John Dewey in a *New*

Republic series called "The New Education Ten Years After." See *The New Republic*, Vol. LXIII (1930), pp. 61–64; 93–96; 123–25; 145–46; 172–76; 204–6.

58. I am using the term here as Whitehead uses it in referring to inert ideas. The inertness was probably partly a price of success (Where do progressives go from here?) and partly a reaction to the more conservative temper which gradually enveloped the nation during the later forties. In any case, progressive education after 1945 too frequently became "right thinking" or "best thinking"—another orthodoxy—among the initiated. Dewey, himself, had noted the tendency as early as 1938 in *Experience and Education*. The fact that new generations of students who had never participated in developing these ideas were now taking them over—frequently as unexamined jargon—in Education courses across the country only compounded the difficulty.

59. The PEA (renamed the American Education Fellowship in 1944) succumbed in the summer of 1955; *Progressive Education* magazine continued under the sponsorship of the John Dewey Society for two more years.

60. True they were almost universally badly reviewed in both the progressive and the conservative press. But the PEA was as uninterested in Sinclair's problem as it was in Sinclair. Witness the similar reception given several years later to John Kirkpatrick's less polemical study, *The American College and Its Rulers*. New York: New Republic, 1926, and to George S. Counts's analysis of *The Social Composition of Boards of Education*, Chicago: University of Chicago Press, 1927.

61. Similarly the PEA ignored a lively criticism of the American college sponsored by *The New Republic* in 1929. See *The Students Speak Out: A Symposium from 23 Colleges*. New York: New Republic 1929. Only later in the thirties did the reform of higher education begin to command the Association's interest. See, for example, *Progressive Education*, Vol. XIV (1937), No. 5.

62. In a Ph.D. Thesis on New Deal policies in education now being written at Teachers College, Columbia University, Harry Zeitlin finds that neither the Association nor the "social frontier" group at Teachers College exercised appreciable influence on educational policy-making in Washington. *Progressive Education* did carry articles on the New Deal youth programs, but somehow one never derives the feeling that these programs are "progressive education." See, for example, the essays by Arthur Linden and Aubrey Williams in *Progressive Education*, Vol. XII (1935), No. 8.

3
Inside the System: The Character of Urban Schools, 1890–1940

David B. Tyack

One August day early in the century, Helen Todd climbed the long stairs of a converted warehouse on Lake Street in Chicago. When she reached the attic, the smell of turpentine and the blast of heat from the cement furnace nauseated her. Inside were fourteen girls aged fourteen or fifteen sitting on stools and lacquering canes. After inspecting the room she sat down to talk with some of them: "How can you stand it here, children?" she asked. "Why don't you little girls go to school?" "School!" cried one who had given her name as Tillie Isakowsky, aged fourteen years and three months, shaking her head until her red bows trembled. "School is de fiercest t'ing youse kin come up against. Factories ain't no cinch, but schools is worst." All over the city in her rounds as factory inspector, Helen Todd heard similar stories. She asked 500 children this question in 1909: "If your father had a good job and you didn't have to work, which would you rather do—go to school or work in a factory?" Of these 500, 412 said they preferred the factory. Bewildered, Todd jotted down their reasons:

> "Because it's easier to work in a factory than 'tis to learn in school."
> "They ain't always pickin' on you because you don't know things in a factory."
> "The children don't holler at ye and call ye a Christ-killer in a factory."
> "They're good to you at home when you earn money."
> "What ye learn in school ain't no good. Ye git paid just as much in the factory if ye never was there."

In the basement of a building in the stockyards, Inspector Todd stumbled over a thirteen-year-old boy who had huddled there, hoping she would not discover him. He wept bitterly when told he would have to go to school, blurting between his sobs that "they hits ye if yer don't learn, and they hits ye if ye whisper, and they hits ye if ye have string in yer pocket, and they hits ye if yer seat squeaks, and they hits ye if ye don't stan' up in time, and they hits ye if yer late, and they hits ye if ye ferget the page." Again and again she heard the same story: 269 children said they preferred factory to school because no one hit them there. They were more "push-outs" than "drop-outs."[1]

At the turn of the century Chicago was the center of a movement to humanize schooling and to train teachers to understand the natural learning processes of children. The charismatic progressive Francis Parker taught hundreds of teachers at the Cook County Normal School in the years from 1896 to 1899, showing them his techniques for employing the child's curiosity as the easy and pleasant path of instruction. John Dewey was developing his progressive philosophy and practice of teaching at his famous Laboratory School at the University of Chicago. "What the best and wisest parent wants for his own child," he told an audience in Chicago in 1899, "that must the community want for all of its children. Any other ideal for our schools is narrow and unlovely; acted upon, it destroys our democracy." One of Dewey's strongest advocates, Ella Flagg Young, became superintendent of the Chicago schools in 1909. Barely five feet tall, a woman of great courage, intelligence, and compassion, she taught teachers about Dewey's "new education" when she served as instructor at the Normal School from 1905 to 1909. Like her friend Jane Addams, she was most concerned about reaching the children of the slums, largely second generation immigrants (67 percent of Chicago pupils in 1909 were children of foreign-born parents).[2]

Obviously there was a gap between what leaders intended and what children perceived.

The view from the top and the view from the bottom sometimes was different in New York, too. Although imposing and stern in appearance, with his frock-coat and walrus moustache, Superintendent William Maxwell felt deeply about the suffering of the poor. He knew that thousands of children came hungry to school each day and that stomach pains gnawed at them as they tried to study; he thought providing cheap lunches in schools the "most pressing of all school reforms." He proudly told of a principal on the lower east side who was so loved and respected that as she picked her way through the crowds and the pushcarts on the street, children smiled at her, older boys tipped their caps, and bearded men greeted her. He helped to install baths in schools so that children who had no water in their flats could get clean. He marveled at the ability of teachers who instructed pupils who could speak no English; in one school alone there were twenty-nine different languages or dialects. He stayed in the city during the steaming summer months partly to encourage those teaching in the vacation schools, where hundreds of thousands of children went voluntarily to learn crafts and nature study. Maxwell told with delight about a little girl, Leah, who invited her teacher home to eat at a table set just like the one in the picture in a magazine her teacher had lent to her.[3]

But for all this dedication, the response from "crowded, ignorant, prejudiced, and highly excitable people" was often distrust. In 1907, Maxwell said teachers in an East Side school faced a riot in which "frenzied mothers and fathers by the thousands besieged the school." The reason: parents thought that "the children's throats were being cut." The school had 150 children whose adenoids were enlarged—a condition assumed to contribute to mental retardation. When eighty parents refused to take their children to clinics to have the adenoids removed, the principal decided to bring in a surgeon to operate on the children in the school. For days thereafter, whenever a health board doctor appeared in the ghetto, "it was a signal for a mob to storm the gates of the schoolhouse." To these Jewish parents the school was capable of genocide.[4]

Different perceptions of urban schools were equally meaningful to different people—to school managers, educational scientists, black parents, first and second generation immigrants, teachers, and the heterogeneous millions of children and youth called students.

For the administrators at the top of city school systems, together with their mentors in universities and lay allies, the years from 1890 to 1940 represented largely a success story whose plot was apparent early in the twentieth century, though details sometimes were in doubt. As Cubberley taught in his popular history of public education, the public school was part of a larger social evolution whose beneficence was not to be doubted by the faithful. Challenges like Americanization of immigrants abounded, to be sure, but the strategies to respond to them were to be found in "science," in administrative efficiency, and professional specialization. For leading schoolmen it was mostly an age of confidence inspired by a dream of social efficiency.[5]

The administrative progressives believed that they knew what was wrong with the old one best system which Philbrick and his peers had labored to create: it was too "bookish," rigid, and undiversified, ill-adapted to the great variety of students flooding the upper grades of elementary schools and the secondary schools and poorly serving the needs of the economy for specialized manpower. The modernized one best system should "meet the needs of the children," but these needs and social demands could be assessed scientifically and the system reshaped accordingly. Intelligence testing and other forms of measurement provided the technology for classifying children. Nature-nurture controversies might pepper the scientific periodicals and magazines of the intelligentsia, but schoolmen found IQ tests invaluable means of channeling children; by the very act of channeling pupils, they helped to make the IQ prophecies self-fulfilling. Likewise, the differentiation of secondary education into tracks and the rise of vocational schooling represented a profound shift in the conception of the functions of universal education.[6]

In one respect, however, the administrative progressives continued and indeed accentuated one of the earlier purposes of public schooling: the Americanization of the foreign-born and their children. In the two decades bracketing World War I, especially, concern for homogenizing American beliefs and behavior reached a fever pitch. Just as it was the educator who decided which differences among children were significant in the tracking of children into a differentiated system, so it was leading schoolmen and powerful native-American interest groups that determined the proper pattern of socialization to American norms. With but few dissenters, policy-makers in these years saw pluralism as a peril.[7]

Although for purposes of official policy pupils were members of a "unitary community" of persons who differed in ways measurable individually by the tester and significant to the psychologically trained counselor or administrator, they were also members of different ethnic and religious and class groups. Just as welfare workers were trained to think in psychological ways and to regard their "cases" as individual problems, so teachers and administrators often came under the spell of the individualistic orientation of the psychologists who dominated educational thought. Educators often failed to see that many problems children faced in school were sociological and economic in character and were, in C. Wright Mills's terms, "public issues" rather than "personal troubles." Early in the century, as now, the culture of the school poorly fit the culture of certain subgroups in the population. That Italian-American children, for example, scored an average of eighty-five on IQ tests and dropped out of school in droves indicated not a plethora of individual problems but a mismatch of institutional demands and group norms and behavior. To explore this phenomenon it is useful to look at two groups—Italians and Jews—who differed markedly in their response to schooling.[8]

It makes little sense to malign the intentions of schoolmen in their campaign to differenti-ate the structure of schools, to classify students, to socialize in uniform ways. With but few exceptions their motives were good, their belief in the objectivity of their "scientific" proce-dures manifest, their achievements in the face of massive challenges impressive. But some unforeseen consequences of administrative progressivism become most clear when one looks at the educational experience of those citizens at the bottom of the social structure, in partic-ular those who became victims without "crimes," black Americans.[9]

The changes in schooling affected teachers as much as students. As persons in the middle of the growing school bureaucracies, teachers were often restive. When they became better edu-cated and learned a rhetoric of professionalism, they more and more objected to being func-tionaries. As they seized power here and there in their unions and professional associations, they demanded greater security, autonomy, and pay. Women, especially, gained new assur-ance and won equal pay and greater influence. But the tensions of being "professionals" at low levels within hierarchical organizations persisted, largely unresolved.[10]

1. Success Story: The Administrative Progressives

Looking back in 1930 on the previous quarter century in city school administration, George D. Strayer of Teachers College, Columbia, saw twenty-five years of steady progress. The keys to this success were "the application of the scientific method" and "the professional training of school executives," he believed. At the beginning of the century "a relatively powerful and able group" of administrators had been dubious about the benefits of educational science, he said, but by 1930 almost all influential schoolmen had become converts. The results were every-where apparent: "better organization of the administrative and supervisory" employees into line and staff categories; the differentiation of the "traditional elementary school and senior high school" into institutions like junior high schools, vocational schools, and junior colleges that "provide unique opportunities for boys and girls who vary greatly in their ability to acquire skill and knowledge"; grouping of pupils by scientific tests; the expansion of high schools with multiple tracks until they enrolled 50 percent of students of high school age; extensive revision of the curriculum; the keeping of detailed records on students, from IQ's to physical history and vocational and recreational interests; and rapid upgrading of the stan-dards of training for all professional personnel. The principle underlying such progress was "recognition of individual differences" and the consequent attempt "to adjust our schools to the needs and capacities of those who are registered in them."[11]

Statistics revealed the magnitude of the transformation and suggested the character of the challenges schoolmen faced as education became increasingly universal through the high school years. The costs of city schools in 1910 were twice as high as in 1900, three times higher than 1890. From 1890 to 1918 there was, on the average, more than one new high school built for every day of the year. Attendance in high schools increased during that period from 202,963 to 1,645,171, an increase of 711 percent while the total population increased only 68 percent. The curve of secondary school enrollment and graduation continued to soar: in 1920, 61.6 percent of those fourteen to seventeen were enrolled, and high school graduates repre-sented 16.8 percent of youths seventeen years old; in 1930, the figures were 73.1 percent and 29 percent; in 1940, 79.4 percent and 50.8 percent. As these statistics suggest, during the first two decades of the twentieth century compulsory schooling laws were increasingly effective. From

1900 to 1920 educators became less ambivalent about coercion than they had often been during the nineteenth century. Gradually school accommodations began to catch up with demand, the size of classes diminished, and the gospel of social efficiency helped create a commitment to universal education as an achievable goal. State aid increasingly was tied to average daily attendance, and thus stimulated the pursuit of truants. School leaders joined muckraking journalists, foes of child labor, and elite reformers in political campaigns to translate their concerns into compulsory schooling and child labor laws. In part as a consequence of the new laws, school systems developed new officials whose sole purpose was to insure universal attendance (usually to age fourteen). Members of these new bureaucracies—school census takers, truant officers, statisticians, and school social workers—became experts in "child accounting."[12]

As city systems grew in size and bureaucratic complexity, the number of specialized administrative offices and administrators expanded dramatically. In 1889 the U.S. Commissioner of Education first included data on officers "whose time is devoted wholly or principally to supervision." The category was new enough to cause confusion—and indeed statistics on the number of administrators and their nonteaching staffs are still hard to determine. That year 484 cities reported an average of only 4 supervisors per city. But from 1890 to 1920 the number of "supervisory officers" jumped from 9 to 144 in Baltimore, 7 to 159 in Boston, 31 to 329 in Detroit, 58 to 155 in St. Louis, 235 to 1,310 in New York, 10 to 159 in Cleveland, and 66 to 268 in Philadelphia. Robert and Helen Lynd pointed out that in 1890 in Middletown the superintendent was the only person in the system who did not teach, but by the 1920s there was between the teacher and superintendent "a whole galaxy of principals, assistant principals, supervisors of special subjects, directors of vocational education and home economics, deans, attendance officers, and clerks, who do no teaching but are concerned in one way or another with keeping the system going." Problems were met "not by changes in its foundation but by adding fresh stories to its superstructure."[13]

Schoolmen created special programs for retarded, deaf, blind, delinquent, gifted, anemic, and other groups of children, and specialized tracks and schools for vocational and other special training. With such differentiation came dozens of new job categories, programs of professional preparation, and many new bureaus and officials. Specialists of all sorts formed their own professional associations: superintendents, secondary school principals, elementary school principals, counselors, curriculum directors, vocational education teachers, high school teachers of art, music, English, social studies, and many others. Together with the rapidly expanding college and university departments and schools of education, professional associations helped to persuade state legislatures to pass laws requiring certificates for the various specializations. Replacing the earlier licenses based on examinations, the new certificates were based on completion of professional training and legitimized specialists by *level*—kindergarten, elementary school, junior high school, high school, and so on—and by *function*—principal, guidance counselor, school librarian, supervisor, or teacher of vocational subjects, and so forth. In 1900 only two states had specialized credentials; by 1930 almost all states had elaborate certification laws. In the decade following 1912, fifty-six cities created research departments that kept track of the new credentials and bureaus, tested the "intelligence" and achievement of pupils, helped to channel students, and amassed statistics for "child accounting" and business management.[14]

In the half century following 1890, then, there was a vast influx into urban schools of youth who previously might have gone to work or roamed the streets, pushed into the classroom by child labor laws and compulsory attendance or attracted by new curricula, activities, and facilities. At the same time, the structure of urban schools became enormously complex and differentiated for diverse groups in the population.

Differentiated education was not a new phenomenon in city schools, of course. We have seen that schoolmen sometimes treated groups like the Irish poor or black children in a manner different from the mainstream of children in the common school. But the goal of uniform education had been an attractive one in the nineteenth century both for practical and ideological reasons. Many of the innovations designed to offer differentiated schooling in the nineteenth century stemmed not so much from career educators as from wealthy philanthropists, merchants, and industrialists. Influential lay people, for example, founded private kindergartens for poor children in cities as far apart as Boston and San Francisco; in a number of cities they privately funded the first public trade schools and commercial high schools, as well as "industrial schools" for the children of the poor; they supported the first program of vocational guidance; they created "parental schools" and other institutions for truants and predelinquents; and they sometimes subsidized municipal research bureaus, which were the forerunners of research departments of city school systems. Through these programs the elites sought to reach children bypassed by the public schools or to provide skills or services absent in the one best system. Thus kindergartens or industrial schools had taken children off the slum streets; commercial or trade schools had taught skills which industrialists or merchants wanted; vocational counselors in settlement houses had helped boys and girls find jobs. Piece by piece such new agencies were added to the public school structure.[15]

But the administrative progressives were not content with piecemeal reform, however much they might agree with the specific changes pioneered by lay elites. After all, the corporate model of school governance was predicated on the idea that experts should design and run the system. Education professors like Strayer, Judd, and Cubberley were training superintendents at Columbia, Chicago, and Stanford. The new "school executives" were taking control of big cities and the professional associations. Together they were developing new strategies for public schooling as well as differentiated structures. A group of such educational leaders formed the "Cleveland Conference," which agreed at a meeting in 1918 that the time was ripe for "a radical reorganization" of schooling and concluded that changes would "go on in the haphazard fashion which has characterized our school history unless some group gets together and undertakes in a cooperative way to coordinate reforms."[16]

The administrative progressives were convinced that "traditional education"—the old one best system—was profoundly anachronistic and flawed. In their journals, they attacked the old uniform curriculum, the undifferentiated structure, the recitation methods, and the skimpy training of teachers typical in nineteenth-century city schools as rigid, unscientific, wasteful, and inhumane. They were evangelists for new educational goals of science and social efficiency. They still wanted a one best system, but it was to be a more complex, differentiated organization adapted to new social and economic conditions.[17]

Social efficiency demanded a new relationship between school and society. The administrative progressives believed that the schools should better prepare students for the tasks they would face in life. To them the old idea that a common school grounding in the three R's would suffice for any career and that public education could train any boy to be President of the United States was clearly absurd. Cubberley wrote that urban schools should "give up the exceedingly democratic idea that all are equal, and that our society is devoid of classes," and should adapt the school to the existing social structure. "Increasing specialization . . . has divided the people into dozens of more or less clearly defined classes," he wrote, "and the increasing centralization of trade and industry has concentrated business in the hands of a relatively small number. . . . No longer can a man save up a thousand dollars and start in business for himself with much chance of success. The employee tends to remain an employee; the wage earner tends to remain a wage earner." It was clear that "success is higher up the ladder now than it was a generation ago, while the crowd about the bottom increases every year." Simple realism decreed that the public schools should prepare some students directly for subordinate roles in the economy while it screened out those fit for further training in higher education. As we shall see, the "science" of psychological measurement would enable schoolmen to retain their traditional faith in *individual* opportunity while in fact the intelligence tests often were unintentionally biased against certain groups.[18]

The vocational education movement clearly expressed the type of reform Cubberley had in mind. During the nineteenth century some educators regarded industrial education as appropriate for low status people, and they experimented with different versions of skill training in reform schools and in institutions for black and Indian youth.[19] But specific vocational preparation spread to other segments of the population, especially when private donors founded commercial and trade high schools in large cities. In city after city businessmen decided that the regular school curriculum did not provide skills they needed in industry or commerce. They gave large sums to establish special schools; in New York, for example, J. P. Morgan endowed the New York Trades Schools with $500,000. By the early twentieth century most such commercial and technical schools founded by philanthropists had been absorbed into the public system, and businessmen in the National Association of Manufacturers and Chambers of Commerce were calling for greatly expanded vocational instruction in urban schools. By 1910 the movement had won broad support, with endorsements from the NEA and the American Federation of Labor (which had long been suspicious of the trade schools as sources of scab labor, but which apparently joined the movement in the hope of sharing in its control and improving the earnings of skilled labor). By 1918 the advocates of vocational training helped to secure federal funds through the Smith-Hughes Act.[20]

As Norton Grubb and Marvin Lazerson argue, the vocational education movement was significant not so much for the numbers of students who actually enrolled in industrial curricula or courses—normally under 10 percent—but because it represented an increasing conviction "that the primary goal of schooling was to prepare youth for the job market" and that the way to do this was through vocational guidance and testing, junior high schools, and differentiated curricula. Most arguments over the character of vocational education concerned who should control it—the existing school boards or new governing groups—and whether industrial schools were "simply a mechanism of social class stratification offering second-class education." By and large educators successfully fought separate boards of control, and instead they included vocational schools, tracks, or courses within the comprehensive system. The question of stratification proved more complex, as the vocational program often became a dead-end side track for lower-class youth.[21]

William H. Dooley, principal of Technical High School in Fall River, Massachusetts, described in 1916 how industrial education could serve the student he described as the "ne'er-do-well" (educators have been prolific in names for the "laggard," "slow learner," "retarded," "reluctant," "hand-minded," "disadvantaged," child who does not fit the system). Dooley maintained that schooling should be mostly adapted to the 85 percent of pupils who would become workers in industry and commerce and who were in danger of becoming cogs in the machine. Untrained, such people might become technologically unemployed, a condition that "breeds discontent that threatens the existence of our government." The old patterns of learning to work on a farm or through apprenticeship no longer worked for city children, nor did the older forms of moral socialization operate effectively. Now a child might wake up in the morning to find his parents off to the mill, go to school dirty and hungry, and "spend the day and evening on the streets, with the result that the dormant vicious tendencies are allowed to develop instead of being stifled by proper parental influence." Schools that teach an abstract curriculum and promote students on the basis of a literary test fail the "motor-minded" child. An efficient school, on the other hand, will measure and account for every child, providing different opportunities depending on his or her needs.

"Unskilled and socially inefficient" children of new immigrants constituted a particularly troublesome subset of the "ne'er-do-well" class. It would be unwise to forbid such children to work in factories between the ages of fourteen and sixteen, thought Dooley, for "they have descended from ancestors who mature early in life and have intensely practical ideas, and therefore should develop useful industrial habits during the early part of adolescence." It is only misguided "groups of social workers in this country attempting to tear down our institutions" who would force "unjust legislation on the community, such as compulsory full-time education for children up to sixteen years of age or over." No, what these children need is the industrial discipline of a job supplemented by a vocational part time school. However harsh Dooley's attitude may appear today, his concern for the millworker's child was genuine and his proposal for a continuation school was at least an advance over a ten-hour day of unbroken drudgery.[22]

Not all administrative progressives agreed with Dooley's particular specifications for the proletarian child or with Cubberley's open avowal of class-based education, of course. But the underlying principle of differentiating schooling to meet the needs of different classes of pupils—as determined by the educational expert in the light of the presumed career of the student—almost all would have accepted. This was the heart of the doctrine of social efficiency. It was partly for this reason that the educational sociologist David Snedden so admired the experiments possible in reform schools, for there the experts had a preselected population over whom they had virtually total social control.[23]

The school survey became a favorite technique to spread the program of the administrative progressives. Hollis Caswell reported that there were sixty-seven surveys of city school systems by outside experts published during the period from 1910 to 1919 and 114 in the years from 1920 to 1927. During the first years of the survey movement it was common for laymen in elite organizations like a Chamber of Commerce to bring in experts to point out faults in the schools and to propose the corporate model of reform. This gave administrative progressives an opportunity to castigate "traditional education" and the village model of school governance, but it was a bit hard on incumbent board members and school employees.[24]

Two such surveys were one conducted under the direction of Harvard's Paul Hanus in New York City in 1911–12 and the study of Portland, Oregon, written by a task force under Cubberley and published in 1913. The Hanus staff claimed that the uniform curriculum in New York represented the "idealism" of an earlier time and was quite out of place under modern economic conditions. The surveyors claimed that mental independence became a form of insubordination and that the hierarchy had created "bureaucratic control all along the line," from the superintendent on down, rather than professional "cooperation under leadership." Principals and supervisors were mere inspectors, certifying compliance with the rules; most teaching, not surprisingly, was mechanical.[25] In Portland Cubberley's team found similar conditions. They concluded that "the most fundamental principle observed in the conduct of the Portland school system is the maintenance unchanged of a rigidly prescribed, mechanical system, poorly adapted to the needs of either the children or the community." Since both principals and teachers had no chance to make decisions, the result was "a uniformity that is almost appalling." The curriculum was "vivisected with mechanical accuracy into fifty-four dead pieces." Because authority was so diffused in the board's subcommittees, the superintendent was reduced to a drill sergant.[26]

The script was a familiar one, and insulted superintendents like New York's Maxwell and Portland's Rigler could justly claim that the "experts" had made up their minds before coming, that they had misinterpreted what they saw, and that they had neglected many achievements of recent vintage. Because of some of the early attacks on traditional educators by administrative progressives, surveys earned a bad reputation in some quarters, especially among those superintendents, like Rigler, who were deposed. But as the movement matured, it became increasingly a device for "progressive" superintendents to enlist the aid of outsiders to make changes they wanted anyway. By the late 1920s most of the superintendents not only survived the surveys but applauded them. When Leonard Koos sent inquiries to twenty-five superintendents whose cities had been surveyed, fourteen of the eighteen who replied said that they favored the studies.[27]

Supporting the survey movement was a network of university professors, administrative progressives in the city school systems, the U.S. Bureau of Education, lay reformers in civic organizations, and foundations. Rockefeller's General Education Board set up its own division of school surveys, which did studies of Gary, Indiana, and several states. The Russell Sage Foundation supported numerous surveys, including one comparing "efficiency" of education in the forty-eight states. The Cleveland Foundation backed a large-scale study of schools in that city. In 1917 a writer in the annual report of the U.S. Commissioner of Education commented that in doing surveys "private philanthropy has taken the initiative, as so often, in doing work for which the Government was not yet ready," but added that the Bureau of Education was by then ready to perform that service. For a brief period the Bureau and state education departments conducted the most surveys, but by the early 1920s the customary agency was a special bureau for survey research located in a college of education.[28]

Raymond Moley reported that more than three-quarters of the recommendations of the Cleveland education survey were rapidly put into effect. Caswell found that many innovations favored by the administrative progressives were incorporated in city systems after surveys, often as a direct result of the study. The administrative progressives saw success in such statistics and good reason to believe that their influence on the structure and processes of American urban education was growing. Few were the voices raised in public dissent against their general program. And the administrative progressives found articulate allies across a wide political spectrum.[29]

In the *New Republic*, the liberal intellectual Randolph Bourne applauded Cubberley's Portland survey, saying that "it stirs enthusiasm because it shows the progress that has been made in clarifying the current problems and the ideals which must be realized if the public school is to prepare the child of to-day for intelligent participation in the society of which he will form a part." Traditional education in Portland, he wrote, "seems more like the ritual of some primitive tribe than the deliberate educational activity of an enlightened American community," yet precisely that is "the type that still prevails in the majority of our cities."[30]

Scott Nearing, a professor of economics who would soon be fired for his liberal views, was as impressed as Bourne with the program of the administrative progressives. In his book *The New Education* he described the changes in the Cincinnati schools wrought by Superintendent Dyer and his staff. Dyer, he said, tried the radical experiment of trusting his principals and teachers to adapt the curriculum to the children. "Up here on the hill, in a wealthy suburban district," Dyer told his staff, "is a grammar school. Its organization, administration and course of study must necessarily differ from that other school, located in the heart of the factory district." It was up to the principals to adapt the school to the people.

What this might mean became clear in the Oyler School, on the wrong side of the railroad tracks and surrounded by factories and little houses. There the principal appealed to the factory owners to support a manual training program. Later with the help of Dyer he set up prevocational programs in which "subnormal" elementary pupils could spend a whole day a week, while others spent a smaller proportion of their time in shop work and domestic science. The boys turned out marketable products in workrooms patterned on real factories. A manufacturer told Nearing that he supported the schools gladly because they made good citizens and because he believed "that the material prosperity of a people is directly related to the mental and manual equipment of its people." At the Oyler School the principal worked through the mothers' club to change patterns of child-raising and to upgrade the appearance of the neighborhood. Discipline problems vanished, more children went to high school, the school became a center of "community"—it was Nearing's model of the "new education."[31]

Then as now, personal concern and energy could sometimes transform a school and thereby change the lives of children. For writers like Nearing and Bourne, who lived by words, rhetoric like "meeting the needs of children" and "cooperation" distinguished the new education from the old and predisposed them to praise what they called "progressivism." They saw a challenge to the schools in the new floods of children entering classrooms, a crisis of urban community, a traditional education that had outgrown its inspiration and calcified its routines.

But "progressivism" in education was a label that was loosely applied to diverse reformers, philosophies, and practices. I have argued that one wing of reformers, whom I have called "administrative progressives," constituted a political-educational movement with an elitist philosophy and constituency. They tried to transfer control of urban education to a centralized board and expert superintendent under a corporate model of governance. Within the system they focused upon differentiating the structure and fulfilling the goals of social efficiency and social control. Thus they were primarily concerned with organizational behavior and the linkage of school and external control, with aggregate goals rather than individual development of students.

These administrative progressives had little in common in aim either with the small libertarian wing of educational progressivism or with the small group of social reconstructionists who dreamed in the 1930s of using the schools to construct a new social order. In some ways the forerunners of A.S. Neill and the free school advocates of today, the libertarians sought to make the school conform to the trajectory of the individual child's growth. They drew on Freud and avant-garde artists and intellectuals to criticize the repressiveness of the traditional school structure and curriculum and to urge the individual self-expression of the child instead. The social reconstructionists—whose ideas were stated most forcefully by George

Counts in *Dare the School Build a New Social Order?* (1932)—argued that schools should undermine the capitalistic system by instilling left-liberal ideology in schoolchildren. Although their writings are fascinating to read, the libertarians and radicals had little practical impact on urban schools.[32]

The administrative progressives found little admirable in either of these versions of educational progressivism. They did, however, often pay attention to innovations advocated by philosophers, psychologists, and curriculum theorists in schools of education, who translated John Dewey's ideas into classroom procedures. These "pedagogical progressives" spoke about the "project method," the "activity curriculum," and other ways to "meet individual needs" of children by subverting the hegemony of established school subjects. The curricular reformers who advanced such ideas normally took the hierarchical structure of differentiated schooling as a given and concentrated on inspiring the teacher to change her philosophy, her curriculum, and her methods in the classroom. In the hortatory, individualistic style of these pedagogical progressives there was little threat to the established power of the school managers; indeed, as David Swift has said, by promoting more subtle techniques of teaching students and less overt control of teachers, the "new education" probably made both more tractable. And the broadened views of what should be learned in school made schoolmen less accountable for Philbrick's old goal of inculcating "positive knowledge."[33]

It was difficult, indeed, to express the spirit of John Dewey's version of cooperative, democratic schooling within a hierarchical bureaucracy, and for the reason Dewey stated in 1902: "it is easy to fall into the habit of regarding the mechanics of school organization and administration as something comparatively external and indifferent to educational purposes and ideals." We forget, he said, that it is such matters as the classifying of pupils, the way decisions are made, the manner in which the machinery of instruction bears upon the child "that really control the whole system." It was no accident that when Dewey and his daughter Evelyn described teachers who exemplified his ideals of democratic, active education in *Schools of Tomorrow*, they concentrated on small and private schools rather than large and public systems. A gifted teacher in a one-room country school house might alone turn her class into Dewey's model of social learning, but changing a large city system was more difficult, for Dewey's ideas of democratic education demanded substantial autonomy on the part of teachers and children—an autonomy which, as we shall see, teachers commonly lacked. Predictably, the call for a "new education" in urban school systems often brought more, not less, red tape and administration, more forms to fill out and committees to attend, more supervisors, new tests for children to take, new jargon for old ideas. The full expression of Dewey's ideal of democratic education required fundamental change in the hierarchical structure of schools—and that was hardly the wish of those administrative progressives and their allies who controlled urban education. As Robert and Helen Lynd concluded in their report on abortive "progressivism" in Middletown, "in the struggle between quantitative administrative efficiency and qualitative educational goals . . . the big guns are all on the side of the heavily concentrated controls behind the former."[34]

Notes

1. Todd, "Why Children Work," 73–78.
2. Dewey, *School and Society*, 33; Herrick, *Chicago Schools*, 114–15, 74; McCaul, "Dewey's Chicago."

3. Maxwell, "Teachers," 11878–79.
4. Ibid., 11877–80; A. Shaw, "Spread of Vacation Schools."
5. Cremin, *Cubberley; Krug, High School*.
6. Lazerson, *Urban Schools*, ch. ix; Katz, *Class, Bureaucracy, and Schools*, 114–18.
7. Hartmann, *Movement to Americanize the Immigrant*.
8. Lubove, *Professional Altruist*, chs. iv, vii; H. Miller and Smiley, eds., *Education in the Metropolis*, 1–13; Mills, *Sociological Imagination*, 9.
9. The study of Thorndike by Geraldine Joncich Clifford, *The Sane Positivist*, gives a detailed and sympathetic view of educational scientists as they saw themselves and their world.
10. Strachan, *Equal Pay*; Reid, "Professionalization of Public School Teachers."
11. Strayer, "Progress in City School Administration," 375–78.
12. U.S. Commissioner of Education, *Report for 1889*, II, 709; Counts, *Selective Character of American Education*, 1; U.S. Bureau of the Census, *Historical Statistics*, 207, 214; Stambler, "Effect of Compulsory Education and Child Labor Laws"; Haney, *Registration of City School Children*; Ensign, *Compulsory School Attendance*.
13. Lynd and Lynd, *Middletown*, 210; U.S. Commissioner of Education, *Report for 1889*, II, 772; *Report for 1890*, II, 1318–48; *Biennial Survey, 1920–22*, II, 94–114.
14. Wesley, *NEA*, 278–79; Kinney, *Certification in Education*, ch. vi; Martens, "Organization of Research Bureaus."
15. Lazerson, *Urban School*, ch. ii; A.G. Wirth, *Education in Technological Society*, chs. ii, v; Riis, *Children of the Poor*.
16. Letter from Charles Judd to members of the Cleveland Conference, Jan. 14, 1918, Edward C. Elliott Papers, Purdue University, courtesy of Dr. Walter Drost.
17. Krug, *High School*; Spring, *Education and the Corporate State*.
18. Cubberley, *Changing Conceptions of Education*, 56–57; Karier, Violas, and Spring, *Roots of Crisis*, ch. vi. I am indebted to Professor Karier and to Russell Marks for their powerful insights into the social philosophy of some of the testers.
19. Cubberley, *Public School Administration*, 338.
20. Wirth, *Education in Technological Society*, ch. i; Curti, *Social Ideas of American Educators*, chs. vi, viii; Chicago City Council, *Recommendations*, 107–12.
21. Grubb and Lazerson, *Education and Industrialism*, "Introduction"; S. Cohen, "Industrial Education Movement."
22. Dooley, *Ne'er-Do-Well*, 8, 13–14, 16–18, 21, 27–28.
23. Snedden, *Reform Schools*, ch. xii.
24. Caswell, *City School Surveys*, 26.
25. Committee on School Inquiry, *Report*, I, 57; Hanus, *Adventuring in Education*, ch. xii.
26. Cubberley, *Portland Survey*, 125, 40, 128, 41–42, 46; Cubberley's colleagues were education professors and school administrators, including Edward C. Elliott, Frank E. Spaulding, J.H. Francis, and Lewis Terman.
27. Koos, "School Surveys," 35–41.
28. U.S. Commissioner of Education, *Report for 1917*, I, 19–21; Pritchett, "Educational Surveys," 118–23; Caswell, *City School Surveys*, 32.
29. Moley, "Cleveland Surveys," 229–31; Caswell, *City School Surveys*, 60–72.
30. Bourne, "Portland Survey," 238.
31. Nearing, *New Education*, 128, 126, 165–69.
32. Cremin, *Transformation of the School*, ch. vi; Bowers, *Progressive Educator and the Depression*.
33. Swift, *Ideology and Change in the Public Schools*.
34. Dewey, *Educational Situation*, 22–23; Lynd and Lynd, *Middletown in Transition*, 241; Dewey, *Democracy and Education*; Katz, *Class, Bureaucracy, and Schools*, 113–25.

Part II
The Politics of Education

4
Broken Promises: School Reform in Retrospect

Samuel Bowles and Herbert Gintis

We shall one day learn to supercede politics by education.
—Ralph Waldo Emerson

Democracy and Technology in Educational Theory

The minds . . . of the great body of the people are in danger of really degenerating, while the other dements of civilization are advancing, unless care is taken, by means of the other instruments of education, to counteract those effects which the simplifications of the manual processes has a tendency to produce.

—James Mill, 1824

Scholars abhor the obvious. Perhaps for this reason it is often difficult to find a complete written statement of a viewpoint which is widely accepted. Such is the case with modern liberal educational theory. Discovering its conceptual underpinnings thus requires more than a little careful searching. What exactly is the theory underlying the notion of education as "panacea"? In reviewing the vast literature on this subject, we have isolated two intellectually coherent strands, one represented by John Dewey and his followers—the "democratic school"—and the other represented by functional sociology and neoclassical economics—the "techno-cratic-meritocratic school." These approaches are best understood by analyzing the way they deal with two major questions concerning the limits of educational policy. The first concerns the compatibility of various functions schools are supposed to perform. The second concerns the power of schooling to perform these functions. We shall treat each in turn.

In the eyes of most liberal reformers, the educational system must fulfill at least three functions. First and foremost, schools must help integrate youth into the various occupational, political, familial, and other adult roles required by an expanding economy and a stable polity. "Education," says John Dewey in *Democracy and Education,* probably the most important presentation of the liberal theory of education, "is the means of [the] social continuity of life." We refer to this process as the "integrative" function of education.

Second, while substantial inequality in economic privilege and social status are believed by most liberals to be inevitable, giving each individual a chance to compete openly for these privileges is both efficient and desirable. Dewey is representative in asserting the role of the school in this process:

> It is the office of the school environment . . . to see to it that each individual gets an opportunity to escape from the limitations of the social group in which he was born, and to come into living contact with a broader environment.[1]

Many liberal educational theorists—including Dewey—have gone beyond this rather limited objective to posit a role for schools in equalizing the vast extremes of wealth and poverty. Schooling, some have proposed, cannot only assure fair competition, but can also reduce the economic gap between the winners and the losers. We shall refer to this role of schooling in the pursuit of equality of opportunity, or of equality itself, as the "egalitarian" function of education.

Lastly, education is seen as a major instrument in promoting the psychic and moral development of the individual. Personal fulfillment depends, in large part, on the extent, direction, and vigor of development of our physical, cognitive, emotional, aesthetic, and other potentials. If the educational system has not spoken to these potentialities by taking individual development as an end in itself, it has failed utterly. Again quoting Dewey:

> The criterion of the value of school education is the extent in which it creates a desire for continued growth and supplies the means for making the desire effective in fact. . . . The educational process has no end beyond itself: it is its own end.[2]

We refer to this as the "developmental" function of education.

For Dewey, the compatibility of these three functions—the integrative, the egalitarian, and the developmental—derives from basic assumptions concerning the nature of social life. First, he assumed that occupational roles in capitalist society are best filled by individuals who have achieved the highest possible levels of personal development. For Dewey, personal development is economically productive. Second, Dewey assumed that a free and universal school system can render the opportunities for self-development independent of race, ethnic origins, class background, and sex. Hence the integrative, egalitarian, and developmental functions of schooling are not only compatible, they are mutually supportive. . . .

Dewey argues the necessary association of the integrative, egalitarian, and developmental functions of education in a democracy. A more recent liberal perspective argues only their mutual compatibility. This alternative view is based on a conception of the economy as a technical system, where work performance is based on technical competence. Inequality of income, power, and status, according to this technocratic-meritocratic view, is basically a reflection of an unequal distribution of mental, physical, and other skills. The more successful individuals, according to this view, are the more skillful and the more intelligent. Since cognitive and psychomotor development are vital and healthy components of individual psychic development and can be provided equally according to the "abilities" of the students upon their entering schools, the compatibility of these three functions of the educational system in capitalism is assured.

The popularity of the technocratic-meritocratic perspective can be gleaned from the policy-maker's reaction to the "rediscovery" of poverty and inequality in America during the decade of the 1960s. Unequal opportunity in acquiring skills was quickly isolated as the source of the problems.[3] Moreover, in assessing the efficacy of the educational system, both of preschool enrichment and of other school programs, measures of cognitive outcomes—scholastic achievement, for example—have provided the unique criteria of success.[4] Finally, the recent failure of educational policies significantly to improve the position of the poor and minority groups has, among a host of possible reappraisals of liberal theory, raised but one to preeminence: the nature-nurture controversy as to the determination of "intelligence."[5]

This technocratic-meritocratic view of schooling, economic success, and the requisites of job functioning supplies an elegant and logically coherent (if not empirically compelling) explanation of the rise of mass education in the course of industrial development. Because modern industry, according to this view, consists in the application of increasingly complex and intellectually demanding production technologies, the development of the economy requires increasing mental skills on the part of the labor force as a whole. Formal education, by extending to the masses what has been throughout human history the privilege of the few, opens the upper levels in the job hierarchy to all with the ability and willingness to attain such skills. Hence, the increasing economic importance of mental skills enhances the power of a fundamentally egalitarian school system to equalize economic opportunity. . . .

The modern technocratic-meritocratic perspective avoids Mann's [Horace Mann was the father of the Common School movement in the 19th century who viewed schools as a great equalizer] class analysis but retains his basic assertions. According to the modern view, the egalitarianism of schooling is complemented by the meritocratic orientation of industrial society. Since in this view ability is fairly equally distributed across social class, and since actual achievement is the criterion for access to occupational roles, differences of birth tend toward economic irrelevance. Since whatever social-class based differences exist in an individual's "natural" aspirations to social status are minimized by the competitive orientation of school-ing, expanding education represents a potent instrument toward the efficient and equitable distribution of jobs, income, and status. If inequalities remain at the end of this process, they must simply be attributed to inevitable human differences in intellectual capacities or patterns of free choice.

Thus as long as schooling is free and universal, the process of economic expansion will not only be consistent with the use of education as an instrument for personal development and social equality; economic expansion, by requiring educational expansion, will necessarily enhance the power of education to achieve these ends. So the argument goes.[6]

If we accept for the moment the compatibility of various functions of education, we are con-fronted with a second group of questions concerning the power of education to counteract opposing tendencies in the larger society. If the educational system is to be a central social cor-rective, the issue of its potential efficacy is crucial to the establishment of the liberal outlook. Dewey does not withdraw from this issue:

> . . . The school environment . . . establishes a purified medium of action. . . . As society
> becomes more enlightened, it realizes that it is responsible not to transmit and conserve

the whole of its existing achievements but only such which make for a better future society. The school is its chief agency for the accomplishment of this end.[7]

But such generalizations cannot substitute for direct confrontation with the thorny and somewhat disreputable facts of economic life. In the reality of industrial society, can the school environment promote either human development or social equality? Self-development may be compatible with ideal work roles, but can education change the seamy realities of the workaday world? Equality may be compatible with the other functions of education, but can the significant and pervasive system of racial, class, and sexual stratification be significantly modified by "equal schooling"?

* * *

This approach became a fundamental tenet of educational reformers in the Progressive Era. Education, thought Dewey, could promote the natural movement of industrial society toward more fulfilling work, hence bringing its integrative and developmental functions increasingly into a harmonious union.

To complete our exposition of liberal theory, we must discuss the power of the educational system to promote social equality. For Dewey, of course, this power derives from the necessary association of personal growth and democracy—whose extension to all parts of the citizenry is a requisite of social development itself. In the technocratic version of liberal theory, however, the egalitarian power of the educational system is not automatically fulfilled. Were economic success dependent on race or sex, or upon deeply rooted differences in human character, the ability of schooling to increase social mobility would of course be minimal. But according to the modern liberal view, this is not the case. And where equal access is not sufficient, then enlightened policy may devise special programs for the education of the poor: job training, compensatory education, and the like.

Poverty and inequality, in this view, are the consequences of individual choice or personal inadequacies, not the normal outgrowths of our economic institutions. The problem, clearly, is to fix up the people, not to change the economic structures which regulate their lives. This, indeed, is the meaning of the "social power" of schools to promote equality.

Despite persistent setbacks in practice, the liberal faith in the equalizing power of schooling has dominated both intellectual and policy circles. Education has been considered not only a powerful tool for self-development and social integration; it has been seen, at least since Horace Mann coined the phrase well over a century ago, as the "great equalizer."

Education and Inequality

> Universal education is the power, which is destined to overthrow every species of hierarchy. It is destined to remove all artificial inequality and leave the natural inequalities to find their true level. With the artificial inequalities of caste, rank, title, blood, birth, race, color, sex, etc., will fall nearly all the oppression, abuse, prejudice, enmity, and injustice, that humanity is now subject to.
>
> —Lester Frank Ward, *Education* c. 1872

Much of the content of education over the past century and a half can only be construed as an unvarnished attempt to persuade the "many" to make the best of the inevitable. The unequal

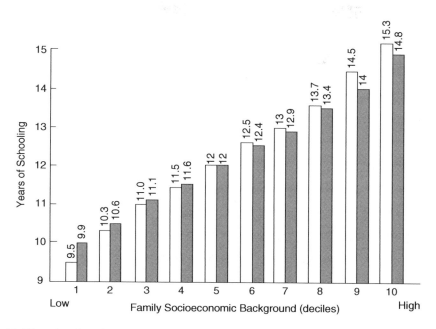

Figure 4.1 Educational attainments are strongly dependent on social background even for people of similar childhood IQs.

Source: Bowles, S. & Nelson V.I. (1974). 'The Inheritance of IQ,' and the Intergenerational Transmission of Economic Inequality. *The Review of Economics and Statistics*, 56(1),39–51. Copyright © by the President and Fellows of Harvard College and the Massachusetts Institute of Technology. Reprinted with permission.

contest between social control and social justice is evident in the total functioning of U.S. education. The system as it stands today provides eloquent testimony to the ability of the well-to-do to perpetuate in the name of equality of opportunity an arrangement which consistently yields to themselves disproportional advantages, while thwarting the aspirations and needs of the working people of the United States. However grating this judgment may sound to the ears of the undaunted optimist, it is by no means excessive in light of the massive statistical data on inequality in the United States. Let us look at the contemporary evidence.

We may begin with the basic issue of inequalities in years of schooling. The number of years of schooling attained by an individual is strongly associated with parental socioeconomic status. This figure presents the estimated distribution of years of schooling attained by individuals of varying socioeconomic backgrounds. If we define socioeconomic background by a weighted sum of income, occupations, and educational level of the parents, a child from the ninetieth percentile may expect, on the average, five more years of schooling than a child in the tenth percentile.[8]

A word about our use of statistics is in order. Most of the statistical calculations which we will present have been published with full documentation in academic journals. . . . Those interested in gaining a more detailed understanding of our data and methods are urged to consult our more technical articles.

The data, most of which was collected by the U.S. Census Current Populations Survey in 1962, refers to "non-Negro" males, aged 25–64 years, from "non-farm" background in the experienced labor force.[9] We have chosen a sample of white males because the most complete statistics are available for this group. Moreover, if inequality for white males can be documented, the proposition is merely strengthened when sexual and racial differences are taken into account.

Additional census data dramatize one aspect of educational inequalities: the relationship between family income and college attendance. Even among those who had graduated from high school in the early 1960s, children of families earning less than $3,000 per year were over six times as likely *not* to attend college as were the children of families earning over $15,000.[10] Moreover, children from less well-off families are *both* less likely to have graduated from high school and more likely to attend inexpensive, two-year community colleges rather than a four-year B.A. program if they do make it to college.[11]

Not surprisingly, the results of schooling differ greatly for children of different social backgrounds. Most easily measured, but of limited importance, are differences in scholastic achievement. If we measure the output of schooling by scores on nationally standardized achievement tests, children whose parents were themselves highly educated outperform the children of parents with less education by a wide margin. Data collected for the U.S. Office of Education Survey of Educational Opportunity reveal, for example, that among white high school seniors, those whose parents were in the top education decile were, on the average, well over three grade levels in measured scholastic achievement ahead of those whose parents were in the bottom decile.[12]

Given these differences in scholastic achievement, inequalities in years of schooling among individuals of different social backgrounds are to be expected. Thus one might be tempted to argue that the close dependence of years of schooling attained on background displayed in the left-hand bars of Figure 4.1 is simply a reflection of unequal intellectual abilities, or that inequalities in college attendance are the consequences of differing levels of scholastic achievement in high school and do not reflect any additional social class inequalities peculiar to the process of college admission.

This view, so comforting to the admissions personnel in our elite universities, is unsupported by the data, some of which is presented in Figure 4.1. The right-hand bars of Figure 4.1 indicate that even among children with identical IQ test scores at ages six and eight, those with rich, well-educated, high status parents could expect a much higher level of schooling than those with less-favored origins. Indeed, the closeness of the left-hand and right-hand bars in Figure 4.1 shows that only a small portion of the observed social class differences in educational attainment is related to IQ differences across social classes.[13, 14] The dependence of education attained on background is almost as strong for individuals with the same IQ as for all individuals. Thus, while Figure 4.1 indicates that an individual in the ninetieth percentile in social class background is likely to receive five more years of education than an individual in the tenth percentile, it also indicated that he is likely to receive 4.25 more years schooling than an individual from the tenth percentile with the same IQ. Similar results are obtained when we look specifically at access to college education for students with the same measured IQ. Project Talent data indicates that for "high ability" students (top 25 percent as measured by a composite of tests of "general aptitude"), those of high socioeconomic background (top 25 percent as measured by a composite of family income, parents' education, and occupation) are nearly twice as likely to attend college than students of low socioeconomic background (bottom 25 percent). For "low ability" students (bottom 25 percent), those of high social background are more than four times as likely to attend college as are their low social background counter-parts.[15]

Inequality in years of schooling is, of course, only symptomatic of broader inequalities in the educational system. Not only do less well-off children go to school for fewer years, they are treated with less attention (or more precisely, less benevolent attention) when they are there. These broader inequalities are not easily measured. Some show up in statistics on the different levels of expenditure for the education of children of different socioeconomic backgrounds. Taking account of the inequality in financial resources for each year in school and the inequal-ity in years of schooling obtained, Jencks estimated that a child whose parents were in the top fifth of the income distribution receives roughly twice the educational resources in dollar terms as does a child whose parents are in the bottom fifth.[16]

The social class inequalities in our school system, then, are too evident to be denied. Defenders of the educational system are forced back on the assertion that things are getting better; the inequalities of the past were far worse. And, indeed, there can be no doubt that some of the inequalities of the past have been mitigated. Yet new inequalities have apparently devel-oped to take their place, for the available historical evidence lends little support to the idea that our schools are on the road to equality of educational opportunity. For example, data from a recent U.S. Census survey reported in Spady indicate that graduation from college has become no less dependent on one's social background. This is true despite the fact that high-school graduation is becoming increasingly equal across social classes.[17] Additional data confirm this impression. The statistical association (coefficient of correlation) between parents' social sta-tus and years of education attained by individuals who completed their schooling three or four decades ago is virtually identical to the same correlation for individuals who terminated their schooling in recent years.[18] On balance, the available data suggest that the number of years of school attained by a child depends upon family background as much in the recent period as it did fifty years ago.

Thus, we have empirical reasons for doubting the egalitarian impact of schooling. But what of those cases when education has been equalized? What has been the effect. We will investigate three cases: the historical decline in the inequality among individuals in years of school attained, the explicitly compensatory educational programs of the War on Poverty, and the narrowing of the black/white gap in average years of schooling attained.

Although family background has lost none of its influence on how far one gets up the edu-cational ladder, the historical rise in the minimum legal school-leaving age has narrowed the distance between the top and bottom rungs. Inequality of educational attainments has fallen steadily and substantially over the past three decades.[19] And has this led to a parallel equaliza-tion of the distribution of income? The reduction in the inequality of years of schooling has not been matched by an equalization of the U.S. income distribution.[20] In fact, a recent U.S. Labor Department study indicates that as far as labor earnings (wages and salaries) are con-cerned, the trend since World War II has been unmistakably away from equality. And it is pre-cisely inequality in labor earnings which is the target of the proponents of egalitarian school reforms.[21] But does the absence of an overall trend toward income equality mask an equalizing thrust of schooling that was offset by other disequalizing tendencies? Perhaps, but Jacob Mincer and Barry Chiswick of the National Bureau of Economic Research, in a study of the determinants of inequality in the United States, concluded that the significant reduction in schooling differences among white male adults would have had the effect—even if operating in isolation—of reducing income inequality by a negligible amount.[22]

Next, consider that group of explicitly egalitarian educational programs brought together in the War on Poverty. In a systematic economic survey of these programs, Thomas Ribich concludes that with very few exceptions, the economic payoff to compensatory education is low.[23] So low, in fact, that in a majority of cases studied, direct transfers of income to the poor would have accomplished considerably more equalization than the education programs in question. The major RAND Corporation study by Averch came to the same conclusion.

Lastly, consider racial inequalities. In 1940, most black male workers (but a minority of whites) earned their livelihoods in the South, by far the poorest region; the education gap between nonwhites and whites was 3.3 years (38 percent of median white education).[24] By 1972, blacks had moved to more affluent parts of the country, and the education gap was reduced to 18 percent (4 percent for young men aged 25–34 years).[25] Richard Freeman has shown that this narrowing of the education gap would have virtually achieved black/white income equality had blacks received the same benefits from education as whites.[26] Yet the income gap has not closed substantially: The income gap for young men is 30 percent, despite an education gap of only 4 percent.[27] Clearly as blacks have moved toward educational (and regional) parity with whites, other mechanisms—such as entrapment in center-city ghettos and suburbanization of jobs, and perhaps increasing segmentation of labor markets—have intensified to maintain a more or less constant degree of racial income inequality. Blacks certainly suffer from educational inequality, but the root of their exploitations lies outside of education, in a system of economic power and privilege in which racial distinctions play an important role.

The same must be concluded of inequality of economic opportunity between men and women. Sexual inequality persists despite the fact that women achieve a level of schooling (measured in years) equivalent to men.

We conclude that U.S. education is highly unequal, the chances of attaining much or little schooling being substantially dependant on one's race and parents' economic level. Moreover, where there is a discernible trend toward a more equal educational system—as in the narrowing of the black educational deficit for example—the impact on the structure of economic opportunity is minimal at best. As we shall presently see, the record of the U.S. school system as a promoter of full human development is no more encouraging.

Education and Personal Development

While the educational practice of regimentation of children has persisted, the fundamentalist conception of a child as immoral or savage has given way, through various stages, to a more appreciative view. To modern educators, the child appears as the primitive embodiment of the good and the natural—the noble savage, if you will. Children are spontaneous and joyful, unpredictable and trusting—traits to be cherished but sadly evanescent in the path toward maturity.[28]

At the same time, the educator's view of the family has changed. Once the trusted engine of moral training for youth, to which the school was considered a complement and ballast, the family increasingly appears in the writings of educators as the source of the child's inadequacy. Thus in the thought of the culture of poverty and cultural deprivation advocates, the school has been elevated to the status of family surrogate in the well engineered Society.[29] The social roots of this transformed concept of the family-school relationship have little to do with any alteration in family structure, and less to do with any heightening of the public morality. The impetus stems rather from the professional educator's profound mistrust of, and even fear of, the families of black and poor children, and in an earlier period, of Irish and other immigrant families.[30] Nor is this mistrust alien to the logic of social control. For all its nobility, the noble savage remains savage, and integration into the world of adults requires regimentation.

The most striking testimonial to the hegemony of the social-control ideology is perhaps its clear primacy even among those who opposed such obvious manifestations of the authoritarian classroom as corporal punishment and teacher-centered discussion. The most progressive of progressive educators have shared the commitment to maintaining ultimate top-down control over the child's activities. Indeed, much of the educational experimentation of the past century can be viewed as attempting to broaden the discretion and deepen the involvement of the child while maintaining hierarchical control over the ultimate processes and outcomes of the educational encounter. The goal has been to enhance student motivation while withholding effective participation in the setting of priorities.

Hence, like the view of the child, the concept of discipline has itself changed. Two aspects of this change are particularly important. First, the once highly personalized authority of the teacher has become a part of the bureaucratic structure of the modern school. Unlike the teachers in the chaotic early nineteenth-century district schools, modern teachers exercise less personal power and rely more heavily on regulations promulgated by higher authorities. Although frequently prey to arbitrary intervention by parents and other community members, the nineteenth-century teacher was the boss of the classroom. The modern teacher is in a more ambiguous position. The very rules and regulations which add a patina of social authority to his or her commands at the same time rigidly circumscribe the teacher's freedom of action.

Second, the aim of discipline is no longer mere compliance: The aim is now "behavior modification." Prompt and obedient response to bureaucratically sanctioned authority is, of course, a must, but sheer coercion is out of keeping with both the modern educator's view of the child and the larger social needs for a self-controlled not just controlled-citizenry and work force. Discipline is still the theme, but the variations more often center on the "internalization of behavioral norms," on equipping the child with a built-in supervisor than on mere obedience to external authority and material sanctions.[31]

The repressive nature of the schooling process is nowhere more clearly revealed than in the system of grading, the most basic process of allocating rewards within the school. We will have gone some distance toward comprehending the school as it is—in going behind the educational rhetoric—if we can answer the question: Who gets what and why?

Teachers are likely to reward those who conform to and strengthen the social order of the school with higher grades and approval, and punish violators with lower grades and other forms of disapproval, independent of their respective academic and cognitive accomplishments. This fact allows us to investigate exactly what personality traits, attitudes, and behavioral attributes are facilitated by the educational encounter.

Outside of gross disobedience, one would suspect the student's exhibition of creativity and divergence of thought to be most inimical to the smooth functioning of the hierarchical classroom. For the essence of the modern educational encounter is, to use Paolo Freire's words, that teaching:

> . . . becomes an act of depositing, in which the students are the depositories and the teacher is the depositor. Instead of communicating, the teacher issues communiques and makes deposits which the students patiently receive, memorize, and repeat. This is the "banking" concept of education. . . . The teacher teaches and the students are taught. . . . The teacher chooses and enforces his choice and the students comply. The teacher acts and the students have the illusion of acting through the action of the teacher.[32]

Others refer to this conception as the "jug and mug" approach to teaching whereby the jug fills up the mugs.

Thus the hostility of the school system to student behavior even approaching critical consciousness should be evident in the daily lives of students. Getzels and Jackson[33] have shown that high school students perceive this to be the case. They subjected a group of 449 high school students to an IQ test and a battery of exams which purport to measure creativity.[34] They found no appreciable correlation between measured IQ and measured "creativity." The top 20 percent in IQ on the one hand, and in creativity on the other, were singled out and asked to rank certain personality traits (a) on the degree to which they would like to have these traits, and (b) on the degree to which they believed teachers would like the student to have. There was virtually complete agreement by the high IQ and the high creatives on which traits are preferred by teachers; in other words, these students view the demands made upon them in a similar way. However, the two groups disagreed on what traits they themselves would like to have: The correlation between the two groups' ratings of the personality traits "preferred for oneself" was quite low.[35] Most striking of all, however, was the finding that, while the high IQs' "preferred traits" correspond closely to their perception of the teachers' values, the high creatives ranking of preferred traits was actually inversely related to the perceived teachers' ranking.[36] The high creatives do not fail to conform; rather they do not wish to conform.[37]

Getzel and Jackson's is but one of the many studies which link personality traits to school grades. We have undertaken a review of this literature, the results of which support the following interpretation.[38] Students are rewarded for exhibiting discipline, subordinancy, intellectually as opposed to emotionally oriented behavior, and hard work independent from intrinsic task motivation. Moreover, these traits are rewarded independently of any effect of "proper demeanor" on scholastic achievement.

Rather than plowing through this mass of data, we shall present the results of the most extensive of our sources. In the early 1960s, John L. Holland undertook a study of the determinants of high school success among a group of 639 National Merit Scholarship finalists—males for the most part in the top 10 percent of students in IQ and the top 15 percent in class rank.[39] Holland collected four objective measures of cognitive development from his subjects' College Entrance Examination Board tests.[40] In addition, he collected some sixty-five measures of personality, attitude, self-concept, creativity, and home life through testing the students, their parents, and obtaining various ratings from their teachers.[41]

We have extensively analyzed this massive body of data.[42] Our first conclusion is that, while the group's high academic rank is doubtless related to their above-average IQs, differences in scholastic achievement among them were not significantly related to their grades, despite a good deal of variation in both achievement and grades within the group. More telling, however, is the fact that many of the personality variables were significantly and positively related to grades. Most important were the teachers' ratings of the students' *Citizenship* and the students' self evaluation of *Drive to Achieve*.[43] Neither of these variables had any significant impact on actual achievement measures!

These results are not in themselves surprising. It is to be expected that students will be rewarded for their conformity to the social order of the school *(Citizenship)* as well as their personal motivation to succeed within the nexus of this social order *(Drive to Achieve)*. Only the most naive would expect school grades to depend on scholastic achievement alone.

But what do *Citizenship* and *Drive to Achieve* really reflect? In a liberated educational encounter, we would expect these traits to embody some combination of diligence, social popularity, creativity, and mental flexibility. Yet statistical analysis of the Holland data reveals a strikingly different pattern. Students who are ranked by their teachers as high on *Citizenship* and *Drive to Achieve* are indeed more likely to be diligent (e.g., they are high on such measures as *Deferred Gratification, Perseverance*, and *Control*) and socially popular (e.g., they are high on *Social Leadership* and *Popularity*). But they are, in fact, significantly below average on measures of creativity and mental flexibility (e.g., they are low on such measures as *Cognitive Flexibility, Complexity of Thought, Originality, Creativity*, and *Independence of Judgment*).[44] Moreover, further statistical analysis shows that these same traits of creativity and mental flexibility are directly penalized in terms of school grades, holding constant test scores, *Citizenship*, and *Drive to Achieve*.

The conclusions from this body of data seem inescapable. Conformity to the social order of the school involves submission to a set of authority relationships which are inimical to personal growth. Instead of promoting a healthy balance among the capacity for creative autonomy, diligence, and susceptibility to social regulation, the reward system of the school inhibits those manifestations of personal capacity which threaten hierarchical authority.

We have emphasized elements on the "hidden curriculum" faced in varying degrees by all students. But schools do different things to different children. Boys and girls, blacks and whites, rich and poor are treated differently. Affluent suburban schools, working-class schools, and ghetto schools all exhibit a distinctive pattern of sanctions and rewards. Moreover, most of the discussion here has focused on high-school students. In important ways, colleges are different; and community colleges exhibit social relations of education which differ sharply from those of elite four-year institutions. In short, U.S. education is not monolithic.

Why do schools reward docility, passivity, and obedience? Why do they penalize creativity and spontaneity? Why the historical constancy of suppression and domination in an institution so central to the elevation of youth? Surely this is a glaring anomaly in terms of traditional liberal educational theory. The naive enthusiasm of the contemporary free-school movement suggests the implicit assumption that no one had ever tried to correct this situation—that the ideal of liberated education is simply a new conception which has never been tried. Even sophisticated critics, such as Charles Silberman, tend to attribute the oppressiveness of schooling to simple oversight and irrationality:

What is mostly wrong with public schools is not due to venality or indifference or stupidity but to mindlessness . . . It simply never occurs to more than a handful, to ask why they are doing what they are doing to think seriously or deeply about the purposes or consequences of education.[45]

Yet, the history of the progressive-education movement attests to the intransigence of the educational system to "enlightened change" within the context of corporate capitalism.

Progressivism has been the keynote of modern educational theory embracing such pillars of intellect and influence as John Dewey, Charles W. Elliot, Alfred North Whitehead, William James, and G. Stanley Hall. The birth of the Association for the Advancement of Progressive Education in 1918 was merely the political codification of an already active social movement whose aim, in the words of its founder Stanwood Cobb, "... had little of modesty. ... We aimed at nothing short of changing the entire school system of America."[46] Subscribing to Dewey's dictum that "... education is the fundamental method of social reform, ..." the statement of principles of the Association for the Advancement of Progressive Education had its aim to be "... the truest and fullest development of the individual, based upon the scientific study of his mental, physical, spiritual, and social characteristics and needs."[47] However avant-garde today's liberal educationists feel themselves to be, they envision little more than did the Progressives in the dawning years of the century. Schooling was to provide the child with the freedom to develop "naturally" with a teacher as guide, not taskmaster. Intrinsic interest not external authority was to motivate all work. The leitmotif of the day was "taking the lid off kids," and the aim was to sublimate natural creative drives in fruitful directions rather than to repress them. Emotional and intellectual development were to hold equal importance, and activity was to be "real life" and "student directed."

The mass media dramatically attest to the ideological victory of the Progressives: Professional journals, education textbooks, and even the various publications of the U.S. Office of Education mouthed the rhetoric of Progressivism. As Lawrence A. Cremin, a foremost historian of the Progressive Movement in education, notes:

> There is a "conventional wisdom" ... in education ... and by the end of World War II progressivism had come to be that conventional wisdom. Discussions of educational policy were liberally spiced with phrases like "recognized individual differences," "personality development," "the whole child," "the needs of learners," "intrinsic motivation," "persistent life situations," "bridging the gap between home and school," "teaching children, not subjects," "adjusting the school to the child," "real-life experiences," "teacher pupil relationships," and "staff planning." Such phrases ... signified that Dewey's forecast of the day when progressive education would eventually be accepted as good education had now finally come to pass.[48]

Yet the schools have changed little in substance.

Thus we must reject mindlessness along with venality, indifference, and stupidity as the source for oppressive education. A more compelling explanation of the failure to combat repression in U.S. schooling is simply that progressive education, though triumphant in educational theory, was never given a chance in practice. Indeed, this argument is often used by those adhering to the liberal perspective. Thus Raymond E. Callahan traces the failure of Progressivism to the growing preoccupation with order and efficiency in educational practice at the same time that progressive education was capturing hearts and minds in educational theory. Callahan argues that:

. . . Very much of what has happened in American education since 1900 can be explained on the basis of the extreme vulnerability of our schoolmen to public criticism and pressure and that this vulnerability is built into our pattern of local support and control.[49]

The direction the formal educational system took in this situation was dictated by the power of business interests and the triumphant ideology of "efficient management." Again Callahan:

What was unexpected (in my investigation) was the extent not only of the power of the business-industrial groups, but of the strength of the business ideology. I had expected more professional autonomy and I was completely unprepared for that extent and degree of capitulation by administrators to whatever demands were made upon them.[50]

This vulnerability had great implications for student, teacher, and administrator alike. "Business methods" in schools meant that administrators were to be recruited from the ranks of politicians and especially businessmen, rather than professional educators, and their orientation was toward cost-saving and control rather than quality of education. Business methods also meant that the teacher was to be reduced to the status of a simple worker, with little control over curriculum, activities, or discipline, and whose accountability to the administrator again involved classroom authority rather than the quality of classroom experience. Lastly, the student was reduced to an "object" of administration, "busy-work," and standardized tests coming to prevail over play and self-development.

In short, the history of twentieth-century education is the history not of Progressivism but of the imposition upon the schools of "business values" and social relationships reflecting the pyramid of authority and privilege in the burgeoning capitalist system. The evolution of U.S. education during this period was not guided by the sanguine statements of John Dewey and Jane Addams, who saw a reformed educational system eliminating the more brutal and alienating aspects of industrial labor. Rather, the time motion orientation of Frederick Taylor and "Scientific Management," with its attendant fragmentation of tasks, and imposition of bureaucratic forms and top-down control held sway.

Thus there are some grounds for the opinion that the modern liberal view of the self-development capacities of schooling has not been falsified by recent U.S. experience; rather it has never been tried. A historian of Progressivism in U.S. education might well echo Gandhi's assessment of Western civilization: "It would be a good idea."

A Preface to the Critique of Liberal Educational Reform

Ignorance is the mother of industry as well as of superstition. Reflection and fancy are subject to err; but a habit of moving the hand or the foot is independent of either. Manufacture, accordingly, prospers most where the mind is least consulted, and where the workshop may . . . be considered an engine, the parts of which are men.—Adam Ferguson, *An Essay on the History of Civil Society,* 1767

Decades of broken promises cast strong doubt on modern liberal educational theory. But the anomalies which arise when theory and practice are juxtaposed cannot lay it finally to rest. As Thomas Kuhn has noted, even in the physical sciences, only a recognizably superior alternative seals the fate of faulty but generally accepted dogma.[51]

All the more true is this observation in the social sciences. In the case of liberal educational theory, the failures of educational reform we have presented are by no means decisive. The "necessary connection" among the integrative, egalitarian, and developmental functions of education may appear only in the long run. Capitalism may still be young, and does seem to promote a rhetoric of tolerance and egalitarianism, as well as a supreme emphasis on individualism and human development. That this rhetoric is consistently thwarted in practice may simply represent a perverse institutional inertia. While educational policy has failed in the past, maturity and increased expertise may render it vastly more potent in the future. No one ever claimed reform to be easy—only ultimately possible with proper dedication. Finally, there may be tangible limits—technologically determined—to the degree of social mobility, due to inherent differences in mental ability. The possibility has been asserted forcefully by such writers as Arthur Jensen and Richard Herrnstein.[52]

In short, decent respect for liberal theory demands it be critiqued on theoretical grounds as well as in terms of the social outcomes it predicts, and, preferably with an alternative in mind. This will be our goal. While detailed presentation of our alternative will await future chapters, our argument may be summarized simply enough here: the failure of progressive educational reforms stems from the contradictory nature of the objectives of its integrative, egalitarian and developmental functions in a society whose economic life is governed by the institutions of corporate capitalism.

Both the democratic and technocratic versions of liberal education theory focus on the relationships into which individuals enter upon adulthood. In Dewey's democratic version, political life is singled out as central, while for the technocratic version, the technical aspects of production hold the honored position. Both have been blind to—or at least treated in quite unrealistic manner—the social relationships of capitalist production. Dewey's overall framework seems eminently correct. His error lies in characterizing the social system as democratic, whereas, in fact, the hierarchical division of labor in the capitalist enterprise is politically autocratic. Moreover, his central thesis as to the economic value of an educational system devoted to fostering personal growth is untrue in capitalist society. Dewey's view requires that work be a natural extension of intrinsically motivated activity. The alienated work of corporate life is inimical to intrinsic motivation.

In corporate capitalist society, the social relations of production conform, by and large, to the "hierarchical division of labor," characterized by power and control emanating from the top downward through a finely gradated bureaucratic order.[53] The social relationships of the typically bureaucratic corporate enterprise require special attention because they are neither democratic nor technical.

For Dewey, democracy is, in essence, ". . . a mode of conjoint communicative experience . . ." which ". . . repudiates the principle of external authority . . . in favor of voluntary disposition and interest." In this sense, the dominant forms of work for which the educational system prepares youth are profoundly antidemocratic. Under capitalism, work is characterized not by conjoint, but by hierarchical "communicative experience," and rigid patterns of dominance and subordinacy, where personal interaction is dictated primarily by rules of procedure set by employers: Dewey's "voluntary disposition" of the worker extends only over the decision to work or starve.

Dewey is of course aware of the undemocratic control of production in capitalist society; indeed, he refers explicitly to ". . . those in control of industry—those who supply its aims." But he avoids the fatal consequence of this admission for his theory by de-emphasizing democratic process and focusing on outcomes: the quality of the decision made by industrial aristocrats. The dehumanized nature of work in Dewey's time, exemplified by Taylorism and time-motion studies, and today, by the "human relations" school of organizational theory—is attributed to their "one-sided stimulations of thought," and hence responsive to liberal educational exposure. Here Dewey exhibits in raw form the liberal proclivity to locate the source of systemic failures in the shortcomings of individuals aim to propose "expert" solutions which respect—even reinforce—the top-down control of social life under corporate capitalism.[54] Surely he could not have been unaware of the forces in a market-oriented economy forcing managerial decision continually toward profit maximization to which end secure hierarchical authority and flexible control of the enterprise from the top are prime requisites.[55]

Similarly, the technocratic version of liberal educational theory suffers from an extremely partial characterization of the capitalist system. The major error in the technocratic school is its overemphasis on cognitive skills as the basic requirement of job adequacy. We shall show that cognitive requirements are by no means determinant, and indeed, can account for little of the association of education and economic success. Had the technocratic school looked at the social rather than the technical relations of production, it might have been more circumspect in asserting the compatibility of the integrative, egalitarian, and developmental functions of schooling. Indeed, it might have found that the way in which the school system performs its integrative function—through its production of stratified labor force for the capitalist enterprise—is inconsistent with its performance of either developmental or egalitarian functions. Focusing on cognitive variables, it cannot even entertain the idea that the correspondence between the social relations of production and the social relations of education—the essential mechanism of the integrative function of schooling—might preclude an egalitarian or truly humanistic education.

Thus the modern economy is a product of a social as well as a technical revolution. In the development of productive organization from precapitalist forms, through the relativity simple entrepreneur-worker relationship of the early factory system based on piecework, immediate supervision, and direct worker assessment to the modern complex, stratified, and bureaucratically ordered corporation or governmental organ, not simply the technical demands of work, but its social organization have changed drastically. Seen from the present, the Industrial Revolution may appear as a simple upgearing of the pace of technological change. From the point of view of those experiencing it, however, it constituted a thorough-going social upheaval involving not only radically new institutions in the governance of economic activity, but a radically different pattern of social interactions with demanding and pervasive requirements on the level of individual psychic functioning. Values, beliefs, modes of personal behavior, and patterns of social and economic loyalties were formed, transformed, and reproduced in the process of bringing the individual into line with the needs of capital accumulation and the extension of the wage labor system.

Conclusion

Of manufactures, of commerce, of both individual and national prosperity, nay even of science itself, the extended and abundant increase tends to complete the fatal circle: and, by decay, convulsion, anarchy, and misery, to produce a new and renovated order of things. In an advanced state of society, where the meridian is attained or passes, nothing can prevent or even protract the evil day, except the revivifying influence of education.—Thomas Bernard, "Extract from an account of the Mendip Schools," *Report of the Society for the Better Condition of the Poor,* 1799

The record of actual successes and failures of education as reform is not sufficient either to accept or to reject the liberal outlook. But it must be a point of departure in any serious inquiry into its potential contribution to social improvement. The record, as we have shown, is not encouraging. First, despite the concerted efforts of progressive educators of three generations, and despite the widespread assimilation of their vocabulary in the United States, schools, by and large, remain hostile to the individual's needs for personal development. Second, the history of U.S. education provides little support for the view that schools have been vehicles for the equalization of economic status or opportunity. Nor are they today. The proliferation of special programs for the equalization of educational opportunity had precious little impact on the structure of the U.S. education, and even less on the structure of income and opportunity in the U.S. economy. It is clear that education in the United States is simply too weak an influence on the distribution of economic status and opportunity to fulfill its promised mission as the Great Equalizer. Schooling remains a meager instrument in promoting full participation of racial minorities in the United States—indeed, even the expensive pilot projects in this direction seem to have failed rather spectacularly.

The educational system serves—through the correspondence of its social relations with those of economic life—to reproduce economic inequality and to distort personal development. Thus under corporate capitalism, the objectives of liberal educational reform are contradictory: It is precisely because of its role as producer of an alienated and stratified labor force that the educational system has developed its repressive and unequal structure. In the history of U.S. education, it is the integrative function which has dominated the purpose of schooling, to the detriment of the other liberal objectives.

More fundamentally, the contradictory nature of liberal educational reform objectives may be directly traced to the dual role imposed on education in the interests of profitability and stability; namely, enhancing workers' productive capacities and perpetuating the social, political, and economic conditions for the transformation of the fruits of labor into capitalist profits. It is these overriding objectives of the capitalist class—not the ideals of liberal reformers—which have shaped the actuality of U.S. education, had left little room for the school to facilitate the pursuit of equality or full human development. When education is viewed as an aspect of the reproduction of the capitalist division of labor, the history of school reforms in the United States appears less as a story of an enlightened but sadly unsuccessful corrective and more as an integral part of the process of capitalist growth itself.

We cannot rule out the possibility that a future dramatic and unprecedented shift toward equality of educational opportunity might act as a force for equality. Nor do we exclude the possibility that open classrooms and free schools might make a substantial contribution to a more liberating process of human development. Indeed, we strongly support reforms of this type as part of a general strategy of social and economic transformation. But to consider educational change in isolation from other social forces is altogether too hypothetical. The structure of U.S. education did not evolve in a vacuum; nor will it be changed, holding other things constant. Education has been historically a device for allocating individuals to economic positions, where inequality among the positions themselves is inherent in the hierarchal division of labor, differences in the degree of monopoly power of various sectors of the economy, and the power of different occupational groups to limit the supply or increase the monetary returns to their services. Thus equalization of educational outcomes, rather than reducing inequality, would more likely simply shift the job of allocating individuals to economic positions to some other "institution." Similarly, a less repressive educational system will produce little more than the "job blues" unless it can make an impact upon the nature of work and the control over production.

This much, at least, we can say with some certainty: Repression, individual powerlessness, inequality of incomes, and inequality of opportunity did not originate historically in the educational system, nor do they derive from unequal and repressive schools today. The roots of repression and inequality lie in the structure and functioning of the capitalist economy. Indeed, we suggest that they characterize any modern economic system—including the socialist state—which denies people participatory control of economic life.

Notes

1. John Dewey, *Democracy and Education* (New York: The Free Press, 1966), p. 20.
2. *Ibid.,* pp. 50–53.
3. Theodore W. Schultz, "Investment in Poor People," Seminar on Manpower Policy and Programs, Office of Manpower Policy Evaluation Research, Washington: Department of Labor, 1966.
4. Harvey Averch *et al.,* "How Effective Is Schooling: A Critical Review and Synthesis of Research Findings" (Santa Monica: The Rand Corporation, 1972).
5. Samuel Bowles and Herbert Gintis, "IQ in the U.S. Class Structure," in *Social Policy,* November–December 1972 and January–February 1973.
6. Arthur A. Jensen, "How Much Can We Boost IQ and Scholastic Achievement?" *Harvard Educational Review,* Vol. 39, No. 1, 1969; Richard Herrnstein, "IQ," *Atlantic Monthly,* Vol. 228, No, 3, September 1971; Edward C. Banfield, *The Unheavenly City* (Boston: Little, Brown and Company, 1968); Daniel P. Moynihan and Nathan Glazer, *Beyond the Melting Pot* (Cambridge, Mass.: MIT Press, 1970).
7. Dewey (1966), *op. cit.,* p. 20.
8. This calculation is based on data reported in full in Samuel Bowles and Valerie Nelson, "The 'Inheritance of IQ' and the Intergenerational Transmission of Economic Inequality," *The Review of Economics and Statistics,* Vol. LVI, No.1, February 1974. It refers to non-Negro males from non-farm backgrounds, aged 35–44 years. The zero-order correlation coefficient between socioeconomic background and years of schooling was estimated at 0.646. The estimated standard deviation of years of schooling was 3.02. The results for other age groups are similar.
9. See Bowles and Nelson (1974), *op. it.* Peter Blau and Otis D. Duncan, *The American Occupational Structure* (New York: John Wiley, 1967); Otis D. Duncan, D.C. Featherman, and Beverly Duncan, *Socioeconomic Background and Occupational Achievement, Final Report,* Project No. S-0074 (EO-191) (Washington, D.C.: Department of Health, Education and Welfare, Office of Education, 1968); Samuel Bowles, "Schooling and Inequality from Generation to Generation," *The Journal of Political Economy,* Vol. 80, No.3, Part II, May–June 1972.
10. These figures refer to individuals who were high-school seniors in October, 1965, and who subsequently graduated from high school. College attendance refers to both two- and four-year institutions. Family income is for the twelve months preceding October 1965. Data is drawn from U.S. Bureau of the Census, *Current Population Reports,* Series P-60, No. 183, May 1969.

11. For further evidence, see U.S. Bureau of the Census (1969), *op. cit.*, and Jerome Karabel, "Community Colleges and Social Stratification," *Harvard Educational Review,* Vol. 424, No. 42, November 1972.

12. Calculation based on data in James S. Coleman *et al., Equality of Educational Opportunity* (Washington, D.C.: U.S. Government Printing Office, 1966), and Bowles and Gintis (1972), *op. cit.*

13. The data relating to IQ are from a 1966 survey of veterans by the National Opinion Research Center; and from N. Bayley and E.S. Schaefer, "Correlations of Material and Child Behaviors with the Development of Mental Ability: Data from the Berkeley Growth Study," *Monographs of Social Research in Child Development,* 29, 6 (1964).

14. This figure is based on data reported in full in Bowles and Nelson (1974), *op. cit.* The left -hand bars of each pair were calculated using the estimated corrdation coefficient between socioeconomic background and education of 0.65. The results for other age groups were similar: 0.64 for ages 25–34 and 44–54, and 0.60 for ages 55–64 years. The right-hand bars were calculated from the normalized regression coefficient on socioeconomic background from an equation using background and early childhood IQ to predict years of schooling, which was estimated at 0.54. The results for other age groups were similar: 0.54 for ages 25–34 and 45–54, and 0.48 for ages 55–64. Socioeconomic background is defined as normalized sum of father's education, father's occupational status, and parents' income. The mean and standard deviation of years of schooling were estimated at 11.95 and 3.02, respectively.

15. Based on a large sample of U.S. high-school students as reported in: John C. Flannagan and William. W. Cooley, *Project Talent, One Year Follow-up Study,* Cooperative Research Project, No. 2333, University of Pittsburgh: School of Education, 1966.

16. Christopher Jencks *et al., Inequality: A Reassessment of the Effects of Family* and *Schooling in America* (New York: Basic Books, 1972), p.48.

17. William L. Spady, "Educational Mobility and Access: Growth and Paradoxes," in *American Journal of Sociology,* Vol. 73, No. 3, November 1967; and Blau and Duncan, *op. cit.* (1967).

18. Blau and Duncan (1967), *op. cit.*

19. We estimate the coefficient of variation of years of schooling at about 4.3 in 1940 (relying on Barry Chiswick and Jacob Mincer, "Time Series Changes in Personal Income Inequality in the U.S." *Journal of Political Economy,* Vol. 80, No. 3, Part II [May–June 1972], Table 4 for the standard deviation of schooling and the Decennial Census for the mean), and at 2.95 in 1969 (relying on Chiswick and Mincer [1972] Table B10).

20. Calculated from Table B1 and Table B10 in Chiswick and Mincer (1972), *op. cit.*

21. Peter Henle, "Exploring the Distribution of Earned Income," *Monthly Labor Review,* Vol. 95, No. 12, December 1972. Inequalities in income (profit, rent interest, and transfer payments plus labor earnings) may also have increased if the unmeasured income from capital gain and other tax shelters for the rich are taken into acount. See Jerry Cromwell, "Income Inequalities, Discrimination and Uneven Development," unpublished Ph.D. dissertation, Harvard University, May 1974.

22. Chiswick and Mincer (1972), *op. cit.*

23. Thomas I. Ribich, *Education and Poverty* (Washington, D.C.: Brookings Institution, 1968).

24. United States Bureau of the Census, *Current Population Reports,* Series P-60, October 1970, Table 75, p. 368.

25. United States Bureau of the Census, *Current Population Reports,* series P-60, November, 1972, Table 1, p. 14.

26. Michael Reich, *Racial Discrimination and the Distribution of Income,* Ph.D. dissertation, Harvard University, May 1973.

27. United States Bureau of the Census, *op. cit.* (December 1973), Table 47, p. 114.

28. Whence e. e. cummings' sharp lines: "... the children knew, but only a few/ and down they forgot as up they grew." e. e. cummings, *Poems, 1923–1954* (New York: Harcourt, Brace and World, 1954), p. 370.

29. cf. Charles Valentine, *Culture and Poverty* (Chicago: University of Chicago Press, 1968). Early in the nineteenth century, Robert Dale Owen, the renowned utopian, had proposed that the interests of social equality dictated that the children of the poor be raised in public institutions.

30. Tyack (1967), *op. cit.;* Katz (1971), *op. cit.*

31. We argue that both changes in the approach to discipline reflect the changing social relationships of production in the corporate capitalist economy.

32. Paulo Freire, *Pedagogy of the Oppressed* (New York: Herder and Herder, 1972), pp. 58–59.

33. J.W. Getzels and P.W. Jackson, "Occupational Choice and Cognitive Functioning," in *Journal of Abnormal and Social Psychology,* February 1960.

34. For a general discussion of the content and meaning of creativity tests, see Michael W. Wallach, *The Intelligence of Creativity Distinction* (New York: General Learning Corporation, 1971).

35. The exact correlation was $r = 0.41$.

36. The correlations between own and teacher's desired personality traits were $r = 0.67$ for the high IQs and $r = 0.25$ for the high creatives.

37. Both groups had similar scores on tests of achievement motivation—McClelland n-ach and Strodtbeck V-score.

38. Herbert Gintis, "Education, Technology, and the Characteristics of Worker Productivity," *American Economic Review,* May 1971.

39. John L. Holland, "Creative and Academic Performance Among Talented Adolescents," *Journal of Educational Psychology,* No. 52, 1961.

40. Verbal and Mathematical sections of the Scholastic Achievement Test, Humanities and Scientific Comprehension.

41. The interested reader should consult Holland (1961), *op. cit.* and Herbert Gintis, *Alienation and Power,* Ph.D. dissertation for Harvard University, May 1969.

42. Gintis (1969), *op. cit.* and (1971), *op. cit.*

43. Holland's personality measures will be presented in italics. Unless otherwise indicated, all are statistically significant at the 1 percent level.

44. In addition to the good citizenship—externally motivated student, a small portion of the high *Drive to Achieve* students exhibit a set of personality traits quite similar to those of the *Deviant Creatives* described in Getzel and Jackson's study, already presented. These students, high on *Artistic Performance and Creative Activities,* evidently reject the pressure to define their personal goals in terms compatible with high grades and teacher approbation, and their positive personality traits are uniformly penalized in terms of grades and teacher ratings for *Citizenship.*

45. Charles Silberman (1971), *op. cit.*

46. As quoted in Lawrence Cremin (1964), *op. cit.,* p. 241.

47. *Ibid.,* pp. 240–241.

48. *Ibid.,* p. 328.

49. Raymond Callahan, *Education and the Cult of Efficiency* (Chicago: The University of Chicago Press, 1962), preface.

50. *Ibid.*

51. Thomas S. Kuhn, *The Structure of Scientific Revolutions* (Chicago: The University of Chicago Press, 1962), p. 53.

52. Arthur A. Jensen, *Educability and Group Differences* (New York: Harper & Row, 1973); and Richard Herrnstein, *IQ in the Meritocracy* (Boston: Little, Brown and Company, 1973).

53. For a more complete discussion, see Richard C. Edwards, Michael Reich, and Thomas Weisskopf, *The Capitalist System* (Englewood Cliffs, NJ: Prentice-Hall, 1972); André Gorz, "Technical Intelligence and the Capitalist Division of Labor," *Telos,* Summer 1972.

54. Clarence Karier, *Shaping the American Educational State: 1900 to the Present* (New York: The Free Press, 1975); and Clarence Karier, Joel Spring, and Paul C. Violas (1973), *op. cit.*

55. Indeed, it has been pointed out to us by Dr. F. Bohnsack in a personal communication that Dewey did begin to revise his views, especially after World War I:

> For this later time, at least, I would doubt whether we could say he characterized the social system as democratic. He saw and criticized the totalitarian features of existing society and the missing ". . . intrinsic growth orientation of education." As self development and equality of opportunity, to him, were inconsistent with preparing workers for existing [alienated] jobs, he criticized such a preparation and wanted to change existing industrial education as well as industrial work.

See A.G. Wirth, *The Vocational-Liberal Studies Controversy between John Dewey and Others (1900–1917)* (Washington, D.C., 1970), and John Dewey, "Education vs. Trade-training," *The New Republic,* Vol. 3, No. 15, May 1915.

As Virginia Held has pointed out to us, Dewey, in his mature work, *Art as Experience* (New York: Minton, Balch and Company, 1934), went further to claim:

> The labor and employment problem of which we are so acutely aware cannot be solved by mere changes in wage, hours of work, and sanitary conditions. No permanent solution is possible save in a radical alteration, which affects the degree and kind of participation the worker has in the production and social disposition of the wares he produces. (p. 343)

5

What "Counts" as Educational Policy? Notes toward a New Paradigm

Jean Anyon

In my first article as a young PhD, which was published in the *Harvard Educational Review*, I argued that high school U.S. history curriculum, as represented in widely used textbooks, excises and thereby defines out of existence radical responses American workers have had to the problems they face on the job and in their communities (Anyon, 1979). This educational excision is one way that schooling mitigates against the development of working-class consciousness.

In empirical and theoretical work since then, I have investigated knowledge and pedagogical experiences made available to students in different social-class contexts (1980, 1981), and have attempted to understand the consequences of ways we conceptualize urban education, urban school reform, and neighborhood poverty. Recent arguments have aimed at unseating simplistic notions of the causes of urban poverty and low achievement in city districts, and explicating unexplored relations between urban education and movements for social change (e.g., 1995, 1997, 2005).

In this chapter I think about education policy over the seventy-five years of *Harvard Educational Review* publication. During these decades, many K–12 policies have been written and implemented by federal, state, and local governments. Some of these have aimed at improving education in America's cities and are my primary focus. Over the years, dominant strategies called upon to improve urban schools have included curricular, administrative, and funding reforms, as well as increases in educational opportunity and district/school accountability.

A historical examination of policies can inform decisions we make today. Policy failures, for example, may demonstrate that we need to rethink strategies we choose in our long-term attempts to solve the problems of school and student achievement in urban districts. Indeed, I will argue that the quality of education in city schools is a complex problem, and education policy as historically conceived has not been adequate to the task of increasing urban school achievement to acceptable levels. Academic learning in city schools is undoubtedly higher than in, say, 1900, yet there is still no large urban district that can demonstrate high achievement in even half its students or schools. Noting this failure of educational policy to render most urban schools high-quality institutions, I ask, what *should* count as educational policy? As in any attempt to resolve complex issues, workable solutions can only be generated by an understanding of underlying causes.

The diagnosis I provide is based on analyses completed for my book, *Radical Possibilities: Public Policy, Urban Education, and a New Social Movement* (Anyon, 2005). In this book I examine federal and regional mandates that affect economic and social opportunities available to the urban poor. I find that despite stated intentions, federal and metropolitan policies and arrangements generally restrict opportunities available to city residents and neighborhoods. I show how job, wage, housing, tax, and transportation policies maintain minority poverty in urban neighborhoods, and thereby create environments that overwhelm the potential of educational policy to create systemic, sustained improvements in the schools. For example, policies such as minimum wage statutes that yield full-time pay below the poverty level, and affordable housing and transportation policies that segregate low-income workers of color in urban areas but industrial and other job development in far-flung suburbs where public transit routes do not reach, are all culpable.

In order to solve the systemic problems of urban education, then, I argue in the book—and will argue here—that we need not only better schools but also the reform of these public policies. Rules and regulations regarding teaching, curriculum, and assessment certainly are important, but policies to eliminate poverty-wage work and housing segregation (for example) should be part of the educational policy panoply as well, for these have consequences for urban education at least as profound as curriculum, pedagogy, and testing.

In the sections that follow I describe major K–12 education policies that have been implemented over the years to attempt to improve urban education, and then discuss several federal and metro-area policies and practices that limit the potential and success of these strategies. I also report hopeful new research suggesting that even modest income and other family supports typically improve low-income students' academic achievement. I end by arguing that, given this power of economic access to influence educational outcomes, strategies to support economic opportunity and development for urban residents and neighborhoods should be among the policies we consider in our attempts to improve urban schools and districts. Just as in affluent suburban districts where economic strength is the engine of educational reform, so it would be in urban districts where resident and neighborhood affluence would support and retool the schools. I begin with an overview of education policy as typically conceived.

Education Policies

Over the last seventy-five years or so, federal policies have attempted various strategies to improve city education. The first federal policy aimed at working-class populations was the Smith-Hughes Act of 1917, which provided funds to prepare students in industrialized areas for working-class jobs through vocational programs. Variants of this policy continued throughout the twentieth century, in the Vocational Education Acts of 1963, 1984, and 1998, and in the School-to-Work Opportunity Act of 1994 and the later federal legislation in which it was subsumed.

Some federal education policies have attempted to improve urban education by making funding available for increased curriculum materials and libraries, early childhood classes, and various types of programmatic innovations in city schools. Head Start in 1965, Follow Through in 1967, and, to a lesser extent, Title IX, which banned sex discrimination in 1972, brought and instigated new curricula and programs into city districts.[1] These policies were intended to increase student access and/or achievement by upgrading curricular resources and experiences.

Other federal K–12 policies have aimed specifically at increasing educational equity. The 1954 *Brown* decision (which committed the federal government to desegregation as a policy stance), the Elementary and Secondary Education Act of 1965 (ESEA), the Bilingual Act in 1968, Title IX in 1972, and the Education for All Handicapped Children Act in 1975 opened doors to academic experiences for previously underserved K–12 students. These policies are generally thought to have expanded urban students' educational opportunities.

More recent federal education policies to improve schooling—with urban students and teachers often a target—have called for increased academic standards and requirements, standardized testing, and professional development of teachers. These policies were recommended by the influential report *A Nation at Risk,* commissioned by President Ronald Reagan and published in 1983. The emphasis on increased academic standards was part of an effort to support business needs for well-prepared workers and employees. The report's recommendations for higher standards and increased testing were introduced as policy in 1994 and 1996 as part of the Goals 2000 legislation. In 2001 these goals were instantiated as federal mandates in the No Child Left Behind Act (NCLB). Privatization of education via nonpublic providers when K–12 schools fail is a subtextual education policy in NCLB (Conley, 2003; Cross, 2004; Stein, 2004).

It is important to note that federal education policies intended to improve urban schools did not take aim at the economic arrangements and practices that themselves produced the poverty in which city schools were embedded. Despite increases in educational opportunity, the effects of almost a century of educational policies on urban school and student achievement have, by most accounts, been disappointing.

The first state policies regarding the education of America's urban (and rural) poor emerged earlier than federal ones. What has counted as state education policy regarding poor students can be said to have begun with mid-to late-nineteenth century insertions into state constitutions of the right of all students to a free, "thorough," "efficient," or "useful" education (Odden & Picus, 1992). Following these insertions and until the 1970s, however, most state education policies did not focus specifically on urban education. State mandates typically set regulations and requirements for school systems, teacher and administrator preparation, and school funding (through property taxes). During the 1970s and 1980s, lawsuits challenging state education funding systems brought increased attention to city schools and districts. State urban education policy in these decades involved various kinds of efforts, including school-based management and basic skills mandates. In the 1990s, state policies attempted to align education standards and regulations with federal ones, mandated curriculum and teacher licensure reform, and closely monitored urban districts. As legal challenges to state systems have led to increased funding of city schools, states have imposed stricter academic and graduation requirements, as well as multigrade and multisubject standardized testing. Quasi-privatization policies supporting charter schools, vouchers, and other school choice programs have also been a state strategy to attempt to improve the education of urban children by offering them a choice of schools to attend (Conley, 2003).

Over the decades, federal and state policies codified an increasing number of requirements that urban schools and districts must meet. Local governments and educational bureaucracies have undertaken a plethora of programs to attempt to meet those guidelines. Local districts have also mounted school reform projects in response to local social conditions and political pressure from parents and communities. Most local initiatives have been curricular, pedagogical, and administrative.

During the Progressive Era, cities consolidated and professionalized their school systems and personnel, introduced programs like the Gary Plan to prepare students for the industrial experience, increased access to high school, organized educational opportunities for immigrant parents, and sometimes fed, bathed, and clothed poor children. During the decade of the Great Depression, most large cities retrenched and severely cut educational social service and academic programs, as local tax receipts plummeted and banks that offered loans demanded broad cuts in education. During the 1960s, many urban districts were weakened further as most remaining businesses and jobs moved to the suburbs, decimating the urban property tax base (Anyon, 1997; Ravitch, 2000; Tyack, 1974; Wrigley, 1982).

Since the 1970s, in response to federal, judicial, and state mandates, urban districts have bused students to meet racial integration guidelines, decentralized authority to increase community participation, and created magnet schools to attempt to attract middle-class parents. Other local policies that have been attempted to improve achievement are a multitude of reform programs or "school improvement projects," student retention services, privatization of educational offerings, vouchers and magnets, mayoral control, small schools, and curriculum standardization and evaluation through testing. The social context of these policies has included pressure to be accountable in the wake of increased funding, as well as community and corporate demands for better schools. None of the local policies has focused on the poverty of families or neighborhoods.

One way to evaluate this long run of education policy is to compare the achievement of urban students at the beginning of the twentieth and twenty-first centuries. Although achievement is higher now in that larger percentages of students remain in school past the elementary years than in 1900, I would argue that the improvement is relative and illusory. That is, while in the early twentieth century relatively few urban poor students went beyond fifth grade, the vast majority did not require further education to find employment in industries that could lead to middle-class income (Anyon, 1997; Ayres, 1909). Currently, relatively few urban poor students go past ninth grade: The graduation rates in large comprehensive inner-city high schools are abysmally low. In fourteen such New York City schools, for example, only 10 percent to 20 percent of ninth graders in 1996 graduated four years later (Fine, 2001; Greene 2001; Miao & Haney, 2004).[2] Despite the fact that low-income individuals desperately need a college degree to find decent employment, only 7 percent obtain a bachelors degree by age twenty-six (Education Trust, 2001; Mishel, Bernstein, & Schmitt, 2001). So, in relation to the needs of low-income students, urban districts fail their students with more egregious consequences now than in the early twentieth century.

Given the plethora of federal, state, and local education policies aimed at urban schools and the current widely acknowledged necessity of high-quality education for all, why have most urban schools and districts not been able to provide such an education for their students?

Barriers to High-Quality Public Education in Cities

There are multiple causes of low-quality schooling in urban areas, and education policies as heretofore conceived address only a few. Education policy has not addressed the neighborhood poverty that surrounds and invades urban schools with low expectations and cynicism. Education policy has not addressed the unemployment and joblessness of families who will have few if any resources for the further education of their children, even if they excel in K–12 classes.

And education policy—even in response to state financial challenges—has not addressed the political economy that largely determines low levels of city district funding. Taxes on wealthy families and corporations are among the lowest on record (Phillips, 2002). Business and government investment in affluent suburban job centers rather than urban areas continues to deprive poor neighborhoods of entry-level jobs and a tax base, and residents' poverty wages further diminish available funding sources (Anyon, 2005; Orfield, 2002; Rusk, 1999). These political-economic constraints on quality schooling are not challenged by current or past education policy. In most U.S. cities, the political leverage of urban parents has not been sufficient to force the funding necessary to overcome outdated buildings, broken computer labs, and overcrowded classrooms.

These economic and political conditions are the building blocks of formidable barriers to systemic, sustainable school quality. Indeed, even when urban school reform succeeds, it fails—when there are no decent jobs a diploma from a successfully reformed school or district will attract, and there is no government or familial funding sufficient for the vast majority of low-income graduates of even good urban high schools to obtain a bachelors degree.

Individual and neighborhood poverty builds walls around schools and classrooms that education policy does not penetrate or scale. In the following section I describe some of the federal and metro-area policies and arrangements that sustain these barriers.

Federal Policy

Analysts typically do not link federal policies to the maintenance of poverty, to the lack of jobs that bedevils American workers, or to the increasingly large portion of employment that pays poverty and near-poverty wages. Yet federal policy is determinative. To take a blatant example, Congress set the first minimum wage in 1938 at $3.05 (in 2000 dollars); it stands in 2005 at $5.15—a mere two dollars more. (Yearly income at this wage is $10,712.) This sum ensures that full-time, year-round, minimum-wage work will not raise people out of poverty (Mishel, Bernstein, & Boushey, 2003). Analysis in 2004 found that minimum-wage standards directly affect the wages of 8.9 percent of the workforce (9.9 million workers); when we include those making one dollar more an hour than the minimum wage, this legislation affects the wages of as much as 18 percent of the workforce (Economic Policy Institute, 2004). Contrary to the claims of those who oppose raising the minimum wage (that an increase will force employers to fire, or hire fewer of those affected by the increase), studies of the 1990–1991 and 1996–1997 minimum-wage increases failed to find any systematic, significant job losses associated with the increases and found no evidence of negative employment effects on small businesses (Economic Policy Institute, 2004).

Almost half the workforce earns what some economists call poverty-*zone* wages (and what I define as up to and including 125 percent of the official poverty level; Anyon, 2005). I analyzed figures provided by the Economic Policy Institute to calculate the overall percentage of people who work full-time year round yet make wages up to and including 125 percent of the official poverty threshold needed to support a family of four at the poverty level. The analysis demonstrates that in 1999, during a very strong economy, almost half of the people at work in the United States (41.3 percent) earned poverty-zone wages—in 1999, $10.24/hour ($21,299/year) or less, working full-time year round (Mishel et al., 2001). Two years later, in 2001, 38.4 percent earned poverty-zone wages working full-time year round (in 2001, 125 percent of the poverty line was a $10.88 hourly wage; Mishel et al., 2003). This suggests that the federal minimum-wage policy is an important determinant of poverty for many millions of U.S. families.

There are other macroeconomic policies that produce hardship. These especially penalize Blacks and Latinos, the majority of whom live in segregated, low-income urban neighborhoods. These policies include the following: job training as a predominant federal antipoverty policy when there have been too few jobs for graduates; ineffective federal implementation of policies that outlaw racial discrimination in hiring and housing; regressive income taxes that charge wealthy individuals less than half the rate charged the rich during most of the first sixty years of the twentieth century, yet substantially raise the payroll taxes paid by the working poor and middle class; and corporate tax policies in recent years that allow 60 percent of large U.S. corporations to pay no federal taxes at all (and in some cases to obtain millions in rebates; Citizens for Tax Justice, 2002; Lafer, 2002; Orfield, 2002; Rusk, 1999).

These federal policies and practices contribute to personal, neighborhood, and educational poverty because they lead to the following problems: There are not enough jobs for poor families who need them; low-income families of color are concentrated in low-resourced urban neighborhoods; and when the wealthy do not contribute equitably to public expenses, funding for services like education declines and the quality of the services tends to be low.

The effects of these policies are compounded by harsh union laws and lack of federal protection for labor organizing; Federal Reserve Bank pronouncements that ignore the portion of its mandate to maintain a high level of employment; and free-trade agreements that send thousands of corporations, and their job opportunities, to other countries. These policies hurt workers of all colors—and in most sectors of the economy—as existing jobs disappear and those remaining pay lower wages, in part because they are not unionized (Anyon, 2005; Citizens for Tax Justice, 2002; Economic Policy Institute, 2002, 2004; Galbraith, 1998; Lafer, 2002; Mishel et al., 2001).

However, there are federal policies we could create that would lower poverty by important margins—including a significantly raised minimum wage, comparable worth laws, and policies to enforce existing regulations that outlaw discrimination in hiring. A raise in the minimum wage that brought workers above poverty would improve the lives of at least a fifth of U.S. workers (Economic Policy Institute, 2004). Paying women the same amount men are paid for comparable work would, according to one analysis, reduce poverty by 40 percent, as such a large percentage of poor people are women in low-wage jobs (Lafer, 2002). And requiring employers to hire without discriminating against Blacks and Latinos would further open opportunities currently denied.

In addition, policies that worked against U.S. poverty in the past could be reinstated: U.S. government regulation of the minimum wage, which kept low-paid workers' income at the median of highly paid unionized workers in the decades after World War II; federal support for union organizing; a federal program of job creation in cities, as during the Great

Depression of the 1930s; and federal programs for urban youth that would support further education, as such policies did for eight million men and women after World War II (Anyon, 2005; Galbraith, 1998). These national policies were important supports of the widespread prosperity of the United States' working and middle classes in the quarter century following 1945 (Galbraith, 1998).

Metropolitan Policy and Practice

Like current federal mandates, there are metro-area policies and practices that increase the problems of urban residents and neighborhoods. Metro areas are shaped by regional markets—for jobs, housing, investment, and production. Metro areas account for over 80 percent of national output and drive the economic performance of the nation as a whole. Each metro area is anchored by one or more cities (Dreier, Mollenkopf, & Swanstrom, 2001).

Today, metropolitan regions are characterized by population growth, extensive inequality, and segregation (Orfield, 2002; Rusk, 1999). The percentage of racial minorities in large metro areas who live in the suburbs jumped from 19 percent to 27 percent during the 1990s. However, a growing share of these families lives in fiscally stressed suburbs, with an increasing number of neighborhoods having poverty levels over 30 percent (Kingsley & Petit, 2003; Orfield, 2002). As in areas of concentrated poverty in the central city, low levels of taxable resources in these "urbanized" segregated suburbs leave services like education lacking in funds.

U.S. metropolitan areas are characterized by the following problems, all of which disadvantage urban minority families and communities: Most entry-level jobs for which adults with low to moderate education levels are qualified are increasingly located in suburbs, rather than in central cities, but public transit systems do not connect these suburban job centers to urban areas, where most low-income minorities live—thus preventing them from access to jobs there. State-allowed local zoning on the basis of income prevents affordable housing in most suburbs where entry-level jobs are located, which means there is little if any housing for low-income families near the suburban job centers. Indeed, as I have mentioned, the failure to enforce antiracial discrimination statutes in housing confines most Blacks and Latinos to housing sites in central cities and segregated suburbs. Finally, even though federal and state taxes are paid by residents throughout metro regions (including inner cities), most tax-supported development takes place in the affluent suburbs rather than in low-income areas. Thus, few jobs exist in most low-income urban neighborhoods (Anyon, 2005; Dreir et al., 2001; Orfield, 2002; Rusk, 1999). These inequitable regional arrangements and policies exacerbate federal wage and job mandates and contribute in important ways to joblessness and poverty in cities and urbanized suburbs, and to the low quality of investment in services such as education there.

Poverty

One consequence of federal and regional policies regarding work, wages, housing segregation, and transportation is that the numbers of poor people approach the figures of 1959—before massive urban poverty became a national issue. Although the percentages are lower now, the numbers are still staggering: There were about as many people officially poor in 1993 (39.2

million) as in 1959 (39.4 million; Harrington, 1963). And in 2003, 35.8 million were officially poor, only 3.5 million fewer than in 1959 (Mishel et al., 2003).

A more realistic measure of poverty than federal guidelines is that those earning incomes up to 200 percent of the official levels are considered poor (Bernstein, Brocht, & Spade-Aguilar, 2000; Citro & Michael, 1995; Short, Iceland, & Garner, 1999). This revised threshold is used by increasing numbers of social scientists. A calculation of the individuals who earned less than 200 percent of the poverty level in 2001 ($17.40/hour, or $36,192/year), demonstrates a much larger percentage of poor employees than is commonly acknowledged: *84 percent of Hispanic workers, 80 percent of Black workers, and 64.3 percent of White workers made wages at or under 200 percent of the official poverty line* (Mishel et al., 2001).

A calculation of *families* living with earnings up to 200 percent of the poverty line reveals that Black and Latino families face the greatest financial hurdles. More than 50 percent of Black and Latino families earn less than 200 percent of the poverty level, compared to only 20.3 percent of White families, even though White families constitute a slight majority (50.5 percent) of families that fall below 200 percent of the poverty level (Mishel et al., 2001). In sum, poverty in the United States is higher than commonly perceived and is maintained in urban areas by federal and metro-area policies and distributions.

Effects of Poverty on Urban Students

Macroeconomic policies that set wages below poverty levels, that train inner-city hopefuls for jobs that do not exist, that do not extract from the wealthy a fair share of social expenses, and that rarely enforce laws that would substantially decrease the economic discrimination of people of color all support persistent poverty and near-poverty among minority urban populations. This economic and social distress can prevent children from developing their full potential and can certainly dampen the enthusiasm, effort, and expectations with which urban children and their families approach K–12 education.

As I will report, a recent national study of young children confirms the potential of impoverished circumstances to prevent students' full cognitive growth before they enroll in kindergarten. Of countervailing power, however, is research demonstrating that when parents obtain better financial resources or better living conditions, the educational achievement of the children typically improves significantly. These findings empirically support the argument that for the urban poor, even with the right educational policies in place, school achievement may await a family's economic access.

I already presented adult poverty figures at the official threshold and noted the alarming increase in numbers when a more realistic assessment is made. The same disparities exist between federal and alternative counts of poor children. Sixteen percent of American children—almost 12 million—lived below the *official* federal poverty line in 2001. Almost half of those children (44 percent, or a little over 5 million) lived in *extreme* poverty (less than half the poverty line, or $7,400 for a family of three in 2001)—including nearly a million African American children. This was a 17 percent increase in the number of children in extreme poverty from 2000, at the end of the economic boom (Cauthen & Lu, 2001; Dillon, 2003; Lu, 2003).

When the more appropriate alternative poverty threshold criterion is applied, however, a full *38 percent* of American children are identified as poor—27 million who lived in families with income up to 200 percent of the official poverty line. These children live in poverty as well—although official statistics do not designate them as such. However, these families experience hardships that are almost as severe as those who are officially poor (Cauthen & Lu 2001; Lu, 2003). *By the revised measure—200 percent of the official poverty cutoff—a full 57 percent of African American children, 64 percent of Latino, and 34 percent of White children were poor in the United States in 2001* (Lu, 2003; Mishel et al., 2003).

It is only in the 1990s that empirical studies focused on why and how poverty affects cognitive development and school achievement. Researchers began to document the specific effects of poverty environments on children's development (Brooks-Gunn, Duncan, Leventhal, & Aber, 1997; Goering & Feins, 2003; Sampson, Morenoff, & Gannon-Rowley, 2002). This body of work documents the correlations between low income, child development, and educational achievement (see Duncan & Brooks-Gunn, 1997, for an overview of studies). For example, poverty has been found to have consistently negative effects on children's cognitive development (Duncan & Brooks-Gunn, 1997; Duncan, Brooks-Gunn, & Klebanov, 1994; McLoyd, 1998). Longitudinal studies that have been carried out also demonstrate that "family income consistently predicts children's academic and cognitive performance, even when other family characteristics are taken into account" (Duncan & Brooks-Gunn, 1997). Persistent and extreme poverty has been shown to be more detrimental to children than temporary poverty (Bolger & Patterson, 1995; Duncan et al., 1994). Family income may influence children through both lack of resources and parental emotional stress (Bradley, 1984; McLoyd & Jartayne, 1994; Smith, Brooks-Gunn, & Klebanov, 1997; Sugland, Zaslow, Brooks-Gunn, & Moore, 1995). Poor children have more health and behavior difficulties than those from more affluent families, which mitigates against educational success (Duncan & Brooks-Gunn, 1997; Houser, Brown, & Prosser, 1998; Klerman, 1991/2003; Korenman & Miller, 1997). Studies collected by Duncan and Brooks-Gunn teased out some of the variables within the effects of income. In summarizing research reported in their 1997 volume *Consequences of Growing up Poor*, they point out the following:

1. Income matters for the cognitive development of preschoolers "because it is associated with the provision of a richer learning environment" (p. 601). This is true in part because family income is a "significant determinant of child care environments, including center-based childcare (p. 601). . . . Income allows parents to provide their children with safer, more stimulating home environments; to live in communities with better schools, parks, and libraries and more challenging peers; to afford tuition and other expenses associated with higher education; to purchase or otherwise gain access to higher-quality health care; and in many other ways to buy the things that promote the health and development of their children" (p. 14).

2. "A variety of income measures—income [relative to needs] . . . income loss, the ratio of debts to assets, and unstable work—are associated with family economic pressure" (p. 602). Economic pressure has been found to be associated with depression (and stress) in parents, which can affect parenting, and thus school achievement.

3. "Family income is usually a stronger predictor of ability and achievement outcomes than are measures of parental schooling or family structure [e.g., single parenthood]" (p. 603). Many studies have shown that children raised in low-income families score lower than children from more affluent families do on assessments of health, cognitive

development, and positive behavior. "In general, the better the measure of family income and the longer the period over which it is measured, the stronger the association between the family's economic well-being and children's outcomes" (p. 14).

It is important to understand that these findings do not suggest that poor students are of low intelligence; rather, the studies point to the power of the economy—and of economic hardship—to place extremely high hurdles to full development in front of children who are poor. It is of course possible—although it is not the norm—that education over time mitigates the effects of SES (Hout, 1988; Jencks & Phillips, 1998).

In 2002, Valerie Lee and David Burkham published the results of a large-sample assessment of the effects of poverty on cognitive development. They utilized data from the United States Department of Education's early childhood longitudinal kindergarten cohort, which is a comprehensive dataset that provides a nationally representative portrait of kindergarten students. Lee and Burkham (2002) explored differences in young children's achievement scores in literacy and mathematics by race, ethnicity, and socioeconomic status (SES) as they began kindergarten. They also analyzed differences by social background in an array of children's homes and family activities.

The study demonstrates that inequalities in children's cognitive ability by SES are substantial even before children begin kindergarten and that poverty has a detrimental impact on early intellectual achievement. Importantly, it demonstrates that the disadvantages of being poor outweigh by far the race or family structure of children as causes of the cognitive disadvantages.

Details of the national assessment include the following:

1. Before children enter kindergarten, the average cognitive scores of children in the highest SES group are 60 percent above the scores of the lowest SES group.
2. Cognitive skills are much *less* closely related to race/ethnicity after accounting for SES. After taking racial differences into account, children from different SES groups achieve at different levels—before they begin kindergarten.
3. The impact of family structure on cognitive skills (e.g., being in a single-parent family) is much less than either race or SES.
4. Socioeconomic status is very strongly related to cognitive skills; SES accounts for more of the variation in cognitive scores than any other factor by far.

Lee and Burkham (2002) also found that disadvantaged children not only enter kindergarten with significantly lower cognitive skills than their advantaged peers, but also that low-SES children begin school (kindergarten) in systematically lower-quality elementary schools than their more advantaged counterparts. "However school quality is defined—in terms of higher student achievement, more school resources, more qualified teachers, more positive teacher attitudes, better neighborhood or school conditions, private vs. public schools—the least advantaged United States children begin their formal schooling in consistently lower-quality schools. This reinforces the inequalities that develop even before children reach school age" (p. 3; see also Entwistle & Alexander, 1997; Phillips, Brooks-Gunn, Duncan, Klevanov, & Crane, 1998; Phillips, Crouse, & Ralph, 1998; Stipic & Ryan, 1997; White, 1982).

In their review of studies of poverty's effects on individual development, Duncan and Brooks-Gunn (1997) conclude, "Taken together, [these studies] suggest that programs that raise the incomes of poor families will enhance the cognitive development of children and may improve their chance of success in [education and] the labor market during adulthood. Most important appears to be the elimination of deep and persistent poverty during a child's early years" (p. 608). I now turn to research suggesting that familial financial and other supports do indeed lead to increased educational achievement in children.

Evidence that Familial Supports Raise Educational Achievement

I have been examining relationships among education policy, the economy, and achievement in urban schools. First, I critiqued education policy for its lack of attention to urban poverty, which, I argued, is maintained by policies and decisions made at the federal and metropolitan levels. I provided evidence of some of the egregious consequences of federal and regional policies and practices for urban families, neighborhoods, students, and schools. In particular, I demonstrated that child poverty creates obstacles to full development and educational achievement, especially when low-income minority children attend low-resourced schools—which most do. In this section I provide indirect and direct research evidence that increased family supports such as financial resources and less segregated neighborhoods raise educational achievement.

Indirect evidence is present in a longitudinal study completed in 2003 that found that improving family income reduces the negative (aggressive) social behavior of children, which in turn is likely to lead to better school behavior and performance. For eight years, researchers studied a representative population sample of 1,420 children ages nine to thirteen in rural North Carolina. A quarter of the children were from a Cherokee reservation. Psychological tests were given at the start of the study and repeated each year (Costello, Compton, Keeler, & Angold, 2003; O'Connor, 2003).

When the study began, 68 percent of the children were living below the official poverty line. On average, the poorer children engaged in more vandalism, stealing, bullying, stubbornness, and outbursts of anger than those who were not poor. But halfway through the study, a local casino began distributing a percentage of its profits to tribal families. Given to each tribal member over eighteen and put in a trust fund for younger members, the payment increased slightly each year, reaching about $6,000 per person for the year 2001. Psychiatric tests administered by researchers for the four years that the funds were being distributed demonstrated that the negative behaviors of children in families who were no longer poor dropped to the same levels found among children whose families had never been poor (decreasing by 40 percent). Parents who moved out of poverty reported having more time to spend with their children, and researchers identified better parenting behavior. Researchers also identified the psychological benefits of not being poor as important to both parents and children. Poverty puts stress on families, which can increase the likelihood of children developing behavioral problems. One parent in the study told researchers that "the jobs [produced by the casino] give people the chance to pull themselves up by their bootstraps and get out of poverty. That carries over into less juvenile crime, less domestic violence, and an overall better living experience for families" (O'Connor, 2003, p. 2).

Other research demonstrates that urban low-income parents are also able to practice more effective parenting strategies when some of the stress of poverty is eased by a higher income.

And the reduction in stress in turn may positively affect the behavior and achievement of low-income children (see information below; also Jackson, Brooks-Gunn, Huang, & Glassman, 2000; Jeremiah, 2003; Seitz, Rosenbaum, & Apfel, 1985).

Direct evidence that income supports improved educational achievement is also available. In March 2001, the Manpower Demonstration Research Corporation (MDRC) published a synthesis of research on how welfare and work policies affect the children of single mothers (Morris, Huston, Duncan, Crosby, & Bos, 2001). This synthesis reviewed data from evaluations of five programs that provided income supplements to poverty-wage workers (Florida's Family Transition Program, the Minnesota Family Investment Program, the National Evaluation of Welfare-to-Work Strategies, Milwaukee's New Hope for Families and Children Program, and the Self-Sufficiency Project). These programs offered supports of differing kinds to poverty-wage workers—income supplements, earnings disregards (rules that allow working welfare recipients to keep more of their income when they go to work), subsidized health care, employment services, counseling, supervised afterschool activities for children and youth, and informal get-togethers with project staff.

MDRC's review of the studies found that even relatively small income supplements to working parents (amounting to about $4,000 per year) improved children's elementary school achievement by about 10 to 15 percent of the average variation in the control groups. These improvements were seen on test scores as well as on ratings by parents and/or teachers. The earning supplements had "consistently positive impacts on children's [school] achievement" (Morris et al., 2001, p. 63). The positive effects were small, but were statistically significant.

Longitudinal studies have found that the achievement and behavior problems of young children can have important implications for their well-being in adolescence and adulthood (Caspi, Wright, Moffit, & Silva, 1998; Masten & Coatsworth, 1995). Moreover, even small differences between children in school achievement early on can translate into larger differences later (Entwistle & Alexander, 1997). Therefore, as the authors of the research synthesis state, "a program's effects on children, even if the effects are small, may continue to have implications over the course of their lives" (Caspi et al., 1998, p. 25).

The earning supplements provided by four of these programs did not, however, bring the families above the poverty level. The improvements in children's school achievement and behavior from even these relatively meager cash supplements for working families suggest that if we were to increase family resources substantially, we could probably improve educational and social outcomes for children substantially.

Indeed, one program that did provide an earning supplement that brought the families above poverty level showed particularly impressive results for children's behavior and achievement. New Hope for Families and Children was run between 1994 and 1998 in two inner-city areas in Milwaukee. Candidates had to live in one of two targeted areas, be eighteen or older, be willing and able to work at least thirty hours per week, and have a household income at or below 150 percent of the federal poverty level (Huston et al., 2001). Almost 90 percent of the adults in the sample were single or separated mothers with children when they entered the study, and 80 percent were receiving public assistance. The program was conceived by a nonprofit community-based organization and provided several benefits: the earnings supplement, subsidized health insurance, and subsidized child care. The program offered help in obtaining a job and provided a community-service job for up to one year for those not able to find work elsewhere, the advice and support of project staff were made available. The annual cost of providing these benefits was $5,300 per family.

New Hope was evaluated at two-year and five-year intervals using a random assignment research design. After conducting outreach in the communities to identify eligible people, the study enrolled over 1,300 low-income adults. Half the applicants were randomly assigned to a program group that received New Hope's benefits, and the other half were randomly assigned to a control group that was not eligible for the benefits.

Both evaluations showed positive results (Bos, Huston, Duncan, Brock, & McLoyd, 1996; Huston et al., 2001). Financial supplements in the New Hope program did reduce the number of families in poverty, but both program and control groups reported similar levels of hardship, such as food insecurity and financial insufficiency. Yet the program had positive effects on parents' wellbeing and coping skills. As Huston et al. (2003) explain:

> Parents in the New Hope group were more aware of available "helping" resources in the community, such as where to find assistance with energy costs or housing problems. More of them also knew about the [Earned Income Tax Credit] and its support, an important source of support for low-income workers. Ethnographic data suggest that a significant number of families intentionally used the Earned Income Tax Credits as a savings plan for making major purchases, reducing debt, and stabilizing rent and other payments. Parents in New Hope also reported better physical health and fewer symptoms associated with depression than did parents in the control group. At the two-year point, New Hope parents reported reduced stress, increased feelings of social support, and increased time pressure. The ethnographic study found that many parents had children with disabilities or behavioral difficulties; New Hope helped the parents achieve a difficult balance among work, services, and parenting. . . . The New Hope parents did report fewer problems controlling their children, and parents of adolescents reported more effective management (better control and less need for punishment). (p. 9)

New Hope improved children's school performance. "At both the two-year and the five-year points, children in the program performed better than control group children on several measures of academic achievement, particularly on reading and literacy tests. After five years, they scored higher on a standardized test of reading skills and their parents reported that they got higher grades in reading skills" (Huston et al., 2001, p. 13). These effects were slightly more pronounced for boys than for girls. Compared with their control group counterparts, boys in New Hope also received higher ratings of academic performance from their teachers and were more likely to expect to attend college at both the two-year and the five-year assessments. "New Hope adolescents reported more engagement with schools, feelings of efficacy, and expectations to finish college than did their control group counterparts" (pp. 13–14). New Hope's effects are consistent with the results of other programs that have improved children's outcomes by providing wage supplements and subsidized child care (Michalopoulos et al., 2002; Morris et al., 2001).

Indeed, the New Hope findings are in line with the increased educational achievement of students that has been identified in large-scale programs that assist low-income minority families by helping them move from inner-city neighborhoods to more affluent and/or less segregated metropolitan areas. The first of these "mobility programs" was the Gautreaux program in the Chicago metropolitan area.

As a result of a victorious lawsuit charging the Chicago Housing Authority with segregation in public housing, the court ordered the housing authority to move families who wanted to live in less segregated areas of the city and suburbs. The Gautreaux program moved over 7,000 families to higher-income areas of the Chicago metropolitan region between 1976 and 1998 (Rubinowitz & Rosenbaum, 2002). Although at first a disproportionate number of the children who moved were placed in classes for the learning disabled by their suburban schools, they ultimately were significantly more likely than their urban counterparts to be in college-bound tracks, in four-year colleges, and were subsequently more likely to be employed in jobs with higher pay and with benefits than children who stayed in the city (Rubinowitz & Rosenbaum, 2002).

The success of the Gautreaux program led to more than fifty other mobility programs, including the Moving To Opportunity program (MTO) begun by the U.S. Department of Housing and Urban Development (HUD) in 1994. The Housing and Community Development Act of 1992 authorized HUD to "assist very low-income families with children who reside in public housing or housing receiving project-based assistance under Section 8 of the Housing and Community Development Act of 1937 to move out of areas with high concentrations of persons living in poverty (40 percent or more) to areas with low concentrations of such persons (less than 10 percent in poverty)" (Goering & Feins, 2003, p. 6). Moving To Opportunity projects were carried out in five cities: Baltimore, Boston, Chicago, Los Angeles, and New York. Congress stipulated that HUD conduct evaluations of the program to determine its effects (Goering & Feins, 2003).

Overall, roughly 5,300 families volunteered to move within the metropolitan area of the city in which they lived. In total, 4,608 families were eligible. They were divided into three groups: the MTO "treatment" or experimental group, which received Section 8 certificates or vouchers that could only be used in areas where 10 percent or less of the residents lived below official poverty levels; they also received counseling assistance in finding private rental units. A second group was given Section 8 certificates with no special restrictions on where they were to move, and no counseling (Section 8 only group). An in-place control group continued to receive housing project assistance in the inner-city neighborhoods where they lived. The families in all three groups of the MTO program tended to be young single mothers (under age 35), African American, with a median income of $8,200. Most stated that their main reason for wanting to move was fear of gangs and violence in the neighborhoods in which they lived.

Social scientists conducted research at all five sites, using HUD data, baseline surveys, follow-up surveys of families, qualitative interviews, and data on juvenile crime, labor-market outcomes, and school performance. Among their findings are the following.

One to three years after the families in the experimental group moved, they lived in significantly more affluent and more racially mixed communities than families in the other two groups. In addition, those who were in the experimental group had median incomes that were 73 percent higher than the median incomes for the control group and 53 percent higher than the Section 8 only group. In 1997, three years after the program began, the MTO experimental group families in all five metropolitan areas lived in less-segregated neighborhoods than either of the other two groups.

Studies of adults in the experimental groups in New York and Boston reported significantly better health and emotional well-being than the Section 8 only and control groups in those cities. Mothers in both the experimental groups were much less likely to report being depressed or stressed. The parents provided more structure for their children's activities and used less restrictive parenting styles. By the third year, 10 percent fewer of the experimental group in New York City were receiving welfare. In Boston, public assistance for MTO families dropped by half, and employment in all MTO sites increased from 27 percent at the beginning of the program to 43 percent three years later. Employment in Boston increased by more than one-half.

The outcomes for children in these experimental groups were also encouraging. They attended schools that had higher pass rates, more affluent student bodies, and more resources than the schools attended by control group children. Ludwig, Duncan, and Ladd (2003) hypothesize that the peer groups in the new schools had more positive attitudes toward school than in the inner city, and this may also have contributed to good outcomes for the children.

Ludwig, Duncan, and Ladd report that young children in the experimental and Section 8 only groups "achieved higher test scores than the controls, and experienced fewer arrests for violent criminal behavior" (2003, p. 164). The authors report in some detail the assessments in Baltimore, and state that they are "largely consistent with evidence from the other MTO sites" (p. 163). Young children in the experimental and Section 8 only groups had Comprehensive Test of Basic Skills (CTBS) reading scores that were on average six to seven percentage points higher than those in the control group (i.e., in low-income urban schools). "This large effect is equal to around one-quarter of the control group mean of 25 percentile points and one-quarter of a standard deviation in the national CTBS math distribution" (p. 165). Children in the experimental group also raised their CTBS math scores about the same amount, and their pass rates on the Maryland Functional Tests' (MFT) reading test were almost double those in the inner-city schools.

High school students in the Baltimore experimental group had a more difficult transition. In the first three years of MTO, they had higher rates of grade retention, disciplinary action, and school dropout rates than the children of families in the other two groups. The authors suggest that these differences may be due to the enforcement of higher behavioral and/or educational standards in more affluent schools (Ludwig et al., 2003).

However, teens who moved from high- to low-poverty neighborhoods were arrested less often than teens in the other groups. For example, 2.7 percent of control group adolescents were arrested during an average three-month period, compared with only 1.4 percent of teens in the experimental group during the same period. Furthermore, there was a 50 percent reduction in the proportion of juveniles in the experimental group who were arrested for violent offenses. For example, in a given quarter, 3 percent of adolescents in the control group were arrested for violent crimes, compared with only 1.4 percent among the experimental group (Ludwig et al., 2003).

Research in the Boston MTO found significantly fewer behavioral and mental health problems among boys in both the experimental and Section 8-only groups, and experimental-group children were less likely to be injured or to experience asthma attacks. Among children with asthma, the number of attacks requiring medical attention fell significantly (Goering & Feins, 2003). Additionally, the children in the experimental group in Boston were less likely to engage in antisocial behavior (Ludwig et al., 2003).

In sum, these results are in general agreement with evaluations of other mobility programs, which have generally led to "substantial improvements in . . . neighborhood conditions, physical and mental health, safety, housing conditions, adult labor-market outcomes (although the findings here are mixed)" (Johnson, Ladd, & Ludwig, 2002, p. 185) and improvements in the children's behavior and educational outcomes of families who moved.

The success of even small family supports and of a move to places of increased opportunity suggests that we should provide a financial and opportunity base for urban families. This in itself will lay the foundation for fuller child development and educational achievement.

A New Education Policy Paradigm

I have outlined a number of federal and regional polices and practices that undermine urban school quality and potential by maintaining large poverty populations in urban neighborhoods. I have also provided evidence that this poverty works against the development and achievement of urban students. Importantly, however, we also see that even modest financial and social supports for poor families enable the children to achieve at higher levels in school. This suggests that policies to counter the devastating effects of macroeconomic and regional mandates and practices should "count" as policies we call on to create equity and quality in urban districts and schools.

As education policymakers and practitioners, we can acknowledge and act on the power of urban poverty, low-wage work, and housing segregation to dwarf most curricular, pedagogical, and other educational reforms. The effects of macroeconomic policies continually trump the effects of education policies.

To remove economic barriers to school quality and consequence, we can legislate a significantly higher living wage; we can create jobs in cities that offer career ladders and prepare low-income residents to fill them. And, like a number of European countries, we can tax wealthy families and corporations to pay for these and other investments. We should enforce federal antidiscrimination measures to integrate segregated housing and create public transit routes so low-income urban residents without cars are not denied access to jobs in the suburbs. Policies like these would create a social foundation on which high-quality schooling would rest. As has been the case in affluent suburbs, economic access creates the financial and political conditions in families and communities for educational commitment and reward.

In this new paradigm, education policies for which we press would take on the larger issues: Education funding reform would include the companion need for financing neighborhood jobs and decent wages. New small schools would be created as an important part of coordinated efforts at neighborhood revitalization for low-income residents. Vocational offerings in high school would link to living-wage campaigns and employers who support them. College graduation would be understood as a continuation of government's financial responsibility for public education. And lawsuits to racially integrate districts would acknowledge housing segregation as fundamental and target legal challenges accordingly.

Policies that set the standards schools must meet would identify the money, materials, teachers, courses, and neighborhood needs that must be filled in order to provide opportunities to learn at high levels. Educational accountability would be conceived as a public undertaking, centrally involving families, communities, and students, in consultation with district and government officials.

In this approach to urban school reform, "policy alignment" would not refer to the fit between education mandates issued by various levels of government and bureaucracy. The fit we would seek is between neighborhood, family, and student needs and the potential of education policies to contribute to their fulfillment.

However, economic strength and political leverage is not all that is required to transform urban education. Good schools require not only good neighborhoods, but—as equity-seeking educational reforms have promised—also the detracking of minority and working-class youth, a culture responsive to students, and assistance to teachers in their struggle to surmount the wall of resignation and defiance that separates many students from the educational enterprise.

A new paradigm of education policy is possible—one that promotes equity-seeking school change and that includes strategies to create conditions that will allow the educational improvements to take root, grow, and bear fruit in students' lives.

Notes

1. The 1958 National Defense Education Act (NDEA) funded and promoted curriculum materials, primarily in science, math, and foreign languages (e.g., the "New Math"), and some of these probably found their way into city districts and classrooms. But the NDEA was aimed at increasing the security and technological prowess of the United States, not at improving urban schools.
2. Graduation rates in large urban high schools are lower than is commonly believed. Jay P. Greene, senior fellow at the Manhattan Institute for Policy Research, calculated graduation rates in all states and large cities for major racial groups. For this calculation he first identified the eighth-grade public school enrollment for each jurisdiction and for each subgroup from the 1993 fall semester, adjusting for student movement into or out of an area. He then obtained counts of the number of regular high school diplomas awarded in the spring of 1998 when the eighth graders should have been graduating. (In calculating the 1998 graduation rate, he did not include later GED or other alternative diplomas, as the federal government does.) He found that the national graduation rate for the class of 1998 was 71 percent. For White students the rate was 78 percent, for African American students it was 56 percent, and for Latinos, 54 percent. In fifteen of forty-five large (mostly urban) districts for which there were data, fewer than 50 percent of African American students graduated; and in twenty-one of thirty-six large, mostly urban districts for which there were data, fewer than 50 percent of Latino students graduated (Greene, 2001, pp. 1–5).

References

Anyon, J. (1979). Ideology and U.S. history textbooks. *Harvard Educational Review, 49,* 361–386.

Anyon, J. (1980). Social class and the hidden curriculum of work. *Journal of Education, 162,* 7–92.

Anyon, J. (1981). Social class and school knowledge. *Curriculum Inquiry, 11,* 3–42.

Anyon, J. (1995). Race, social class, and educational reform in an inner city school. *Teachers College Record, 97,* 69–94.

Anyon, J. (1997). *Ghetto schooling: A political economy of urban educational reform.* New York: Teachers College Press.

Anyon, J. (in press). *Radical possibilities: Public policy, urban education, and a new social movement.* New York: Routledge.

Ayres, L. (1909). *Laggards in our schools: A study of retardation and elimination in city school systems.* New York: Russell Sage.

Bernstein, J., Brocht, C., & Spade-Aguilar, M. (2000). *How much is enough? Basic family budgets for working families.* Washington, DC: Economic Policy Institute.

Bolger, K., & Patterson, C. (1995). Psychosocial adjustment among children experiencing persistent and intermittent family economic hardship. *Child Development, 66*, 1107–1129.

Bos, J., Huston, A.C., Duncan, G.J., Brock, T., & McLoyd, V. (1996). *New hope for people with low incomes: Two-year results of a program to reduce poverty and reform welfare.* New York: Manpower Demonstration Research Corporation.

Bradley, R. (1984). One hundred, seventy-four children: A study of the relation between the home environment and early cognitive development in the first 5 years. In A. Gottfried (Ed.), *The home environment and early cognitive development* (pp. 5–56). Orlando, FL: Academic Press.

Brooks-Gunn, J., Duncan, G., Leventhal, T., & Aber, L. (1997). Lessons learned and future directions for research on the neighborhoods in which children live. In J. Brooks-Gunn, G. Duncan, & L. Aber (Eds.), *Neighborhood poverty, volume 1: Contexts and consequences for children* (pp. 279–298). New York: Russell Sage.

Caspi, A., Wright, B., Moffit, E., & Silva, T. (1998). Early failure in the labor market: Childhood and adolescent predictors of unemployment in the transition to adulthood. *American Sociological Review, 63*, 424–451.

Cauthen, N., & Lu, H. (2001, August). *Living on the edge: Employment alone is not enough for America's low-income children and families* (Research Brief No. 1, Mailman School of Public Health, National Center for Children in Poverty). New York: Columbia University.

Citizens for Tax Justice. (2002). *Surge in corporate tax welfare drives corporate tax payments down to near record low.* Washington, DC: Author.

Citro, C., & Michael, R. (Eds.). (1995). *Measuring poverty: A new approach.* Washington, DC: National Academy Press.

Conley, D. (2003). *Who governs our schools? Changing roles and responsibilities.* New York: Teachers College Press.

Costello, J., Compton, S., Keeler, G., & Angold, A. (2003). Relationships between poverty and psychopathology: A natural experiment. *Journal of the American Medical Association, 290*, 2023–2029.

Cross, C. (2004). *Political education: National policy comes of age.* New York: Teachers College Press.

Dillon, S. (2003, April 30). Report finds number of black children in deep poverty rising. *New York Times*, p. 18A.

Dreier, P., Mollenkopf, J., & Swanstrom, T. (2001). *Place matters: Metropolitics for the 21st century.* Lawrence: University Press of Kansas.

Duncan, G., & Brooks-Gunn, J. (Eds.). (1997). *Consequences of growing up poor.* New York: Russell Sage.

Duncan, G., Brooks-Gunn, J., & Klebanov, P. (1994). Economic deprivation and early childhood development. *Child Development, 65*, 296–318.

Economic Policy Institute. (2002). *Economic snapshots.* Washington, DC: Author.

Economic Policy Institute. (2004). *EPI issue guide: Minimum wage.* Washington, DC: Author.

Education Trust. (2001). *The funding gap: Low-income and minority students receive fewer dollars.* Washington, DC: Author.

Entwistle, D., & Alexander, K. (1997). *Children, schools, and inequality.* Boulder, CO: West-view Press.

Fine, M. (2001, May). *Comparative analysis of the organization of high schools 1996–97, NYC Board of Education.* Findings presented at the Spencer Conference, New York. Document available at www.nysed.gov.80/emsc/docs4-99NYStrategy.ppt.3.

Galbraith, J. (1998). *Created unequal: The crisis in American pay.* New York: Free Press.

Goering, J., & Feins, J. (Eds.). (2003). *Choosing a better life? Evaluating the Moving To Opportunity social experiment.* Washington, DC: Urban Institute Press.

Greene, J. (2001). *High school graduation rates in the United States.* Washington, DC: Black Alliance for Educational Options and the Manhattan Institute.

Harrington, M. (1963). *The other America: Poverty in the United States.* Baltimore: Penguin.

Houser, R.M., Brown, B.V., & Prosser, W.R. (1998). *Indicators of children's well-being.* New York: Russell Sage.

Hout, M. (1988). More universalism, less structural mobility: The American occupational structure in the 1980s. *American Journal of Sociology, 93*, 1358–1400.

Huston, A.C., Duncan, G.J., Granger, R., Bos, J., McLoyd, V.C., Mistry, R., Crosby, D.A., Gibson, C., Magnuson, K., Romich, J., & Ventura, A. (2001). Work-based anti-poverty programs for parents can enhance the school performance and social behavior of children. *Child Development, 72*, 318–336.

Huston, A.C., Miller, C., Richburg-Hayes, L., Duncan, G.J., Eldred, C.A., Weisner, T.S., Lowe, E., McLoyd, V.C., Crosby, D.A., Ripke, M.N., & Redcross, C. (2003). *Summary report, New Hope for families and children: Five-year results of a program to reduce poverty and reform welfare.* New York: Manpower Demonstration Research Corporation.

Jackson, A., Brooks-Gunn, J., Huang, C., & Glassman, M. (2000) Single mothers in low-wage jobs: Financial strain, parenting, and preschoolers' outcomes. *Child Development 71*, 1409–1423.

Jencks, C., & Phillips, M. (1998) *The Black/White test score gap.* Washington, DC: Brookings Institution Press.

Jeremiah, L. (2003). *Family support programs and academic achievement: Lessons for Seattle.* Unpublished manuscript. Available online at http://www.evans.washington.edu/research/psclinic/pdf/02-03dp/Jeremiahdp.pdf.

Johnson, M., Ladd, H., & Ludwig, J. (2002). The benefits and costs of residential mobility programs. *Housing Studies 17*, 125–138.

Kingsley, T., & Petit, K. (2003). *Concentrated poverty? A change in course.* Neighborhood change in urban America series. Washington, DC: Urban Institute.

Klerman, L. (1991; 2003 Reprint edition). The health of poor children: Problems and programs. In A.C. Huston (Ed.), *Children and poverty: Child development and public policy* (pp. 136–157). New York: Cambridge University Press.

Korenman, S., & Miller, J. (1997). Effects of long-term poverty on physical health of children in the national longitudinal survey of youth. In G. Duncan & J. Brooks-Gunn (Eds.), *Consequences of growing up poor* (pp. 70–99). New York: Russell Sage.

Lafer, G. (2002). *The job training charade.* Ithaca, NY: Cornell University Press.

Lee, V., & Burkham, D. (2002). *Inequality at the starting gate: Social background and achievement at kindergarten entry.* Washington, DC: Economic Policy Institute.

Lu, H. (2003). *Low-income children in the United States.* New York: Columbia University, Mailman School of Public Health.

Ludwig, J., Duncan, G., & Ladd, H. (2003). The effects of moving to opportunity on children and parents in Baltimore. In J. Goering & J. Feins (Eds.), *Choosing a better life?* (pp. 153–177). Washington, DC: Urban Institute Press.

Masten, A., & Coatsworth, D. (1995). The structure and coherence of competence from childhood through adolescence. *Child Development, 66*, 1635–1659.

McLoyd, V. (1998). Socioeconomic disadvantage and child development. *American Psychologist, 53*, 185–204.

McLoyd, V., & Jartayne, T. (1994). Unemployment and work interruption among African-American single mothers: Effects on parenting and adolescent socio-emotional functioning. *Child Development, 65*, 562–589.

Miao, J., & Haney, W. (2004). High school graduation rates: Alternative methods and implications. *Education Policy Analysis Archives, 12*(55). Available online at http:// epaa.asu.edu/epaa/v12n55.

Michaloupolos, C., Tattri, D., Miller, C., Robins, P.K., Morris, P., Gyarmati, D., Redcross, C., Foley, K., & Ford, R. (2002). *Making work pay: Final report on the self-sufficiency project for long-term welfare recipients.* New York: Manpower Demonstration Research Corporation.

Mishel, L., Bernstein, J., & Boushey, H. (2003). *The state of working America: 2002/2003.* Ithaca, NY: Cornell University Press.

Mishel, L., Bernstein, J., & Schmitt, J. (2001). *The state of working America: 2000/2001.* Ithaca, NY: Cornell University Press.

Morris, P., Huston, A.C., Duncan, G.J., Crosby, D., & Bos, J. (2001). *How welfare and work policies affect children: A synthesis of research.* Washington, DC: Manpower Demonstration Research Corporation.

O'Connor, A. (2003, October 21). Rise in income improves children's behavior. *New York Times*, p. F5.

Odden, A., & Picus, L. (1992). *School finance: A policy perspective*. New York: McGraw-Hill.

Orfield, M. (2002). *American metropolitics: The new suburban reality*. Washington, DC: Brookings Institute.

Phillips, K. (2002). *Wealth and democracy: A political history of the American rich*. New York: Broadway Books.

Phillips, M., Brooks-Gunn, J., Duncan, G., Klevanov, P., & Crane, J. (1998). Family background, parenting practices, and the Black/White test score gap. In C. Jencks & M. Phillips (Eds.), *The Black/White test score gap* (pp. 103–145). Washington, DC: Brookings Institution Press.

Phillips, M., Crouse, J., & Ralph, J. (1998). Does the Black/White test score gap widen after children enter school? In C. Jencks & M. Phillips (Eds.), *The Black/White test score gap* (pp. 229–272). Washington, DC: Brookings Institution Press.

Ravitch, D. (2000). *The great school wars: A history of the New York City public schools*. Baltimore: Johns Hopkins University Press.

Rubinowitz, L., & Rosenbaum, J. (2002). *Crossing the class and color line: From public housing to White suburbia*. Chicago: University of Chicago Press.

Rusk, D. (1999). *Inside game/outside game: Winning strategies for saving urban America*. Washington, DC: Brookings Institution.

Sampson, R., Morenoff, J., & Gannon-Rowley, T. (2002). Assessing "neighborhood effects": Social processes and new directions in research. *Annual Review of Sociology, 28*, 443–478.

Seitz, V., Rosenbaum L., & Apfel, N. (1985). Effects of family support intervention: A ten-year follow-up. *Child Development 56*, 376–391.

Short, K., Iceland, J., & Garner, T. (1999). *Experimental poverty measures: 1998*. Washington, DC: U.S. Census Bureau.

Smith, J., Brooks-Gunn, J., & Klebanov, P. (1997). Consequences of living in poverty for young children's cognitive and verbal ability and early school achievement. In G. Duncan & J. Brooks-Gunn (Eds.), *Consequencs of growing up poor* (pp. 132–189). New York: Russell Sage Foundation.

Stein, S. (2004). *The culture of educational policy*. New York: Teachers College Press.

Stipic, D., & Ryan, R. (1997). Economically disadvantaged preschoolers: Ready to learn but further to go. *Developmental Psychology, 33*, 711–723.

Sugland, B., Zaslow, M., & Brooks-Gunn, J. (1995). The early childhood HOME inventory and HOME short form in differing socio-cultural groups: Are there differences in underlying structure, internal consistency of subcases, and patterns of prediction? *Journal of Family Issues, 16*, 632–663.

Tyack, D. (1974). *The one best system: A history of American urban education*. Cambridge, MA: Harvard University Press.

White, K. (1982). The relationship between socioeconomic status and academic achievement. *Psychological Bulletin, 91*, 46–81.

Wrigley, J. (1982). *Class politics and public schools: Chicago 1900–1950*. New Brunswick, NJ: Rutgers University Press.

6
The Democratic-Liberal Tradition Under Attack

Diane Ravitch

During the past decade or so, the democratic-liberal tradition in American education has come under sharp attack, particularly from radical critics. In dozens of books and articles, radical writers have charged that American educational institutions have not played the democratic, benevolent role that educators have traditionally claimed for them. On the contrary, assert these critics, the schools are themselves oppressive institutions which regiment, indoctrinate, and sort children, either brutally or subtly crushing their individuality and processing them to take their place in an unjust social order. Indeed, say these critics, the major function of the schools is to mask the "oppressive" features of an undemocratic society.

Criticism of the schools, radical or otherwise, is nothing new. In every generation the schools have had vociferous critics. Religious leaders have complained either that the schools were morally neutral and therefore irreligious, or that they covertly advanced the interests of one sect over another. Political groups have condemned the schools either because they failed to inculcate patriotism or pacifism, or because they were indoctrinating children to a particular political perspective. Conservatives have denounced the schools both for their extravagance and their egalitarian pretensions. Radicals have long dismissed the schools as a tool of the capitalist economy which distracts attention from the need for fundamental change. And liberals have perennially despaired of ever getting enough money, skilled personnel, and public support to make the schools achieve their full potential as a mechanism to promote both individual development and social equality. As Richard Hofstadter observed, the history of educational commentary in America is "a literature of acid criticism and bitter complaint."[1]

In every society there is an integral, reciprocal relationship between education and politics; the kind of education available (however broadly it is defined) influences the nature of politics and society, just as the nature of politics and society has a determinative effect on educational policy. Nations that rule by coercion require citizens who have been educated to accept coercion. A free society, committed to popular rule, must provide an education that prepares people to think for themselves and to function as free citizens. In its basic values, the democratic-liberal tradition argues for an education that respects the worth and dignity of each individual, that prizes freedom of inquiry and expression, and that enables each person to think and participate and choose independently. Just as freedom of religion is safeguarded by the multiplicity of religious groups in America, so freedom of thought is protected by the plurality of the sources of education and information—not limited to schools—and by the diversity of those who control the various agencies of education, whether public or private.

In recent years, the democratic-liberal tradition has been subject to distortion by some who think of themselves as liberals. It seems worthwhile, therefore, to delineate some of these misconceptions: It is not necessarily "liberal" to spend ever greater amounts of money on education without regard to effectiveness or quality; it is not necessarily "liberal" to transfer power from the private sector to the public sector without concern for the potential increase of bureaucratization, standardization, and coercion in American life; it is not necessarily "liberal" to advocate greater governmental regulation of family and community life. It is not easy to reconcile the often conflicting needs of the collectivity and the individual or to maintain a healthy balance between the private sector and the public sector. Yet a liberal democracy must maintain its commitments both to social welfare and to the pre-eminence of free institutions and individual liberties.

In terms of school policy, the programmatic implications of the democratic-liberal tradition have been gradually, if imperfectly, embodied in practice. If universal education is essential to a democratic society, then schooling should be not only universal, but free, publicly supported, and equally available to all. If talent and intelligence are randomly distributed throughout society, then schools must serve as a means for individuals to develop their fullest potential without regard to race, sex, religion, or other ascriptive factors. Liberals have maintained that equal opportunity in education would prevent the hardening of class lines and facilitate social mobility; that education broadly available would stimulate general progress as well as individual mobility; that only popular education makes possible the formation of a common culture, accessible to all; that political participation is stimulated by the dispersion of education, and politics becomes more democratic as more people participate by creating new publics to express their interests; and, that the freest possible exercise of human reason would contribute to the establishment of a good society. The democratic-liberal theory of education is, then, simultaneously a theory of society, a theory of politics, and a theory of culture.

Conservatives have reacted negatively to this tradition because of its implicit egalitarianism. Education had been associated in Europe with aristocratic privilege, and there was more than rhetoric in the saying that knowledge is power. The suspicion lingered that education spreads discontent, envy, and an unquenchable thirst for equality. On the other hand, radicals have attacked the democratic-liberal tradition precisely because it was not sufficiently egalitarian. Equal opportunity is not the same as equal results, and to radicals, equal opportunity means meritocracy, which they find as reprehensible as aristocracy.

These polar reactions have each had a floodtide in recent decades. Conservative criticism reached a zenith in the 1950s, when opponents of progressive education demanded the elimination of "fads and frills," as well as the purging of "internationalist" and "socialist'" influences, from the public schools' curricula. Educational radicalism became popular in the 1960s, as radical critics assailed the central tenets of liberalism. The schools, they charged, were rigid, repressive institutions whose real purpose was to preserve the social order by inculcating passivity and conformity. Some scorned the idea of public schooling and urged counter-cultural "free" schools instead, while others rejected institutionalized schooling altogether. The radicals raised questions that had seemingly been long settled: Is compulsory schooling a denial of children's liberty? Do adults have the right to impose their values on the younger generation? What is the moral basis for authority in the classroom? Are all educational standards arbitrary? Is schooling simply a sociological cookie-cutter, coercing children into a common mold and readying them for the industrial needs of the capitalist economy?

Underlying such questions is a fundamental divergence between liberals and radicals about the direction of American history. Recalling the reciprocal relationship between education and society, it becomes clear that any scheme of deliberate education represents a choice on the part of the educator, a commitment to a particular view of society. Liberals tend to believe that American society has become more open, more inclusive, and more democratic over time, not accidentally or inevitably, but because of political action by those who sought these goals. Thus, if one believes in the values of a free, democratic society and prefers rational persuasion to coercion, then one must teach what those values mean and how to function in such a society. Radicals, however, tend to believe that the basic trend in American history has been a straight line—unremittingly racist, bureaucratic, exclusive, and undemocratic. Influenced largely by economic determinism, radicals perceive "vested interests" so powerful that no change can take place unless it is sponsored by those interests. Given this understanding, political action is fruitless because it can occur only if it is ineffectual. Educational reform, in this view, merely buttresses an unjust political system by making it operate more efficiently and flexibly.

Since the consequences of any particular change are never entirely predictable, reformers must be risk-takers. When they are effective, reformers become responsible for the changes they institute. And when, at some future date, the reforms need reforming, their original sponsors can be disparaged for not having had the prescience to see what would go wrong. Thus, anyone who gets involved in political action runs the considerable risk of failing, while those who refuse to abandon their utopian ideals never can be held accountable. The liberal reformer who wants to bring about incremental change must negotiate with those who oppose him and, in doing so, may have to compromise some of his original commitment. The radical preserves the purity of his principles by remaining aloof from the system and from any ultimate responsibility for its success or failure. By definition, then, the reformer is one who grapples with political and social problems and seeks solutions, while the radical eschews entanglement with a "corrupt" system, since any incremental improvement would only help secure the social order. And again by definition, anyone who participates politically is predestined to be corrupted, to be a "servant of power," and thus to fail when judged by radical standards.

The democratic-liberal tradition in education has been bound up with the spirit of reform, a sense that education could be consciously arranged to make American society more open, more just, and more democratic. This view has been persistently misrepresented by radical critics to mean that liberals saw the schools as a universal panacea and devoted energies to school reform that should have been directed to economic and social change. Indeed, the radical historians assert that the liberal's promotion of schooling was *intended* to divert attention from more salient issues. This is not, however, a fair reading of the liberal position, at least as it has been expressed by its leading exponents. Thomas Jefferson, certainly no advocate of the school as a universal panacea, wrote clearly about the interconnectedness of the institutions of a free society, and free schools were no more important (indeed, were rather less important) in his concept than a free press and a democratic polity. Though Horace Mann passionately advanced the cause of the public schools (which was scarcely surprising since he was employed by the state of Massachusetts to do so), he was also active on behalf of prison reform, better treatment for the insane, temperance legislation, and abolition. If his faith in the power of schooling now seems naive and excessive, it is a judgment made possible by hindsight. Merle Curti held that

> Mann should not be judged harshly for overemphasizing the ameliorating role of education. Confidence in the efficacy of the school as a means of effecting social change was then in its heyday. Education on a large scale had not been tried for a sufficiently long time to disprove his belief that it would vanquish crime, the excesses of profit-making, and even poverty itself. Finally, the unqualified acceptance of education as a means of remedying social evils was the natural corollary to the dominant belief in individualism which Mann, like almost everyone else, shared.

Like Mann, John Dewey believed that the schools, rightly conceived and organized, might become a lever of social progress, but he did not see the school as the *sole* instrument of social and economic change. It was, he maintained, a necessary though not a sufficient condition in the creation of a better social order. And in the late 1930s, he warned that the schools, as they became more pervasive and efficient, could become instruments controlled by a totalitarian state, as they had in Nazi Germany. He was himself a critic of the naive and simplistic faith in the public schools' automatic goodness:

> after a century of belief that the Common School system was bound by the very nature of its work to be what its earlier apostles called a 'pillar of the republic', we are learning that everything about the public schools, its official agencies of control, organization and administration, the status of teachers, the subjects taught and methods of teaching them, the prevailing modes of discipline, set *problems*; and that the problems have been largely ignored as far as the relation of schools to democratic institutions is concerned.

So much attention had been lavished on the technical side of school questions, he complained, that "the central question"—the relation of schools to democratic institutions—had been obscured.[2]

Schooling, though not necessarily public schooling, was recognized by liberal thinkers as one of the cultural conditions that would nurture a free, democratic society. Schooling was a means, political and social democracy the end. That liberal aspirations have not been fully realized (and have even occasionally been negated) is not an indictment of the aspiration but is rather an acknowledgment of the difficulty of the goal and the stubbornness of human nature and institutions. To be sure, to define the ideal is to become aware of the distance between ideal and practice, though the appropriate analytical question is not whether there is a gap between ideal and practice, but whether the gap is growing larger or smaller. Nonetheless, the ideal remains, even when imperfectly realized, a standard by which to measure practice. The lapses from the standard are all the more conspicuous because they are lapses, exceptions to educational aspirations which are broadly shared even when they are still unattained.

To recount the history of education strictly as an ideological struggle, in which certain seminal thinkers led the way, bringing educational reform in their wake, needlessly sharpens the contrast between rhetoric and reality while serving up a desiccated version of complicated events. There is never a simple cause-and-effect relationship between ideas and events. Men like Jefferson, Mann, and Dewey were not innovators as much as they were articulators of major trends, and their ideas form the mainstream of American educational thought because they correctly analyzed and identified the moving historical forces of their time. Jefferson's 1779 proposal for a pyramidal structure of public education was rejected by the Virginia legislature but eventually became the prototype of American public schooling, not because Jefferson said it should, but because it was what most nearly satisfied the wishes of voters, taxpayers, and legislators. Jefferson's concern for both equality and excellence turned out to have been an accurate prediction, though not necessarily a proximate cause, of the American public school system. Mann is known as the father of the common (public) school movement, but common schools were established in many towns and districts long before Mann became involved in the question. He was the best known advocate of a movement that was already well underway, not its progenitor. The movements with which Mann and Dewey were identified were not created by their pens, but by a confluence of forces within American society. Dewey influenced and inspired the progressive education movement, but he neither invented nor directed it. A comprehensive analysis of educational policy must include not only ideas and ideals but also consideration of the underlying political, economic, and social conditions that cause one set of ideas and not another to come to the fore. Recognizing this, Dewey argued against the reductionist tendency to locate single causes:

> we have to get away from the influence of belief in bald single forces, whether they are thought of as intrinsically psychological or sociological. . . . We have to analyze conditions by observations, which are as discriminating as they are extensive, until we discover specific interactions that are taking place, and learn to think in terms of interactions instead of force. We are led to search even for the conditions which have given the interacting factors the power they possess.[3]

Those who attribute the spread of public schooling solely to Horace Mann's forcefulness, or to the organizing skills of other school reformers, underestimate the objective conditions that persuaded people in diverse communities to tax themselves on behalf of public schooling while prohibiting public funds for sectarian instruction. Sometimes nonsectarianism was simply anti-Catholicism, but it can also be seen as a compromise that permitted people of different sects, none in a majority, to school their children together. The effect of the common school revival in the mid-nineteenth century was to build support for state-enforced educational standards and to promote the cause of public schooling. The economist Albert Fishlow has noted that mass schooling was well established in the New England states by 1830, before the common school revival. Fishlow holds that Mann's activities were directed not merely against indifference to education, but also against a burgeoning of private and semiprivate educational activities. Because historians of education have largely been professional educators, with a special stake in public education, they have traditionally depicted Mann's fight for public schooling as a crusade of principle rather than as a genuine controversy between public and private interests, with a degree of right on both sides.[4]

The subsidiary effect of the common school movement was to formulate a powerful, sometimes evangelistic, ideology for the American public school. Mann was Jeffersonian in the sense that he clearly perceived the interrelationship among education, society, and politics.

But unlike Jefferson, whose concept of a "crusade against ignorance" put no special emphasis on public schooling, Mann argued that the public school was uniquely suited to carry forward the promise of American life. He grounded his plea for the primacy of the common school on generally held assumptions about the beneficial power of education. But not everyone believed, as he did, that the fate of the nation was inextricably tied to the fate of public schools. The view that education was morally uplifting, that it improved character and prevented poverty and vice, was commonplace, in part because of the traditional association of religion and education, but also because of the empirical evidence: criminals and paupers were likelier than not to be unlettered. So reformers of Mann's era shared his belief in the power of universal education without necessarily adopting his commitment to public schooling. Governor William Seward of New York, as dedicated to social reform as Mann, urged public support for Catholic schools as a means of extending the blessings of education to the children of poor Irish Catholics who shunned the publicly supported nonsectarian schools of New York City. Despite their very different opinions about the necessity of cornmon schooling, Mann and Seward both believed that unequal education was the basis of social inequality, and both believed that the state had an obligation to remedy the inequity. The area of agreement between these two contemporaries defines the popular values to which reformers appealed. As political leaders, Mann and Seward were anxious to persuade their publics to adopt their programs and took care to express their ideas in what they hoped would be a convincing fashion. In other words, they clothed their innovative proposals in popular rhetoric. Theirs was an optimistic, individualistic outlook. It said that anyone could overcome his original circumstances by his own effort, that a young man should have no bounds other than his own ability and energy. It assumed that heredity and authority counted for little and that American society ought to be open, democratic, and malleable. Though in some parts of the country blacks, women, and certain other minorities were excluded from participating as equals, the internal dynamic of this outlook contained the eventual destruction of these contradictions.

These were the values of a society bent on self-improvement, a society with fluid class lines, a society where Horatio Alger stories would become popular, a society that would ultimately be compelled by its own democratic creed to confront its prejudices and discriminatory practices and seek to abolish them. In such a society, with its emphasis on self-improvement and getting ahead, educational enterprises of all kinds thrived, not just schools, but museums, libraries, Chautauquas, settlement houses, debating societies, labor unions, political clubs, and countless other activities intended to teach, to learn, to change people's minds or skills or values or sensibilities.

In the midst of all this educational busyness, the public school assumed a special place, not because Mann and other reformers said it should, but because it was there that the rising generation would be systematically instructed. By the time of the Civil War, most American children outside the South attended public schools. The most important fact about the American public schools was that they were popularly controlled. This meant that school policy could not deviate very far from popular dictates and that the schools would largely reflect the aspirations and values of the polity, for better or worse. Reformers might propose this or that change, but they had to win the approval of the local school board, which was either popularly elected or appointed by elected officials. The financing of schools injected another political constraint, either through popular referenda or through the legislative process.

Whatever the issue at hand, reformers had to take into account the necessity of persuading others to agree with them. In other nations, the schools were controlled by the established church or by a powerful centralized state agency. Popular control in the United States meant that school politics was an extension of democratic politics. If the public schools did not satisfy the voters, there were various ways by which their dissatisfaction might be expressed: by voting against the school board, by sending their children to nonpublic schools, by opposing a school bond issue, or by lobbying their elected representatives. The displeasure of a few irate parents might not cause a stir, but mass disaffection could not be ignored.

Because of the interconnection of the schools' politics with the politics of the society at large, the schools generally reflect the society. An electorate will not long support a school system that openly subverts its wishes, values, and interests. School policy usually represents what most people expect of schools at any particular time; a school board that tried to introduce changes that were repugnant to the community would not long survive so long as there were some mechanism of popular control. Because the demands made on them are simultaneously liberal and conservative, the schools are simultaneously liberal and conservative. Indeed, to the frustration of ideological purists, the distinction between that which is liberal and that which is conservative is not always clear, since most people are liberal in one sphere and conservative in another; it is not unusual, for example, to encounter individuals who are politically liberal and pedagogically conservative, as well as the reverse.

This curious intermingling of opposite impulses has been evidenced in other contexts. When Mann sought to persuade people to support public schools more generously, he appealed alternately to those who wanted a more equal society and to those who wanted a more stable society. He argued both that education would be a great equalizer and that it would disarm the poor of their hostility toward the rich. Part of the political potency of the public school idea in the United States has been this simultaneous appeal to disparate interests. The continuing strength of the schools is due to the fact that they have at least partially fulfilled the expectations of their differing constituencies.

This outcome, this blurring and compromising of conflicting demands, is the result of a political process which continually strives for conciliation and coalition-building, for settlements in which the victors are not totally victorious and the losers not totally vanquished. To be sure, this consensual political process is a manifestation of democratic, pluralist politics, in which many groups and individuals press for their own interests and arrive at a resolution which satisfies most of the participants and crushes none. Radicals, believing in the inexorability as well as the desirability of class struggle, see the political process as a way of defusing discontent without sharply altering the status quo.

The difference between them comes down to the radicals' exclusive preoccupation with ends as contrasted with the liberals' concern with means and ends in relation. Carl Becker wrote that "The case for democracy is that it accepts the rational and humane values as ends, and proposes as the means of realizing them the minimum of coercion and the maximum of voluntary assent." An anarchist society, if such a contradiction could exist, would have no compulsion whatever, and very likely have no means of assuring elementary standards of equity; a Marxist society, which places its emphasis on ends, tolerates the maximum of coercion in pursuing its goals. Fundamental to a democratic-liberal society is the recognition that basic values endure but are realized partially, incrementally, and sporadically; that ends and means are inseparable; that one ultimately determines the other, and that inhumane means can never produce humane ends.[5]

Educational politics is not simply a mirror image of the politics of the larger society, though many of the same values permeate both. It involves a wide array of interest groups—teachers, parents, supervisors, students, elected officials, state education agencies, federal officials, foundations, unions, good government groups, and the press. In any particular decision, the interested parties shift in terms of the intensity of their concern. But the process of decision-making—the impact of public opinion, the necessity of discussion and agreement, the negotiations among different constituencies, the constraints of law and the judiciary—is democratic.

To say that the policy process is democratic is not to say that every decision that comes forth is correct. Political solutions are often temporary, expedient, or short-sighted. In the short run, the test of educational policy is whether it works, whether it satisfies most participants, whether it assures majority rule without traducing the rights of the minority. There may be an objectively better way to do things, which may be obvious to those with the perspective of history; but unless the participants can be persuaded of the better way, then it will have to wait for another time, a time when its proponents are more effective in their role as educators of the public.

Because education is so bound up with the interests and values of the public, and because these interests and values of the public, and because these interests and values continually shift over time, educational policy can never be static. It is forever in the process of becoming, forever a subject of proper concern, forever in need of reformation. At some times in our history there has seemed to be a better fit between educational institutions and perceived needs than at other times, and the schools were said to be doing "a good job" and "meeting society's needs." But as American society changes, so must and do the schools. Change never comes easily. Generally, it occurs after much debate, agitation, complaint, and criticism; and it is in this perspective that the radical critics play a useful and important function by prodding educational policymakers to reexamine their assumptions, their intentions, and their effectiveness. To respond to criticism intelligently, without reinventing the wheel, without unknowingly reenacting some cyclical drama, educational policymakers need to understand the aspirations, the values, and the traditions that have shaped American education. They cannot have an adequate sense of the future without having an adequate sense of the past, nor can they judge—what should be without knowing what has been.

A Summing Up: Limitations of the Ideological Approach

Educational history, whether written by intellectual historians, social historians, or economic historians, offers broad vistas for new and significant research into human behavior, social processes, and political decision-making. The issues are complicated, and they go directly to the core of American life and thought. Freed of the Cubberleyan tradition, educational historians are studying, among other things, family and community life, the communications media, religion, race, ethnicity, and group biography. With a perspective informed by the social sciences, historians are using new techniques to reinvestigate old issues and ask new questions. The school is seen as one of a number of educating institutions that influenced the lives of Americans. While this conception of education may seem to derogate the role of the school, it does more nearly approximate the educative experiences of most Americans.

In light of these trends, it becomes increasingly difficult to write about the school historically without setting it within a wide social context. But it is one thing to assess the political,
economic, and social functions of the school and quite another to "discover" these functions
as though they were clandestine purposes, hidden until now by capitalist conspirators. The
difference in emphasis is the difference between a political analysis of history and a politicization of history. The former seeks to understand causes and effects in their historical context,
the latter imposes a particular interpretation on past events.

Politicization has many risks, the greatest of which is that it frequently forces a telescoping
and distortion of the past for the sake of explaining the present. The presentist method
involves projecting one's own ideas onto the past in search of the seeds of present problems.
The more passionate the seeker, the likelier he is to treat the past as a precursor of the great
goodness or great evil of the present, rather than on its own terms. While present-day problems obviously have their origins in the past, the historical inquiry must be informed by a
respect for the importance of context. Nothing that exists today has precisely the same
meaning that it had a century ago; the perceptions of the 1970s are not the same as those of
other eras.

As David Hackett Fischer has pointed out, the impulse to use history for political purposes
is not new; it has been indulged in by scholars of all political persuasions, by communists and
anti-communists, by conservatives and liberals, and most recently, by young radical
historians, who

> regard all aspirations to objectivity as a sham and a humbug, and stubbornly insist that
> the real question is not whether historians can be objective, but which cause they will be
> subjective to. . . . To make historiography into a vehicle for propaganda is simply to
> destroy it. . . . The fact that earlier generations and other ideological groups have com-
> mitted the same wrong does not convert it into a right.[1]

The presentist orientation of the radical historians is freely acknowledged. The authors of
Roots of Crisis aver that if one starts with the assumption that this society is in fact racist, fundamentally materialistic, and institutionally structured to protect vested interests, the past
takes on vastly different meanings. The authors of these essays write from such a conception of
the present, which shapes our own view of the past.

Katz, defending the manifest presentism of *Class, Bureaucracy, and Schools*, states that "Our
concerns shape the questions that we ask and, as a consequence, determine what we select
from the virtually unlimited supply of 'facts'." The conviction that American public schools
are inherently racist, pathologically bureaucratic, and class-biased informs the radicals' decision to read the past into the present and the present into the past. Their stated intention is to
spur radical change in the schools and the larger society, but the effect of their arguments is
quite different. If policymakers heed Katz, they will resist taking initiatives': and "imposing"
reforms on the people; judges too would be restrained from forcing educational change upon
reluctant communities. If they heed Karier, they will abandon any effort to work within a system that is fundamentally "racist and designed to protect class interest." If they heed Bowles
and Gintis, they will see the futility of any educational reform within a capitalist society. If they
heed Spring, they will cease being policymakers altogether. As Sol Cohen has observed, "The
ideological commitment of the radical revisionists, far from being a road to action, has

become a dead end." If reformers in the past have been power-hungry, manipulative, and devious, why trust reformers in the present? If past reforms have served hidden "vested interests" rather than the people, why assume beneficial consequences from present reforms? If class connections are so compelling, what are we to make of the radical revisionists themselves, all of whom are, by professional status and income, members of the same upper middle-class group that has traditionally led reform movements?[2]

Educational history is a particularly tempting arena for politicization because of the ready availability of the public school as a straw man, a panacea that failed. School officials and reformers spoke glowingly of the Great American Public School, the Bulwark of Democracy, that was supposed to make everyone equal and happy and successful. As more people stayed in school longer, society was supposed to become better and wiser. But clearly everyone is not equal and happy and successful, nor have inequality, injustice, war, and corruption vanished with the extension of schooling. Therefore, say the politicized historians, the people who sold us on schooling deceived us; the schools were a fraud from the beginning and intentionally so.

But this is a simplistic rendering of the past. There have been at least two traditions of education commentary that exist side by side. One lauds the greatness of the public school, the other laments its lowly state. The first was the creation of promoters and local officials, waging intensive campaigns for public funds and stressing the accomplishments of the schools. The other was what Richard Hofstadter called "the educational jeremiad" of reformers and critics. The two traditions interacted, for the propagandists knew that the American public had to be convinced of the value of schooling, in terms of their own interest. No one in the nineteenth or early twentieth century was taken in by rhetoric alone, particularly when it contradicted one's own experience. There were plenty of people who had gotten ahead without much schooling. The Horatio Alger rags-to-riches stories were not testimonials to the schools, but to the rewards of hard work, good character, and luck. As Hofstadter showed, Americans have had an anti-intellectual strain that precluded any automatic respect for credentials; typically, schooling was appreciated for its cash value not as an engine of social reconstruction. Schoolmen addressing a skeptical public that held the purse strings, alternately spoke rhapsodically and despairingly of the schools that might be and the schools that were.[3]

From this mixed bag of hope, despair, promise, and complaint, and from a motley company of idealists, pragmatists, cynics, and moralists, the politicized historians select the passages and the quotes that make their case against American schooling and the liberal tradition. A history that is rich with controversy and complexity is reduced to a simple ideological cliché. The school is a failure, they tell us, without giving us a deeper understanding of what the schools have and have not accomplished. Bureaucracy is antihumanistic and unnecessary, they agree, without providing an analysis that would enable us to control and redirect the bureaucratic process, whose reach is enlarged by every new demand for governmental services and regulation.

By contrast, a political analysis of educational history asks a series of open-ended, empirical questions: How was education policy made? What educational issues were involved? Who participated? What was their self-interest and how did they perceive it? How were the issues resolved? How did the participants try to influence the outcome? Who gained what? Who lost what? What alternatives were available? Why were they rejected? How did the press and other influential agencies affect the issue? How did the resolution of the issue affect the original problem? The questions could be multiplied; the important criterion is that the answer is not presumed by the question.

Politicized history, written in reaction to the mood of the moment, becomes dated as the mood of the moment fades. The most useful and most relevant approach to educational history is that which seeks to determine how ideas are translated into policy, how policy is translated into practice, how practice grows into policy, how schools respond or fail to respond to various kinds of aspirations, how families mediate their children's education, how social origins affect educational opportunity, and how political, social, and economic forces interrelate to affect the educational process. The possibilities for study are as boundless as the question of how knowledge, skills, values, and sensibilities are transmitted across time, across generations, and across cultures. An understanding of the democratic political process, a respect for rational inquiry, and a capacity for surprise are necessary equipment for those who attempt to reconstruct a sense of the past and to understand the role of education in it.

The point is that ideas have consequences. History matters, not only because of the importance of the search for knowledge, but because of the uses to which analyses of the past may be put. The interpretation of history can have political implications, and historians know this; they know that their readings of the past, especially when they delve into the origins and effects of contemporary social institutions, can influence public opinion and policymaking. By telling people who they are and what they have done and by telling a nation how its institutions have succeeded or failed, the historian helps us to define the limitations and possibilities of the present and future.

The historian who undertakes to demonstrate that kindergartens and vocational education were intended to "oppress" and "contain" the children of the poor directs his message at present policymakers. The historian who maintains that American rhetoric and American reality are not only far apart but are entirely contradictory has a political purpose, which is not to encourage people to close the gap but to persuade them that the gap can never be closed because American society is inherently flawed. The historian who asserts that reform in American society always fails and that reformers have always been either knaves or fools is in reality insisting on the futility of reform. These are political messages, intended to have a political effect.

Consider the impact of historians who have argued that the "real" purpose of schools is not the cultivation of intelligence but social sorting, and that the "real" value of a degree is not what it represents in terms of learning but what it signifies in the competition for status. These are claims that became self-fulfilling prophecies because they encouraged educators to think of schools as degree-granting custodial institutions. One consequence for policymaking has been to justify a decline in educational standards, as evidenced by policies of automatic promotion in elementary and secondary schools, and at the postsecondary level, by the acceptance of grade inflation, diploma mills, and term-paper factories. These changes did not come about solely because of the way history has been written in recent years, but the repeated assertions by historians and social scientists that schooling was of little or no intrinsic value has had its impact on policymakers.

To the extent that history influences social policy, it should be to enable policymakers to understand the complexity of events and institutions and the tenuousness of causal connections. In the light of historical analysis, the assertion that schools end crime and poverty is as simplistic and naive as the claim that the schools maintain inequality. There is an unfortunate evangelistic tone to educational commentary that leads to either excessive acclamation or excessive denunciation. Thus, the old belief in the school as the great panacea has been replaced by the opposite belief either that the school is utterly impotent and ineffective, or that it is an evil, all-powerful mechanism of social stratification and technological blight. We know from experience that crime and poverty have survived the widespread extension of schooling; we also know that schooling has enabled many people to rise above their social origins and that advanced technology produces not just bombs and pollutants but also the means to cure disease and avert famine. It *is* possible to see American history as something other than a road map to heaven or hell.

If the evangelistic tradition were set aside, then perhaps schools might be understood neither as the single institution most responsible for America's greatness nor as the single institution most responsible for its ills. It might perhaps, be possible to think of schools in terms that are modest and reasonable and that are appropriately related to their capacities. Seen in this light, the American school-teacher might emerge as neither a miracle worker of superhuman dimensions nor as an agent of malevolent forces, but as a rather ordinary citizen with a complicated job to do.

Suppose, for the sake of discussion, that schools do not have cosmic purposes; that they cannot "save" society; that they are neither spearheads of radical change nor instruments of cultural repression. Think instead of institutions whose purposes are circumscribed by the public that supports them, and whose goals are limited and potentially attainable. Universal literacy is one such goal that, despite the massive expansion of schooling both vertically and horizontally, has not yet been achieved; universal access to higher education is another such goal which, with the recent burgeoning of public institutions, has become a virtual reality.

But even universal literacy and universal access to the highest levels of schooling do not solve larger social problems. People with equal amounts of schooling do not earn equal incomes nor does high educational attainment safeguard the degree-bearer against economic misfortune, mental instability, social insecurity, or life's other travails. Education does not guarantee success, however it is defined, but it does offer opportunity. How that opportunity is used depends to a very great extent on the ability and motivation of the individual. This is not to deny the importance of the social and economic problems which are not solved by schooling, but to suggest that they might be more directly and fruitfully attacked in noneducational ways.

Education in a liberal society must sustain and hold in balance ideals that coexist in tension: equality and excellence. While different generations have emphasized one or the other, in response to the climate of the times, schools alone cannot make either ideal a reality, though they contribute to both. The schools are limited institutions which have certain general responsibilities and certain specific capacities; sometimes they have failed to meet realistic expectations, and at other times they have succeeded beyond realistic expectations in dispersing intelligence and opportunity throughout the community. In order to judge them by reasonable standards and in order to have any chance of improving their future performance, it is necessary to abandon the simplistic search for heroes and devils, for scapegoats and panaceas.

Notes

1. Richard Hofstadter, *Anti-intellectualism in American Life* (New York: Random House, Vintage Books, 1962), p. 301.

2. Merle Curti, *The Social Ideas of American Educators* (1935; reprinted ed., Totowa, NJ: Littlefield, Adams, 1971), p. 125; John Dewey, *Freedom and Culture* (New York: G.P. Putnam's Sons, 1939), p. 42.

3. Dewey, *Freedom and Culture*, pp. 39–40.

4. Albert Fishlow, "The American Common School Revival: Fact or Fancy?" in *Industrialism in Two Systems*, ed. Henry Rosovsky (New York: Jon Wiley & Sons, 1966), pp. 40–66.

5. Carl L. Becker, *New Liberties for Old* (New Haven: Yale University Press, 1941), p. 151.

Part III

The Sociology of Education

7

Functional and Conflict Theories of Educational Stratification

Randall Collins

Education has become highly important in occupational attainment in modern America, and thus occupies a central place in the analysis of stratification and of social mobility. This paper attempts to assess the adequacy of two theories in accounting for available evidence on the link between education and stratification: a functional theory concerning trends in technical skill requirements in industrial societies; and a conflict theory derived from the approach of Max Weber, stating the determinants of various outcomes in the struggles among status groups. It will be argued that the evidence best supports the conflict theory, although technical requirements have important effects in particular contexts. It will be further argued that the construction of a general theory of the determinants of stratification in its varying forms is best advanced by incorporating elements of the functional analysis of technical requirements of specific jobs at appropriate points within the conflict model. The conclusion offers an interpretation of historical change in education and stratification in industrial America, and suggests where further evidence is required for more precise tests and for further development of a comprehensive explanatory theory.

The Importance of Education

A number of studies have shown that the number of years of education is a strong determinant of occupational achievement in America with social origins constant. They also show that social origins affect educational attainment, and also occupational attainment after the completion of education (Blau and Duncan, 1967:163–205; Eckland, 1965; Sewell et al., 1969; Duncan and Hodge, 1963; Lipset and Bendix, 1959:189–192). There are differences in occupational attainment independent of social origins between the graduates of more prominent and less prominent secondary schools, colleges, graduate schools, and law schools (Smigel, 1964:39, 73–74, 117; Havemann and West, 1952:179–181; Ladinsky, 1967; Hargens and Hagstrom, 1967).

Table 7.1 Percent of Employers Requiring Various Minimum Levels of Employees, by Occupational
Level

	National Survey, 1937–38					
	Unskilled	Semiskilled	Skilled	Clerical	Managerial	Professional
Less than high school	99%	97%	89%	33%	32%	9%
High school diploma	1	3	11	63	54	16
Some college				1	2	23
College degree				3	12	52
	100%	100%	100%	100%	100%	100%
San Francisco Bay Area, 1967						
Less than high school	83%	76%	62%	29%	27%	10%
High School diploma	16	24	28	68	14	4
Vocational training beyond high school	1	1	10	2	2	4
Some college		2	12	7		
College degree			41	70		
Graduate degree			3	5		
	100%	100%	100%	101%	99%	100%
	(244)	(237)	(245)	(306)	(288)	(240)

Educational requirements for employment have become increasingly widespread, not only
in elite occupations but also at the bottom of the occupational hierarchy (see Table 7.1). In a
1967 survey of the San Francisco, Oakland, and San Jose areas (Collins, 1969), 17% of the
employers surveyed required at least a high school diploma for employment in even unskilled
positions;[1] a national survey (Bell, 1940) in 1937–1938 found a comparable figure of 1%. At
the same time, educational requirements appear to have become more specialized, with 38%
of the organizations in the 1967 survey which required college degrees of managers preferring

Table 7.2 Percentage Educational Attainment in the United States, 1869–1965

Period	High School graduates/pop. 17 yrs. old	Resident college students/ pop. 18–21	B.A.s or 1st prof. degrees/1/10 of pop. 15–24	M.A.s or 2nd prof. degrees/1/10 of pop. 25–34	Ph.D.s 1/10 of pop. 25–34
1869–1870	2.0	1.7			
1879–1880	2.5	2.7			
1889–1890	3.5	3.0			
1899–1900	6.4	4.0	1.66	0.12	0.03
1909–1910	8.8	5.1	1.85	0.13	0.02
1919–1920	16.8	8.9	2.33	0.24	0.03
1929–1930	29.0	12.4	4.90	0.78	0.12
1939–1940	50.8	15.6	7.05	1.24	0.15
1949–1950	59.0	29.6	17.66	2.43	0.27
1959–1960	65.1	34.9	17.72	3.25	0.42
1963	76.3	38.0			
1965			19.71	5.02	0.73

business administration training, and an additional 15% preferring engineering training; such requirements appear to have been virtually unknown in the 1920s (Pierson, 1959:34–54). At the same time, the proportions of the American population attending schools through the completion of high school and advanced levels have risen sharply during the last century (Table 7.2). Careers are thus increasingly shaped within the educational system.

The Technical-Function Theory of Education

A common explanation of the importance of education in modern society may be termed the technical-function theory. Its basic propositions, found in a number of sources (see, for example, B. Clark, 1962; Kerr et al., 1960), may be stated as follows: (1) the skill requirements of jobs in industrial society constantly increase because of technological change. Two processes are involved: (a) the proportion of jobs requiring low skill decreases and the proportion requiring high skill increases; and (b) the same jobs are upgraded in skill requirements. (2) Formal education provides the training, either in specific skills or in general capacities, necessary for the more highly skilled jobs. (3) Therefore, educational requirements for employment constantly rise, and increasingly larger proportions of the population are required to spend longer and longer periods in school.

The technical-function theory of education may be seen as a particular application of a more general functional approach. The functional theory of stratification (Davis and Moore, 1945) rests on the premises (A) that occupational positions require particular kinds of skilled performance; and (B) that positions must be filled with persons who have either the native ability, or who have acquired the training, necessary for the performance of the given occupational role.[2]

The technical-function theory of education may be viewed as a subtype of this form of analysis, since it shares the premises that the occupational structure creates demands for particular kinds of performance, and that training is one way of filling these demands. In addition, it includes the more restrictive premises (1 and 2 above) concerning the way in which skill requirements of jobs change with industrialization, and concerning the content of school experiences.

The technical-function theory of education may be tested by reviewing the evidence for each of its propositions (1a, 1b, and 2).[3] As will be seen, these propositions do not adequately account for the evidence. In order to generate a more complete explanation, it will be necessary to examine the evidence for the underlying functional propositions, (A) and (B). This analysis leads to a focus on the processes of stratification—notably group conflict—not expressed in the functional theory, and to the formalization of a conflict theory to account for the evidence.

Proposition (1a): *Educational requirements of jobs in industrial society increase because the proportion of jobs requiring low skill decreases and the proportion requiring high skill increases.* Available evidence suggests that this process accounts for only a minor part of educational upgrading, at least in a society that has passed the point of initial industrialization. Fifteen percent of the increase in education of the U. S. labor force during the twentieth century may be attributed to shifts in the occupational structure—a decrease in the proportion of jobs with low skill requirements and an increase in proportion of jobs with high skill requirements (Folger and Nam, 1964). The bulk of educational upgrading (85%) has occurred *within* job categories.

Proposition (1b): *Educational requirements of jobs in industrial society rise because the same jobs are upgraded in skill requirements.* The only available evidence on this point consists of data collected by the U.S. Department of Labor in 1950 and 1960, which indicate the amount of change in skill requirements of specific jobs. Under the most plausible assumptions as to the skills provided by various levels of education, it appears that the educational level of the U.S. labor force has changed in excess of that which is necessary to keep up with skill requirements of jobs (Berg, 1970:38–60). Over-education for available jobs is found particularly among males who have graduated from college and females with high school degrees or some college, and appears to have increased between 1950 and 1960.

Proposition (2): *Formal education provides required job skills.* This proposition may be tested in two ways: (a) Are better educated employees more productive than less educated employees? (b) Are vocational skills learned in schools, or elsewhere?

(a) *Are better educated employees more productive?* The evidence most often cited for the productive effects of education is indirect, consisting of relationships between *aggregate* levels of education in a society and its overall economic productivity. These are of three types:

(i) The national growth approach involves calculating the proportion of growth in the U. S. Gross National Product attributable to conventional inputs of capital and labor; these leave a large residual, which is attributed to improvements in skill of the labor force based on increased education (Schultz, 1961; Denison, 1965). This approach suffers from difficulty in clearly distinguishing among technological change affecting productive arrangements, changes in the abilities of workers acquired by experience at work with new technologies, and changes in skills due to formal education and motivational factors associated with a competitive or achievement-oriented society. The assignment of a large proportion of the residual category to education is arbitrary. Denison (1965) makes this attribution on the basis of the increased income to persons with higher levels of education interpreted as rewards for their contributions to productivity. Although it is a common assumption in economic argument that wage returns reflect output value, wage returns cannot be used to prove the productive contribution of education without circular reasoning.

(ii) Correlations of education and level of economic development for nations show that the higher the level of economic development of a country, the higher the proportion of its population in elementary, secondary, and higher education (Harbison and Myers, 1964). Such correlations beg the question of causality. There are considerable variations in school enrollments among countries at the same economic level, and many of these variations are explicable in terms of political demands for access to education (Ben-David, 1963–64). Also, the overproduction of educated personnel in countries whose level of economic development cannot absorb them suggests the demand for education need not come directly from the economy, and may run counter to economic needs (Hoselitz, 1965).

(iii) Time-lag correlations of education and economic development show that increases in the proportion of population in elementary school precede increases in economic development after a takeoff point at approximately 30–50% of the 7–14 years old age-group in school. Similar anticipations of economic development are suggested for increases in secondary and higher education enrollment, although the data do not clearly support this conclusion (Peaslee, 1969). A pattern of advances in secondary school enrollments preceding advances in economic development is found only in a small number of cases (12 of 37 examined in Peaslee, 1969). A pattern of growth of university enrollments and subsequent economic development is found in 21 of 37 cases, but the exceptions (including the United States, France, Sweden, Russia, and Japan) are of such importance as to throw serious doubt on any *necessary* contribution of higher education to economic development. The main contribution of education to economic productivity, then, appears to occur at the level of the transition to mass literacy, and not significantly beyond this level.

Direct evidence of the contribution of education to *individual* productivity is summarized by Berg (1970:85–104, 143–176). It indicates that the better educated employees are not generally more productive, and in some cases are less productive, among samples of factory workers, maintenance men, department store clerks, technicians, secretaries, bank tellers, engineers, industrial research scientists, military personnel, and federal civil service employers.

(b) *Are vocational skills learned in school, or elsewhere?* Specifically vocational education in the schools for manual positions is virtually independent of job fate, as graduates of vocational programs are not more likely to be employed than high school dropouts (Plunkett, 1960; Duncan, 1964). Most skilled manual workers acquire their skills on the job or casually (Clark and Sloan, 1966:73). Retraining for important technological changes in industry has been carried out largely informally on-the-job; in only a very small proportion of jobs affected by technological change is formal retraining in educational institutions used (Collins, 1969: 147–158; Bright, 1958).

The relevance of education for nonmanual occupational skills is more difficult to evaluate. Training in specific professions, such as medicine, engineering, scientific or scholarly research, teaching, and law can plausibly be considered vocationally relevant, and possibly essential. Evidences comparing particular degrees of educational success with particular kinds of occupational performance or success are not available, except for a few occupations. For engineers, high college grades and degree levels generally predict high levels of technical responsibility and high participation in professional activities, but not necessarily high salary or supervisory responsibility (Perrucci and Perrucci, 1970).

At the same time, a number of practicing engineers lack college degrees (about 40% of engineers in the early 1950s; see Soderberg, 1963:213), suggesting that even such highly technical skills may be acquired on the job. For academic research scientists, educational quality has little effect on subsequent productivity (Hagstrom and Hargens, 1968). For other professions, evidence is not available on the degree to which actual skills are learned in school rather than in practice. In professions such as medicine and law, where education is a legal requirement for admission to practice, a comparison group of noneducated practitioners is not available, at least in the modern era.

Outside of the traditional learned professions, the plausibility of the vocational importance of education is more questionable. Comparisons of the efforts of different occupations to achieve "professionalization" suggest that setting educational requirements and bolstering them through licensing laws is a common tactic in raising an occupation's prestige and autonomy (Wilensky, 1964). The result has been the proliferation of numerous pseudo-professions in modern society; nevertheless these fail to achieve strong professional organization through lack of a monopolizable (and hence teachable) skill base. Business administration schools represent such an effort. (See Pierson, 1959: 9, 55–95, 140; Gordon and Howell, 1959:1–18, 40, 324–337). Descriptions of general, nonvocational education do not support the image of schools as places where skills are widely learned. Scattered studies suggest that the knowledge imparted in particular courses is retained only in small part through the next few years

(Learned and Wood, 1938: 28), and indicate a dominant student culture concerned with nonacademic interests or with achieving grades with a minimum of learning (Coleman, 1961; Becker et al., 1968).

The technical-function theory of education, then, does not give an adequate account of the evidence. Economic evidence indicates no clear contributions of education to economic development, beyond the provisions of mass literacy. Shifts in the proportions of more skilled and less skilled jobs do not account for the observed increase in education of the American labor force. Education is often irrelevant to on-the-job productivity and is sometimes counter-productive; specifically, vocational training seems to be derived more from work experience than from formal school training. The quality of schools themselves, and the nature of dominant student cultures suggest that schooling is very inefficient as a means of training for work skills.

Functional and Conflict Perspectives

It may be suggested that the inadequacies of the technical-function theory of education derive from a more basic source: the functional approach to stratification. A fundamental assumption is that there is a generally fixed set of positions, whose various requirements the labor force must satisfy. The fixed demand for skills of various types, at any given time, is the basic determinant of who will be selected for what positions. Social change may then be explained by specifying how these functional demands change with the process of modernization. In keeping with the functional perspective in general, the needs of society are seen as determining the behavior and the rewards of the individuals within it.

However, this premise may be questioned as an adequate picture of the fundamental processes of social organization. It may be suggested that the "demands" of any occupational position are not fixed, but represent whatever behavior is settled upon in bargaining between the persons who fill the positions and those who attempt to control them. Individuals want jobs primarily for the rewards to themselves in material goods, power, and prestige. The amount of productive skill they must demonstrate to hold their positions depends on how much clients, customers, or employers can successfully demand of them, and this in turn depends on the balance of power between workers and their employers.

Employers tend to have quite imprecise conceptions of the skill requirements of most jobs, and operate on a strategy of "satisficing" rather than optimizing—that is, setting average levels of performance as satisfactory, and making changes in procedures or personnel only when performance falls noticeably below minimum standards (Dill et al., 1962; March and Simon, 1958:140–141). Efforts to predict work performance by objective tests have foundered due to difficulties in measuring performance (except on specific mechanical tasks) and the lack of control groups to validate the tests (Anastasi, 1967). Organizations do not force their employees to work at maximum efficiency; there is considerable insulation of workers at all levels from demands for full use of their skills and efforts. Informal controls over output are found not only among production workers in manufacturing but also among sales and clerical personnel (Roy, 1952; Blau, 1955; Lombard, 1955). The existence of informal organization at the managerial level, the widespread existence of bureaucratic pathologies such as evasion of responsibility, empire-building, and displacement of means by ends ("red tape"), and the fact that administrative work is only indirectly related to the output of the organization, suggest that managers, too, are insulated from strong technological pressures for use of technical skills. On all levels, wherever informal organization exists, it appears that standards of performance reflect the power of the groups involved.

In this light, it is possible to reinterpret the body of evidence that ascriptive factors continue to be important in occupational success even in advanced industrial society. The social mobility data summarized at the onset of this paper show that social origins have a direct effect on occupational success, even after the completion of education. Both case studies and cross-sectional samples amply document widespread discrimination against Negroes. Case studies show that the operation of ethnic and class standards in employment based not merely on skin color but on name, accent, style of dress, manners, and conversational abilities (Noland and Bakke, 1949; Turner, 1952; Taeuber et al., 1966; Nosow, 1956). Cross-sectional studies, based on both biographical and survey data, show that approximately 60 to 70% of the American business elite come from upper-class and upper-middle-class families, and fewer than 15% from working-class families (Taussig and Joselyn, 1932:97; Warner and Abegglen, 1955:37–68; Newcomer, 1955:53; Bendix, 1956:198–253; Mills, 1963:110–139). These proportions are fairly constant from the early 1800s through the 1950s. The business elite is overwhelmingly Protestant, male, and completely white, although there are some indications of a mild trend toward declining social origins and an increase of Catholics and Jews. Ethnic and class background have been found crucial for career advancement in the professions as well (Ladinsky, 1963; Hall, 1946). Sexual stereotyping of jobs is extremely widespread (Collins, 1969:234–238).

In the traditional functionalist approach, these forms of ascription are treated as residual categories: carry-overs from a less advanced period, or marks of the imperfections of the functional mechanism of placement. Yet available trend data suggest that the link between social class origins and occupational attainment has remained constant during the twentieth century in America (Blau and Duncan, 1967:81–113); the proportion of women in higher occupational levels has changed little since the late nineteenth century (Epstein, 1970:7); and the few available comparisons between elite groups in traditional and modern societies suggest comparable levels of mobility (Marsh, 1963). Declines in racial and ethnic discrimination that appear to have occurred at periods in twentieth-century America may be plausibly explained as results of political mobilization of particular minority groups rather than by an increased economic need to select by achievement criteria.

Goode (1967) has offered a modified functional model to account for these disparities: that work groups always organize to protect their inept members from being judged by outsiders' standards of productivity, and that this self-protection is functional to the organizations, preventing a Hobbesian competitiveness and distrust of all against all. This argument re-establishes a functional explanation, but only at the cost of undermining the technological view of functional requirements. Further, Goode's conclusions can be put in other terms: it is to the advantage of groups of employees to organize so that they will not be judged by strict performance standards; and it is at least minimally to the advantage of the employer to let them do so, for if he presses them harder he creates dissension and alienation. Just how hard an employer *can* press his employees is not given in Goode's functional model. That is, his model has the disadvantage, common to functional analysis in its most general form, of covering too many alternative possibilities to provide testable explanations of specific outcomes. Functional analysis too easily operates as a justification for whatever particular pattern exists, asserting in effect that there is a proper reason for it to be so, but failing to state the conditions under which a particular pattern will hold rather than another. The technical version of job requirements has the advantage of specifying patterns, but it is this specific form of functional explanation that is jettisoned by a return to a more abstract functional analysis.

A second hypothesis may be suggested: the power of "ascribed" groups may be the *prime* basis of selection in all organizations, and technical skills are secondary considerations depending on the balance of power. Education may thus be regarded as a mark of membership in a particular group (possibly at times its defining characteristic), not a mark of technical skills or achievement. Educational requirements may thus reflect the interests of whichever groups have power to set them. Weber (1968:1000) interpreted educational requirements in bureaucracies, drawing especially on the history of public administration in Prussia, as the result of efforts by university graduates to monopolize positions, raise their corporate status, and thereby increase their own security and power vis-à-vis both higher authorities and clients. Gusfield (1958) has shown that educational requirements in the British Civil Service were set as the result of a power struggle between a victorious educated upper-middle-class and the traditional aristocracy.

To summarize the argument to this point: available evidence suggests that the technical-functional view of educational requirements for jobs leaves a large number of facts unexplained. Functional analysis on the more abstract level does not provide a testable explanation of which ascribed groups will be able to dominate which positions. To answer this question, one must leave the functional frame of reference and examine the conditions of relative power of each group.

A Conflict Theory of Stratification

The conditions under which educational requirements will be set and changed may be stated more generally, on the basis of a conflict theory of stratification derived from Weber (1968:926–939; see also Collins, 1968), and from advances in modern organization theory fitting the spirit of this approach.

A. *Status groups.* The basic units of society are associational groups sharing common cultures (or "subcultures"). The core of such groups is families and friends, but they may be etxended to religious, educational, or ethnic communities. In general, they comprise all persons who share a sense of status equality based on participation in a common culture: styles of language, tastes in clothing and decor, manners and other ritual observances, conversational topics and styles, opinions and values, and preferences in sports, arts, and media. Participation in such cultural groups gives individuals their fundamental sense of identity, especially in contrast with members of other associational groups in whose everyday culture they cannot participate comfortably. Subjectively, status groups distinguish themselves from others in terms of categories of *moral evaluation* such as "honor," "taste," "breeding," "respectability," "propriety," "cultivation," "good fellows," "plain folks," etc. Thus the exclusion of persons who lack the ingroup culture is felt to be normatively legitimated.

There is no *a priori* determination of the number of status groups in a particular society, nor can the degree to which there is consensus on a rank order among them be stated in advance. These are not matters of definition, but empirical variations, the causes of which are subjects of other developments of the conflict theory of stratification. Status groups should be regarded as ideal types, without implication of *necessarily distinct* boundaries; the concepts remain useful even in the case where associational groupings and their status cultures are fluid and overlapping, as hypotheses about the conflicts among status groups may remain fruitful even under these circumstances.

Status groups may be derived from a number of sources. Weber outlines three: (a) differences in life style based on economic situation (i.e., class); (b) differences in life situation based on power position; (c) differences in life situation deriving directly from cultural conditions or institutions, such as geographical origin, ethnicity, religion, education, or intellectual or aesthetic cultures.

B. *Struggle for Advantage.* There is a continual struggle in society for various "goods"—wealth, power, or prestige. We need make no assumption that every individual is motivated to maximize his rewards; however, since power and prestige are inherently scarce commodities, and wealth is often contingent upon them, the ambition of even a small proportion of persons for more than equal shares of these goods sets up an implicit counter-struggle on the part of others to avoid subjection and disesteem. Individuals may struggle with each other, but since individual identity is derived primarily from membership in a status group, and because the cohesion of status groups is a key resource in the struggle against others, the primary focus of struggle is between status groups rather than within them.

The struggle for wealth, power, and prestige is carried out primarily through organizations. There have been struggles throughout history among organizations controlled by different status groups, for military conquest, business advantage, or cultural (e.g., religious) hegemony, and intricate sorts of interorganizational alliances are possible. In the more complex societies, struggle between status groups is carried on in large part *within* organizations, as the status groups controlling an organization coerce, hire, or culturally manipulate others to carry out their wishes (as in, respectively, a conscript army, a business, or a church). Organizational research shows that the success of organizational elites in controlling their subordinates is quite variable. Under particular conditions, lower or middle members have considerable *de facto* power to avoid compliance, and even to change the course of the organizations (see Etzioni, 1961).

This opposing power from below is strengthened when subordinate members constitute a cohesive status group of their own; it is weakened when subordinates acquiesce in the values of the organization elite. Coincidence of ethnic and class boundaries produces the sharpest cultural distinctions. Thus, Catholics of immigrant origins have been the bulwarks of informal norms restricting work output in American firms run by WASPs, whereas Protestants of native rural backgrounds are the main "ratebusters" (O. Coffins et al., 1946). Selection and manipulation of members in terms of status groups is thus a key weapon in intraorganizational struggles. In general, the organization elite selects its new members and key assistants from its own status group and makes an effort to secure lower-level employees who are at least indoctrinated to respect the cultural superiority of their status culture.[4]

Once groups of employees of different status groups are formed at various positions (middle, lower, or laterally differentiated) in the organization, each of these groups may be expected to launch efforts to recruit more members of their own status group. This process is illustrated by conflicts among whites and blacks, Protestants and Catholics and Jews, Yankee, Irish and Italian, etc. found in American occupational life (Hughes, 1949; Dalton, 1951). These conflicts are based on ethnically or religiously founded status cultures; their intensity rises and falls with processes increasing or decreasing the cultural distinctiveness of these groups, and with the succession of advantages and disadvantages set by previous outcomes of these struggles which determine the organizational resources available for further struggle. Parallel processes of cultural conflict may be based on distinctive class as well as ethnic cultures.

C. *Education As Status Culture.* The main activity of schools is to teach particular status cultures, both in and outside the classroom. In this light, any failure of schools to impart technical knowledge (although it may also be successful in this) is not important; schools primarily teach vocabulary and inflection, styles of dress, aesthetic tastes, values and manners. The emphasis on sociability and athletics found in many schools is not extraneous but may be at the core of the status culture propagated by the schools. Where schools have a more academic or vocational emphasis, this emphasis may itself be the content of a particular status culture, providing sets of values, materials for conversation, and shared activities for an associational group making claims to a particular basis for status.

Insofar as a particular status group controls education, it may use it to foster control within work organizations. Educational requirements for employment can serve both to select new members for elite positions who share the elite culture and, at a lower level of education, to hire lower and middle employees who have acquired a general respect for these elite values and styles.

Tests of the Conflict Theory of Educational Stratification

The conflict theory in its general form is supported by evidence (1) that there are distinctions among status group cultures—based both on class and on ethnicity—in modern societies (Kahl, 1957:127–156, 184–220); (2) that status groups tend to occupy different occupational positions within organizations (see data on ascription cited above); and (3) that occupants of different organizational positions struggle over power (Dalton, 1959; Crozier, 1964). The more specific tests called for here, however, are of the adequacy of conflict theory to explain the link between education and occupational stratification. Such tests may focus either on the proposed mechanism of occupational placement, or on the conditions for strong or weak links between education and occupation.

Education as a Mechanism of Occupational Placement. The mechanism proposed is that employers use education to select persons who have been socialized into the dominant status culture: for entrants to their own managerial ranks, into elite culture; for lower-level employees, into an attitude of respect for the dominant culture and the elite which carries it. This requires evidence that: (a) schools provide either training for the elite culture, or respect for it; and (b) employers use education as a means of selection for cultural attributes.

(a) Historical and descriptive studies of schools support the generalization that they are places where particular status cultures are acquired, either from the teachers, from other students, or both. Schools are usually founded by powerful or autonomous status groups, either to provide an exclusive education for their own children, or to propagate respect for their cultural values. Until recently most schools were founded by religions, often in opposition to those founded by rival religions; throughout the 19th century, this rivalry was an important basis for the founding of large numbers of colleges in the U. S., and of the Catholic and Lutheran school systems. The public school system in the U. S. was founded mainly under the impetus of WASP elites with the purpose of teaching respect for Protestant and middle-class standards of cultural and religious propriety, especially in the face of Catholic, working-class immigration from Europe (Cremin, 1961; Curti, 1935). The content of public school education has consisted especially of middle-class, WASP culture (Waller, 1932:15–131; Becker, 1961; Hess and Torney, 1967).

At the elite level, private secondary schools for children of the WASP upper class were founded from the 1880s, when the mass indoctrination function of the growing public schools made them unsuitable as means of maintaining cohesion of the elite culture itself (Baltzell, 1958:327–372). These elite schools produce a distinctive personality type, characterized by adherence to a distinctive set of upper-class values and manners (McArthur, 1955). The cultural role of schools has been more closely studied in Britain (Bernstein, 1961; Weinberg, 1967), and in France (Bourdieu and Passeron, 1964), although Riesman and his colleagues (Riesman, 1958; Jencks and Riesman, 1968) have shown some of the cultural differences among prestige levels of colleges and universities in the United States.

(b) Evidence that education has been used as a means of cultural selection may be found in several sources. Hollingshead's (1949:360–388) study of Elmtown school children, school dropouts, and community attitudes toward them suggests that employers use education as a means of selecting employees with middle-class attributes. A 1945–1946 survey of 240 employers in New Haven and Charlotte, N.C. indicated that they regarded education as a screening device for employees with desirable (middle-class) character and demeanor; white-collar positions particularly emphasized educational selection because these employees were considered most visible to outsiders (Noland and Bakke, 1949:20–63).

A survey of employers in nationally prominent corporations indicated that they regarded college degrees as important in hiring potential managers, not because they were thought to ensure technical skills, but rather to indicate "motivation" and "social experience" (Gordon and Howell, 1959:121). Business school training is similarly regarded, less as evidence of necessary training (as employers have been widely skeptical of the utility of this curriculum for most positions) than as an indication that the college graduate is committed to business attitudes. Thus, employers are more likely to refuse to hire liberal arts graduates if they come from a college which has a business school than if their college is without a business school (Gordon and Howell, 1959:84–87; see also Pierson, 1959:90–99). In the latter case, the students could be said not to have had a choice; but when both business and liberal arts courses are offered and the student chooses liberal arts, employers appear to take this as a rejection of business values.

Finally, a 1967 survey of 309 California organizations (Collins, 1971) found that educational requirements for white-collar workers were highest in organizations which placed the strongest emphasis on normative control over their employees.[5] Normative control emphasis was indicated by (i) relative emphasis on the absence of police record for job applicants; (ii) relative emphasis on a record of job loyalty; (iii) Etzioni's (1961) classification of organizations into those with high normative control emphasis (financial, professional services, government, and other public services organizations) and those with remunerative control emphasis (manufacturing, construction, and trade). These three indicators are highly interrelated, thus mutually validating their conceptualization as indicators of normative control emphasis. The relationship between normative control emphasis and educational requirements holds for managerial requirements and white-collar requirements generally, both including and excluding professional and technical positions. Normative control emphasis does not affect blue-collar education requirements.

Variations in Linkage between Education and Occupation

The conflict model may also be tested by examining the cases in which it predicts education will be relatively important or unimportant in occupational attainment. Education should be most important where two conditions hold simultaneously: (1) the type of education most closely reflects membership in a particular status group, and (2) that group controls employment in particular organizational contexts. Thus, education will be most important where the fit is greatest between the culture of the status groups emerging from schools, and the status group doing the hiring; it will be least important where there is the greatest disparity between the culture of the school and of the employers.

This fit between school-group culture and employer culture may be conceptualized as a continuum. The importance of elite education is highest where it is involved in selection of new members of organizational elites, and should fade off where jobs are less elite (either lower level jobs in these organizations, or jobs in other organizations not controlled by the cultural elite). Similarly, schools which produce the most elite graduates will be most closely linked to elite occupations; schools whose products are less well socialized into elite culture are selected for jobs correspondingly less close to elite organizational levels.

In the United States, the schools which produce culturally elite groups, either by virtue of explicit training or by selection of students from elite backgrounds, or both, are the private prep schools at the secondary level; at the higher level, the elite colleges (the Ivy league, and to a lesser degree the major state universities); at the professional training level, those professional schools attached to the elite colleges and universities. At the secondary level, schools which produce respectably socialized, nonelite persons are the public high schools (especially those in middle-class residential areas); from the point of view of the culture of WASP employers, Catholic schools (and all-black schools) are less acceptable. At the level of higher education, Catholic and black colleges and professional schools are less elite, and commercial training schools are the least elite form of education.

In the United States, the organizations most clearly dominated by the WASP upper class are large, nationally organized business corporations, and the largest law firms (Domhoff, 1967:38–62). Those organizations more likely to be dominated by members of minority ethnic cultures are the smaller and local businesses in manufacturing, construction, and retail trade; in legal practice, solo rather than firm employment. In government employment, local governments appear to be more heavily dominated by ethnic groups, whereas particular branches of the national government (notably the State Department and the Treasury) are dominated by WASP elites (Domhoff, 1967: 84–114, 132–137).

Evidence on the fit between education and employment is available for only some of these organizations. In a broad sample of organizational types (Collins, 1971), educational requirements were higher in the bigger organizations, which also tended to be organized on a national scale, than in smaller and more localistic organizations.[6] The finding of Perrucci and Perrucci (1970) that upper-class social origins were important in career success precisely within the group of engineers who graduated from the most prestigious engineering schools with the highest grades may also bear on this question; since the big national corporations are most likely to hire this academically elite group, the importance of social origins within this group tends to corroborate the interpretation of education as part of a process of elite cultural selection in those organizations.

Among lawyers, the predicted differences are clear: graduates of the law schools attached to elite colleges and universities are more likely to be employed in firms, whereas graduates of Catholic or commercial law schools are more likely to be found in solo practice (Ladinsky, 1967). The elite Wall Street law firms are most educationally selective in this regard, choosing not only from Ivy League law schools but from a group whose background includes attendance at elite prep schools and colleges (Smigel, 1964: 39, 73–74, 117). There are also indications that graduates of ethnically-dominated professional schools are most likely to practice within the ethnic community; this is clearly the case among black professionals. In general, the evidence that graduates of black colleges (Sharp, 1970:64–67) and of Catholic colleges (Jencks and Riesman, 1968:357–366) have attained lower occupational positions in business than graduates of white Protestant schools (at least until recent years) also bolsters this interpretation.[7]

It is possible to interpret this evidence according to the technical-function theory of education, arguing that the elite schools provide the best technical training, and that the major national organizations require the greatest degree of technical talent. What is necessary is to test simultaneously for technical and status-conflict conditions. The most direct evidence on this point is the California employer study (Collins, 1971), which examined the effects of normative control emphasis and of organizational prominence, while holding constant the organization's technological modernity, as measured by the number of technological and organizational changes in the previous six years. Technological change was found to affect educational requirements at managerial and white-collar (but not blue-collar) levels, thus giving some support to the technical-function theory of education. The three variables—normative control emphasis, organizational prominence, and technological change—each independently affected educational requirements, in particular contexts. Technological change produced significantly higher educational requirements only in smaller, localistic organizations, and in organizational sectors not emphasizing normative control. Organizational prominence produced significantly higher educational requirements in organizations with low technological change, and in sectors de-emphasizing normative control. Normative control emphasis produced significantly higher educational requirements in organizations with low technological change and in less prominent organizations. Thus, technical and normative status conditions all affect educational requirements; measures of association indicated that the latter conditions were stronger in this sample.

Other evidence bearing on this point concerns business executives only. A study of the top executives in nationally prominent businesses indicated that the most highly educated managers were not found in the most rapidly developing companies, but rather in the least economically vigorous ones, with highest education found in the traditionalistic financial and utility firms (Warner and Abegglen, 1955:141–143, 148). The business elite has always been highly educated in relation to the American populace, but education seems to be a correlate of their social origins rather than the determinant of their success (Mills, 1963:128; Taussig and Joslyn, 1932:200; Newcomer, 1955:76). Those members of the business elite who entered its ranks from lower social origins had less education than the businessmen of upper and upper-middle-class origins, and those businessmen who inherited their companies were much more likely to be college educated than those who achieved their positions by entrepreneurship (Bendix, 1956:230; Newcomer, 1955:80).

In general, the evidence indicates that educational requirements for employment reflect employers' concerns for acquiring respectable and well-socialized employees; their concern for the provision of technical skills through education enters to a lesser degree. The higher the normative control concerns of the employer, and the more elite the organization's status, the higher his educational requirements.

Historical Change

The rise in educational requirements for employment throughout the last century may be explained using the conflict theory, and incorporating elements of the technical-functional theory into it at appropriate points. The principal dynamic has centered on changes in the supply of educated persons caused by the expansion of the school system, which was in turn shaped by three conditions:

(1) Education has been associated with high economic and status position from the colonial period on through the twentieth century. The result was a popular demand for education as mobility opportunity. This demand has not been for vocational education at a terminal or commercial level, short of full university certification; the demand has rather focused on education giving entry into the elite status culture, and usually only those technically-oriented schools have prospered which have most closely associated themselves with the sequence of education leading to (or from) the classical Bachelor's degree (Collins, 1969:68–70, 86–87, 89, 96–101).

(2) Political decentralization, separation of church and state, and competition among religious denominations have made founding schools and colleges in America relatively easy, and provided initial motivations of competition among communities and religious groups that moved them to do so. As a result, education at all levels expanded faster in America than anywhere else in the world. At the time of the Revolution, there were nine colleges in the colonies; in all of Europe, with a population forty times that of America, there were approximately sixty colleges. By 1880 there were 811 American colleges and universities; by 1966, there were 2,337. The United States not only began with the highest ratio of institutions of higher education to population in the world, but increased this lead steadily, for the number of European universities was not much greater by the twentieth century than in the eighteenth (Ben-David and Zloczower, 1962).

(3) Technical changes also entered into the expansion of American education. As the evidence summarized above indicates: (a) mass literacy is crucial for beginnings of full-scale industrialization, although demand for literacy could not have been important in the expansion of education beyond elementary levels. More importantly, (b) there is a mild trend toward the reduction in the proportion of unskilled jobs and an increase in the promotion of highly skilled (professional and technical) jobs as industrialism proceeds, accounting for 15% of the shift in educational levels in the twentieth century (Folger and Nam, 1964). (c) Technological change also brings about some upgrading in skill requirements of some continuing job positions, although the available evidence (Berg, 1970:38–60) refers only to the decade 1950–1960. Nevertheless, as Wilensky (1964) points out, there is no "professionalization of everyone," as most jobs do not require considerable technical knowledge on the order of that required of the engineer or the research scientist.

The existence of a relatively small group of experts in high-status positions, however, can have important effects on the structure of competition for mobility chances. In the United States, where democratic decentralization favors the use of schools (as well as government employment) as a kind of patronage for voter interests, the existence of even a small number of elite jobs fosters a demand for *large-scale* opportunities to acquire these positions. We thus have a "contest mobility" school system (Turner, 1960); it produced a widely educated populace because of the many dropouts who never achieve the elite level of schooling at which expert skills and/or high cultural status are acquired. In the process, the status value of American education has become diluted. Standards of respectability are always relative to the existing range of cultural differences. Once higher levels of education become recognized as an objective mark of elite status, and a moderate level of education as a mark of respectable middle-level status, increases in the supply of educated persons at given levels result in yet higher levels, becoming recognized as superior, and previously superior levels become only average.

Thus, before the end of the nineteenth century, an elementary school or home education was no longer satisfactory for a middle-class gentleman; by the 1930s, a college degree was displacing the high school degree as the minimal standard of respectability; in the late 1960s, graduate school or specialized professional degrees were becoming necessary for initial entry to many middle-class positions, and high school graduation was becoming a standard for entry to manual laboring positions. Education has thus gradually become part of the status culture of classes far below the level of the original business and professional elites.

The increasing supply of educated persons (Table 7.2) has made education a rising requirement of jobs (Table 7.1). Led by the biggest and most prestigious organizations, employers have raised their educational requirements to maintain both the relative prestige of their own managerial ranks and the relative respectability of middle ranks.[8] Education has become a legitimate standard in terms of which employers select employees, and employees compete with each other for promotion opportunities or for raised prestige in their continuing positions. With the attainment of a mass (now approaching universal) higher education system in modern America, the ideal or image of technical skill becomes the legitimating culture in terms of which the struggle for position goes on.

Higher educational requirements, and the higher level of educational credentials offered by individuals competing for position in organizations, have in turn increased the demand for education by the populace. The interaction between formal job requirements and informal status cultures has resulted in a spiral in which educational requirements and educational attainments become ever higher. As the struggle for mass educational opportunities enters new phases in the universities of today and perhaps in the graduate schools of the future, we may expect a further upgrading of educational requirements for employment. The mobilization of demands by minority groups for mobility opportunities through schooling can only contribute an extension of the prevailing pattern.

Conclusion

It has been argued that conflict theory provides an explanation of the principal dynamics of rising educational requirements for employment in America. Changes in the technical requirements of jobs have caused more limited changes in particular jobs. The conditions of the interaction of these two determinants may be more closely studied.

Precise measures of changes in the actual technical skill requirements of jobs are as yet available only in rudimentary form. Few systematic studies show how much of particular job skills may be learned in practice, and how much must be acquired through school background. Close studies of what is actually learned in school, and how long it is retained, are rare. Organizational studies of how employers rate performance and decide upon promotions give a picture of relatively loose controls over the technical quality of employee performance, but this no doubt varies in particular types of jobs.

The most central line of analysis for assessing the joint effects of status group conflict and technical requirements are those which compare the relative importance of education in different contexts. One such approach may take organization as the unit of analysis, comparing the educational requirements of organizations both to organizational technologies and to the status (including educational) background of organizational elites. Such analysis may also be applied to surveys of individual mobility, comparing the effects of education on mobility in different employment contexts, where the status group (and educational) background of employers varies in its fit with the educational culture of prospective employees. Such analysis of "old school tie" networks may also simultaneously test for the independent effect of the technical requirements of different sorts of jobs on the importance of education. Inter-nation comparisons provide variations here in the fit between types of education and particular kinds of jobs which may not be available within any particular country.

The full elaboration of such analysis would give a more precise answer to the historical question of assigning weight to various factors in the changing place of education in the stratification of modern societies. At the same time, to state the conditions under which status groups vary in organizational power, including the power to emphasize or limit the importance of technical skills, would be to state the basic elements of a comprehensive explanatory theory of the forms of stratification.

Notes

1. This survey covered 309 establishments with 100 or more employees, representing all major industry groups.
2. The concern here is with these basic premises rather than with the theory elaborated by Davis and Moore to account for the universality of stratification. This theory involves a few further propositions: (C) in any particular form of society certain occupational positions are functionally most central to the operation of the social system; (D) the ability to fill these positions, and/or the motivation to acquire the necessary training, is unequally distributed in the population; (E) inequalities of rewards in wealth and prestige evolve to ensure that the supply of persons with the necessary ability or training meshes with the structure of demands for skilled performance. The problems of stating functional centrality in empirical terms have been subjects of much debate.
3. Proposition 3 is supported by Tables 7.1 and 7.2. The issue here is whether this can be explained by the previous propositions and premises.
4. It might be argued that the ethnic cultures may differ in their functionality: that middle-class Protestant culture provides the self-discipline and other attributes necessary for higher organizational positions in modern society. This version of functional theory is specific enough to be subject to empirical test: are middle-class WASPs in fact better businessmen or government administrators than Italians, Irishmen, or Jews of patrimonial or working class cultural backgrounds? Weber suggested that they were in the initial construction of the capitalist economy within the confines of

traditional society; he also argued that once the new economic system was established, the original ethic was no longer necessary to run it (Weber, 1930:180–183). Moreover, the functional explanation also requires some feedback mechanism whereby organizations with more efficient managers are selected for survival. The oligopolistic situation in large-scale American business since the late nineteenth century does not seem to provide such a mechanism; nor does government employment. Schumpeter (1951), the leading expositor of the importance of managerial talent in business, confined his emphasis to the formative period of business expansion, and regarded the large, oligopolistic corporation as an arena where advancement came to be based on skills in organizational politics (1951:122–124); these personalistic skills are arguably more characteristic of the patrimonial cultures than of WASP culture.

5. Sample consisted of approximately one-third of all organizations with 100 or more employees in the San Francisco, Oakland, and San Jose metropolitan areas. See Gordon and Thal-Larsen (1969) for a description of procedures and other findings.

6. Again, these relationships hold for managerial requirements and white-collar requirements generally, both including and excluding professional and technical positions, but not for blue-collar requirements. Noland and Bakke (1949:78) also report that larger organizations have higher educational requirements for administrative positions than smaller organizations.

7. Similar processes may be found in other societies, where the kinds of organizations linked to particular types of schools may differ. In England, the elite "public schools" are linked especially to the higher levels of the national civil service (Weinberg, 1967:139–143). In France, the elite Ecole Polytechnique is linked to both government and industrial administrative positions (Crozier, 1964: 238–244). In Germany, universities have been linked principally with government administration, and business executives are drawn from elsewhere (Ben-David and Zloczower, 1962). Comparative analysis of the kinds of education of government officials, business executives, and other groups in contexts where the status group links of schools differ is a promising area for further tests of conflict and technical-functional explanations.

8. It appears that employers may have raised their wage costs in the process. Their behavior is nevertheless plausible, in view of these considerations: (a) the thrust of organizational research since Mayo and Barnard has indicated that questions of internal organizational power and control, of which cultural dominance is a main feature, take precedence over purely economic considerations; (b) the large American corporations, which have led in educational requirements, have held positions of oligopolistic advantage since the late 19th century, and thus could afford a large internal "welfare" cost of maintaining a well-socialized work force; (c) there are inter-organizational wage differentials in local labor markets, corresponding to relative organizational prestige, and a "wage-escalator" process by which the wages of the leading organizations are gradually emulated by others according to their rank (Reynolds, 1951); a parallel structure of "educational status escalators" could plausibly be expected to operate.

References

Anastasi, Anne, 1967 "Psychology, psychologists, and psychological testing." *American Psychologist* 22 (April): 297–306.

Baltzell, E. Digby, 1958 *An American Business Aristocracy.* New York: Macmillan.

Becker, Howard S., 1961 "Schools and systems of stratification." pp. 93–104 in A.H. Halsey, Jean Floud, and C. Arnold Anderson (eds.), *Education, Economy, and Society.* New York: Free Press.

Becker, Howard S., Blanche Geer, and Everett C. Hughes, 1968 *Making the Grade: The Academic Side of College Life.* New York: Wiley.

Bell, H. M., 1940 *Matching Youth and Jobs.* Washington: American Council on Education.

Ben-David, Joseph, 1963 "Professions in the class systems of present-64 day societies." *Current Sociology* 12:247–330.

Ben-David, Joseph and Awraham Floczower, 1962 "Universities and academic systems in modern societies." *European Journal of Sociology* 31:45–85.

Bendix, Reinhard, 1956 *Work and Authority in Industry.* New York: Wiley.

Berg, Ivar, 1970 *Education and Jobs.* New York: Praeger.

Bernstein, Basil, 1961 "Social class and linguistic development." pp. 288–314 in A.H. Halsey, Jean Floud, and C. Arnold Anderson (eds.), *Education, Economy, and Society.* New York: Free Press.

Blau, Peter M., 1955 *The Dynamics of Bureaucracy.* Chicago: University of Chicago Press.

Blau, Peter M. and Otis Dudley Duncan, 1967 *The American Occupational Structure.* New York: Wiley.

Bourdieu, Pierre and Jean-Claude Passeron, 1964 *Les Heritiers: Les Etudiants et la Culture.* Paris: Les Editions de Minuit.

Bright, James R., 1958 "Does automation raise skin requirements?" *Harvard Business Review* 36 (July–August):85–97.

Clark, Burton R., 1962 *Educating the Expert Society.* San Francisco: Chandler.

Clark, Harold F. and Harold S. Sloan, 1966 *Classrooms on Main Street.* New York: Teachers College Press.

Coleman, James S., 1961 *The Adolescent Society.* New York: Free Press.

Collins, Orvis, Melville Dalton, and Donald Roy, 1946 "Restriction of output and social cleavage in industry." *Applied Anthropology* 5 (Summer): 1–14.

Collins, Randall, 1968 "A comparative approach to political sociology." pp. 42–67 in Reinhard Bendix et al. (eds.), *State and Society.* Boston: Little, Brown.

—— 1969 Education and Employment. Unpublished Ph.D. dissertation, University of California at Berkeley.

—— 1971 "Educational requirements for employment: A comparative organizational study." Unpublished manuscript.

Cremin, Lawrence A., 1961 *The Transformation of the School.* New York: Knopf.

Crozier, Michel, 1964 *The Bureaucratic Phenomenon.* Chicago: University of Chicago Press.

Curti, Merle, 1935 *The Social Ideas of American Educators.* New York: Scribners.

Dalton, Melville, 1951 "Informal factors in career achievement." *American Journal of Sociology* 56 (March): 407–415.

—— 1959 *Men Who Manage.* New York: Wiley.

Davis, Kingsley and Wilbert Moore, 1945 "Some principles of stratification." *American Sociological Review* 10:242–249.

Denison, Edward F., 1965 "Education and economic productivity." pp. 328–340 in Seymour Harris (ed.), *Education and Public Policy.* Berkeley: McCutchen.

Dill, William R., Thomas L. Hilton, and Walter R. Reitman, 1962 *The New Managers.* Englewood Cliffs: Prentice-Hall.

Domhoff, G. William, 1967 *Who Rules America?* Englewood Cliffs: Prentice-Hall.

Duncan, Beverly, 1964 "Dropouts and the unemployed." *Journal of Political Economy* 73 (April):121–134.

Duncan, Otis Dudley and Robert W. Hodge, 1963 "Education and occupational mobility: A regression analysis." *American Journal of Sociology* 68:629–644.

Eckland, Bruce K., 1965 "Academic ability, higher education, and occupational mobility." *American Sociological Review* 30:735–746.

Epstein, Cynthia Fuchs, 1970 *Woman's Place: Options and Limits in Professional Careers.* Berkeley: University of California Press.

Etzioni, Amitai, 1961 *A Comparative Analysis of Complex Organizations.* New York: Free Press.

Folger, John K. and Charles B. Nam, 1964 "Trends in education in relation to the occupational structure." *Sociology of Education* 38:19–33.

Goode, William J., 1967 "The protection of the inept." *American Sociological Review* 32:5–19.

Gordon, Margaret S. and Margaret Thal-Larsen, 1969 *Employer Policies in a Changing Labor Market.* Berkeley: Institute of Industrial Relations, University of California.

Gordon, Robert A. and James E. Howell, 1959 *Higher Education for Business.* New York: Columbia University Press.

Gusfield, Joseph R., 1958 "Equalitarianism and bureaucratic recruitment." *Administrative Science Quarterly* 2 (March):521–541.

Hagstrom, Warren O. and Lowell L. Hargens, 1968 "Mobility theory in the sociology of science." Paper delivered at Cornell Conference on Human Mobility, Ithaca, N.Y. (October 31).

Hall, Oswald, 1946 "The informal organization of the medical profession." *Canadian Journal of Economic and Political Science* 12 (February): 30–44.

Harbison, Frederick and Charles A. Myers, 1964 *Education, Manpower, and Economic Growth.* New York: McGraw-Hill.

Hargens, Lowell and Warren O. Hagstrom, 1967 "Sponsored and contest mobility of American academic scientists." *Sociology of Education* 40:24–38.

Havemann, Ernest and Patricia Salter West, 1952 *They Went to College.* New York: Harcourt, Brace.

Hess, Robert D. and Judith V. Torney, 1967 *The Development of Political Attitudes in Children.* Chicago: Aldine.

Hollingshead, August B., 1949 *Elmtown's Youth.* New York: Wiley.

Hoselitz, Bert F., 1965 "Investment in education and its political impact." pp. 541–565 in James S. Coleman (ed.), *Education and Political Development.* Princeton: Princeton University Press.

Hughes, Everett C., 1949 "Queries concerning industry and society growing out of the study of ethnic relations in industry." *American Sociological Review* 14:211–220.

Jencks, Christopher and David Riesman, 1968 *The Academic Revolution.* New York: Doubleday.

Kahl, Joseph A., 1957 *The American Class Structure.* New York: Rinehart.

Kerr, Clark, John T. Dunlop, Frederick H. Harbison, and Charles A. Myers, 1960 *Industrialism and Industrial Man.* Cambridge: Harvard University Press.

Ladinsky, Jack, 1963 "Careers of lawyers, law practice, and legal institutions." *American Sociological Review* 28 (February):47–54.

—— 1967 "Higher education and work achievement among lawyers." *Sociological Quarterly* 8 (Spring):222–232.

Learned, W.S. and B.D. Wood, 1938 *The Student and His Knowledge.* New York: Carnegie Foundation for the Advancement of Teaching.

Lipset, Seymour Martin and Reinhard Bendix, 1959 *Social Mobility in Industrial Society.* Berkeley: University of California Press.

Lombard, George F., 1955 *Behavior in a Selling Group.* Cambridge: Harvard University Press.

March, James G. and Herbert A. Simon, 1958 *Organizations.* New York: Wiley.

Marsh, Robert M., 1963 "Values, demand, and social mobility." *American Sociological Review* 28 (August): 567–575.

McArthur, C., 1955 "Personality differences between middle and upper classes." *Journal of Abnormal and Social Psychology* 50:247–254.

Mills, C. Wright, 1963 *Power, Politics, and People.* New York: Oxford University Press.

Newcomer, Mabel, 1955 *The Big Business Executive.* New York: Columbia University Press.

Noland, E. William and E. Wight Bakke, 1949 *Workers Wanted.* New York: Harper.

Nosow, Sigmund, 1956 "Labor distribution and the normative system." *Social Forces* 30:25–33.

Peaslee, Alexander L., 1969 "Education's role in development." *Economic Development and Cultural Change* 17 (April): 293–318.

Perrucci, Carolyn Cummings and Robert Perrucci, 1970 "Social origins, educational contexts, and career mobility." *American Sociological Review* 35 (June):45l–463.

Pierson, Frank C., 1959 *The Education of American Businessmen.* New York: McGraw-Hill.

Plunkett, M., 1960 "School and early work experience of youth." *Occupational Outlook Quarterly* 4:22–27.

Reynolds, Lloyd, 1951 *The Structure of Labor Markets.* New York: Harper.

Riesman, David, 1958 *Constraint and Variety in American Education.* New York: Doubleday.

Roy, Donald, 1952 "Quota restriction and goldbricking in a machine shop." *American Journal of Sociology* 57 (March):427–442.

Schultz, Theodore W., 1961 "Investment in human capital." *American Economic Review* 51 (March):1–16.

Schumpeter, Joseph, 1951 *Imperialism and Social Classes*. New York: Augustus M. Kelley.

Sewell, William H., Archibald O. Halter, and Alejandro Portes, 1969 "The educational and early occupational attainment process." *American Sociological Review* 34 (February):82–92.

Sharp, Laure M., 1970 *Education and Employment: The Early Careers of College Graduates*. Baltimore: Johns Hopkins Press.

Smigel, Erwin O., 1964 *The Wall Street Lawyer*. New York: Free Press.

Soderberg, C. Richard, 1963 "The American engineer." pp. 203–230 in Kenneth S. Lynn, *The Professions in America*. Boston: Beacon Press.

Taeuber, Alma F., Karl E. Taeuber, and Glen G. Cain, 1966 "Occupational assimilation and the competitive process: A reanalysis." *American Journal of Sociology* 72:278–285.

Taussig, Frank W. and C.S. Joslyn, 1932 *American Business Leaders*. New York: Macmillan.

Turner, Ralph H., 1952 "Foci of discrimination in the employment of nonwhites." *American Journal of Sociology* 58:247–256.

—— 1960 "Sponsored and contest mobility and the school system." *American Sociological Review* 25 (October):855–867.

Waller, Willard, 1932 *The Sociology of Teaching*. New York: Russell and Russell.

Warner, W. Lloyd and James C. Abegglen, 1955 *Occupational Mobility in American Business and Industry, 1928–1952*. Minneapolis: University of Minnesota Press.

Weber, Max, 1930 *The Protestant Ethic and the Spirit of Capitalism*. New York: Scribner's.

—— 1968 *Economy and Society*. New York: Bedminster Press.

Weinberg, I., 1967 *The English Public Schools*. New York: Atherton.

Wilensky, H.L., 1964 "The professionalization of everyone?" *American Journal of Sociology* 70: 137–158.

8
The Logic of Teacher Sentiments

Dan Lortie

People in a similar line of work are likely to share at least some common thoughts and feelings about that work. Such convergence can arise from the diffusion of a subculture; on the other hand, it may derive from common responses to common contingencies. Whatever the source of the shared sentiments, however, it is essential to know their nature if we are to grasp the ethos of an occupation.

Sentiment is a broad term. We can facilitate analysis, I believe, if we subdivide that idea into three components—preoccupations, beliefs, and preferences. Colleagues are likely to show similar preoccupations—they heed particular aspects of the environment and are indifferent to others. Thus does the world look different to geologists and painters. Beliefs can also vary along occupational lines; members of an occupation develop theories (implicit as well as explicit) to account for events which are important to them. Thus policemen and social workers are likely to use different theories to explain similar behavior. Members of different occupations have different preferences in working arrangements and such: whereas the "big-ticket" salesman is sharply individualistic, ironworkers count heavily on the intimate coorperation of their four-man teams.

What work sentiments do teachers share? That is the first question we shall address in this chapter; we will analyze survey data and open-ended interviews to identify some of their shared preoccupations, beliefs, and preferences. The data will cover a variety of issues including the circumstances teachers associate with high points in their work, the nature of their discontents, and the changes they would like to see in their work context. We will search for general sentiments which permeate different aspects of their work; where we succeed, we should gain insight into teacher perspectives and, quite possibly, teacher behavior.

There is a second major objective for this chapter—a more ambitious one. That goal is to understand as much as we can about the underlying logic of teacher sentiments. The assumption is that teacher sentiments represent an adaptation to their work situation; if we understand the problems of teachers, their sentiments should prove more understandable. We will look for such understanding by connecting our findings on sentiments to what we have already learned about the occupation. More is required, however. We cannot afford to over-look limits imposed on teachers by their particular status. Teacher tasks and teacher status are related, and an examination of teacher sentiments must reflect that relationship.

First, I will recapitulate some of the major points made so far, connecting them with the teacher's stake in school organization; I will draw certain corollaries and test them with survey data. Second, I will analyze teacher tasks and the imperatives which flow from them to see what tensions arise between the tasks teachers perform and the status they occupy.

Priorities of Teacher Allegiance

The argument carries implications for teachers' views on their work setting. We observed that psychic rewards have special significance for teachers and that such rewards are linked to achievement with students. We argued that teacher purposes revolve around classroom events; the problematics we identified arise in the immediate work setting of the teacher. But what about the school and the school system? How do teachers view the organizational con-text in which they work?

If teachers cathect classrooms, it means that other settings and relationships have less importance for them. Two corollaries follow. First, teachers should care less about tasks and activities rooted in organizational matters than about those rooted in classroom matters. Second, when a conflict arises between organizational and classroom demands, teachers should favor those originating in the classroom. We can test these corollaries with data from Dade County.

When asked how they would choose to spend additional work time, Dade County teachers overwhelmingly selected activities related to classroom rather than schoolwide matters. Ninety-one percent of the respondents chose teaching-related activities such as more prepa-ration (40 percent), more teaching (28 percent), counseling students (19 percent), and parent conferences (4 percent).[1] Nine percent gave first choice to committee work on school opera-tions, instruction, and public relations. Their press is toward effort where psychic rewards occur—in work directly connected with their students. (The choices have an interesting side implication; they throw doubt on teachers' allegations about wanting greater control over cur-ricular affairs at the school system level.) It is also interesting that 91 percent of the first choices are individualistic; they are all tasks which teachers normally perform alone. As an indication of preference for classroom versus schoolwide activities, the responses are unambiguous; the vast majority of respondents—5,448 out of 5,991—chose to spend additional time on class-room tasks rather than working with the school at large.

Two kinds of data speak to the question of which claims, organizational or classroom, teachers prefer to meet. The first consists of responses Dade County teachers gave to a ques-tion on school organization.[2] They were asked to choose between more freedom from organi-zational authority and greater efficiency through rules; an attempt was made to balance the evident appeal of freedom by mentioning an explicit benefit of rules. The results were clear-cut: 66 percent chose greater freedom, 29 percent prevailing arrangements, and 4 percent more rules and efficiency. If anything, these teachers want to loosen organizational claims in favor of teacher decision-making in the classroom.

The second set of data consists of answers to a question we discussed previously; we may recall that 59 percent of Dade County teachers said that the good teacher monitors his own efforts in the classroom. By the most generous count, 7 percent of the respondents emphasized superordinate judgments as the most appropriate source of work monitoring. Since the line of vertical authority symbolizes organizational goals and claims, its relegation to such infrequency indicates secondary allegiance to the organization at large.[3]

These data seem to support the corollaries which have been drawn; in the available data, teachers prefer classroom tasks over organizational tasks and classroom claims over organizational initiations. Their impulses are organizationally centrifugal; their primary allegiance is to the classroom. What makes these tendencies interesting (they are understandable given the reward structure) is that teachers are not seen as entrepreneurs seeking psychic rewards; they are defined as employees of school systems and are hired to implement board policies and administrative rulings. As we shall see, the tension between teacher impulses and status realities has consequences for the nature of teacher sentiments.

Task Imperatives and Status Constraints

Since teachers assign priority to classroom tasks, we would expect their sentiments to reflect that concern. The question arises: What circumstances are likely to advance or retard realization of their classroom aims? For if teachers have a stake in task performance, they are likely to be deeply concerned with conditions which affect that performance.

To get a fresh perspective on teaching tasks, let us compare teaching with other occupations which include similar tasks. What is the relationship between rights and obligations and what people must do in their work? More abstractly, how are status realities and task imperatives related? Task imperatives refer here to the necessities involved in performing duties; for example, in order to make arrests, a police officer must be able to use force in overcoming resistance. In teaching, the imperative of maintaining classroom discipline requires that teachers be able to punish other people's children—an unusual right. In this instance, the status of the teacher and his task imperatives are congruent. But as we shall see, alignment is not always present; tension can obtain between task imperatives and status realities.

Teachers strive to "*reach*" students. They *manage* groups of young people at work. Teachers are also expected to *perceive and act on* the needs of individual learners. The foregoing tasks can be found in other occupations. The first requires communication with, and penetration of, a group of people in a face-to-face situation. This requirement occurs in several occupations— we will choose the theater for comparison. The occupation analogous to the second set of tasks, the management of work groups, is more obvious; industrial or business managers perform similar tasks. The need to observe individuals and to prescribe suitable procedures and moniter their progress is similar to the tasks of the psychotherapist.

Although teaching is a long-range, continuing activity, in contrast to the short-range, immediate impact sought in the theater, both teachers and actors face similar task imperatives. They must overcome the influence of distractions and mobilize the attention of initially uninvolved audiences. Without full attention, neither learning nor dramatic experience is likely to take place. In theater work there is a complex division of labor aimed at reaching the audience; directors, stage managers, actors—to say nothing of the playwright—work together. The teacher typically works alone and is forced to play all those roles simultaneously. The theatrical setting, moreover, is usually manipulated to concentrate audience attention; lighting, scenery, properties, and costumes all contribute to monopolizing the audience's attention.

The teacher, on the other hand, works under comparatively humdrum conditions, with fewer resources for riveting attention. (We should also recall that students, unlike theater audiences, have not come voluntarily.) Teachers, in short, face some of the same imperatives as theater people without possessing equal resources.

The teacher has an additional handicap in maintaining attention; unlike the director of a play, the teacher has little "artistic control" over the enterprise. Teachers cannot select or reject scripts; they frequently must follow curricula which bore students or are beyond their capacities. Nor is the classroom a stage over which the teacher can legitimately assert full authority; as part of the school, its activities are subject to review by higher officials. Teachers have difficulty in sealing off disruption. Administrators may intervene and peers may interrupt; students may break the spell a teacher has sought to develop. The teacher must work with supplies furnished by others and may in fact have trouble getting enough. In addition to having fewer resources, the teacher has less control over the situation than those directing theatrical productions. The teacher's status, in short, is less suited to imperatives of communication and penetration.

Although one hears references to "classroom management," teachers are rarely described as managers. Perhaps the position of teachers as subordinates, coupled with the lower prestige accorded to work with minors, accounts for the tendency to overlook similarities between teachers and managers. Both set goals for groups of subordinates and try to lead them toward accomplishment. Both must decide how to allocate time and other scarce resources to get work done. Both must balance task and socioemotional considerations. Both distribute rewards and punishments to those in their charge.

It is a truism of organization that administrators need a degree of autonomy and authority to carry out their responsibilities (Parsons 1958). The statuses of teachers and managers are nowhere more different than here; teachers work *under* administrators—the latter term is used to distinguish managers from teachers. Without the title to identify their managerial functions, teachers do not benefit from the principle of administrative discretion. Nor are they expected to show the personal qualities (e.g., independence in decision-making, aggressiveness) which mark the manager. Teachers rarely have budgetary discretion and the other prerogatives which are part of the manager's working equipment. In status terms, teachers are disadvantaged compared with managers; imperatives which flow from their managerial tasks are likely to be misaligned with their formal status.

Although teachers have difficulty meeting individual needs in the grouped structure of public schools, they are expected to make individual assessments and decisions about students. Such work with people involves considerable judgement; to prescribe particular remedies for learning difficulties, for example, is not a cut-and-dried matter—it involves intuition as well as explicit reasoning. One's judgments, moreover, need time to reveal their merit or inadequacy; others must be willing to extend trust until the results are in. Similar conditions apply to the practice of psychotherapy; diagnoses and treatment interact over time as the therapist tests various possibilities. But although the tasks and imperatives may be similar for teachers and therapists, there is normally a large difference in their prestige. Therapists may be licensed psychologists or physicians; where that is so, their claims to trust are buttressed by impressive qualifications based on protracted study.

Although it would require separate research to find out how willing members of the public are to trust teachers' judgments about individual students, that trust rarely matches that extended to qualified therapists. Teachers are certified to teach in schools without demonstrating expert knowledge of individual psychology. There is evidence, moreover, that parents question teachers' judgments and do not feel constrained to "wait it out"; one hears of administrators overruling teachers' judgments.[4] Again we find that the imperatives of teaching and the status of teachers are misaligned.

In each comparison, we found that persons performing tasks similar to teachers' enjoyed greater status rights. Teachers have fewer resources, and less control over them, than theater directors. Teachers have less discretionary power and fewer resources than managers. Teachers have less formal recognition to support their judgments than do psychotherapists. Teachers therefore can be said to be comparatively poorer in the status resources which facilitate accomplishment of the tasks listed here. Recalling how deeply teachers feel about their psychic rewards, we would expect them to develop ideas about these points of stress and tension. They are inhibited in impulses toward autonomy, more resources, and control over the work situation—that, at least, is a reasonable inference from our analysis so far. On the other hand, teachers have been socialized to a subordinate position within school systems. We know, too, that they are dogged by painful uncertainties.

How do teachers cope with these tensions? Do their sentiments focus on status limitations? Or do they accept such difficulties as unavoidable features of their work?

Preoccupations, Beliefs, and Preferences

The researcher's delight can be the writer's bane. Certain key sentiments appeared and reappeared in several questions I asked Five Towns teachers; that repetition convinced me of their importance. Yet discussion of repetition could prove tedious. I will therefore mention the range of responses to each question but emphasize new themes as they come up.

High Points for Teachers: The Good Day

One of the most useful questions in the Five Towns interviews asked respondents to describe "a good day" in their teaching; the question was developed after pilot research indicated that teachers used the phrase in discussing their work. The question meets the criteria we used in [previously] to assess the quality of interview data: it is personal, concrete, indirect and cathected. The vast majority of respondents gave graphic and detailed answers. Since the material was valuable, it was analyzed in three distinct ways—each tells us something about how teachers see those occasions when things go very well.

Invariant Themes

Lindesmith argued that social scientists should give special attention to invariant findings—that is, occasions where one cannot find exceptions to patterns in one's data (Lindesmith 1947). All respondents made certain points (explicitly and implicitly) in answering this question. Of the three invariant themes identified, two are familiar to us and can be discussed briefly.

The first commonality was that all respondents readily accepted the assumption of variability built into the question and based their answers on that assumption. These teachers evidently see their work as "'up and down'' in nature and view the flow of accomplishment and rewards as erratic. This observation fits in with earlier discussions of teacher rewards and uncertainty.

The second invariant theme was that every teacher, regardless of grade or specialty, based his answer on the same locale. In each instance he focused on events within his immediate work area, whether classroom, gymnasium, woodworking shop, or laboratory. Other settings (e.g., assemblies, lunchrooms, or corridors) were alluded to in negative terms; good things were not linked to them. We have already discussed teachers' cathexis of classrooms and their secondary involvement in other facets of their work; responses to this question underscore that point.

The third similarity in the answers revolves around the actors identified in the events which mark a good day. The pattern is striking; positive events and outcomes are linked to two sets of actors—the teacher and the students. (Students occasionally produce negative references connected with discipline cases.) But *all* other persons, without exception, were connected with undesirable occurrences. Negative allusions were made to parents, the principal, the school nurse, colleagues—in fact, to anyone and everyone who "intrudes" on classroom events. The cathected scene is stripped of all transactions save those between teacher and students.

This third theme introduces sentiments we have not yet discussed. From the evidence of this question, teachers attach great meaning to the boundaries which separate their classrooms from the rest of the school and, of course, the community. Teachers deprecate transactions which cut across those boundaries. Walls are perceived as beneficial; they protect and enhance the course of instruction. All but teacher and students are outsiders. That definition conveys an implicit belief that, on site, other adults have potential for hindrance but not for help.

It's a day when you really have the children to yourself. You accomplish a lot. At the end of the day you feel you've taught them something.

A good day for me . . . is a smooth day. A day when you can close the doors and do nothing but teach. When you don't have to collect picture money or find out how many want pizza for lunch or how many want baked macaroni or how many want to subscribe to a magazine. If you could have a day without those extra duties—that would be a good day.

I think, to me, a day is good without interruption—the several days during the week that I spend mostly in the classroom. There is no gym, no TV, no programs that take the children out of the room, but those days are getting less all the time . . . . I like to be right in the classroom and have the children there. Some days can be rather hectic here. You just don't get that much done. You look up and where is Johnny? He's taking a lesson. Sometimes the children are out of the room and you don't even realize it. It is hard to keep track of some of the things and extras. I think they are extras in some cases and interfere with the teacher's day.

Well, when things you planned go well. For example, you have a subject to teach that's not always an interesting subject but one of the dull factors that has to do with mechanics and suddenly you get results. You see that the youngsters see what you have and get it easily and quickly and apply it and it comes back to you as you want it to come back. I think that is a satisfying day—a day when you feel you've accomplished your job as a teacher. You taught something.

[Could you contrast this with a bad day?]

Well, just the reverse—when everything you do just does not go all right. Sometimes I wonder if the days have to have a great many interruptions and we have those unfortunately. It's a day you're being pushed for reports, you're being pushed for this and you don't feel as though you have the time and sometimes the energy to put across the subject that you need to put across in your classrooms and so your approach is perhaps not as calm as it would have been on a good day and, as a result, you don't get results and you feel it's been a completely frustrating day. I think it usually comes when you're being pressed for reports on time or you have a great many interruptions. Things of that kind. It used to be an extremely difficult day when we used to give the polio shots, for instance, in the gym and this room, this corridor out here, was Grand Central Station. You had youngsters crying, you had mamas, you know, in and out, and mama would see you in the room so she would burst right into the class and say, "Oh, hello Miss———, it's you." A day like that could be a very bad day and yet it was something to be able to do that in itself. A bad day to me is something that you can't do anything about.

All because there are so many interruptions. You start to teach something and one of the teachers might come in, or the principal comes in or a supervisor comes in and before you know it, you've lost their attention entirely and might as well just not bother to even teach. As far as that goes with that particular subject because you're not about to get their attention back and that's my idea of a bad day.

The quotations remind us of the comparisons between teachers and theater people; distraction is the enemy. Teaching can be marred when others interrupt its flow; the teacher may be pulled away to activities which, in his view, have nothing to do with teaching. In the teacher's idyll, there is a continuous, productive exchange between teacher and students; others have little to offer in advancing that exchange. Schoolwide tasks are defined in negative terms—they take energy and attention away from the primary setting, the classroom. It appears that teachers want to establish and maintain a time-bound but definite monopoly over students' attention and involvement. A key belief shown in these responses is that attention and response flourish when the classroom is a bounded, protected space. Teachers clearly prefer boundedness.

In interpreting such sentiments, it is important to remember W.I. Thomas's dictum: it is not objective "truth" but what people believe to be true that affects their outlook. Teachers apparently think that their lives would be happier and their work more effective if they had more occasions when their relationship with the students matched their wants. They strive for a kind of privatization. Yet note that they are reporting on the rarity of such occasions; they are describing *high points* in their work. Teacher status does not ensure conditions they consider favorable to their work; the imperatives they value are infrequently satisfied. The impulse to build boundaries collides with status reality.

The Events of a Good Day

What happens within the classroom on a good day? What do teachers and students experience when all goes well? To answer such questions, responses were analyzed on a sentence-by-sentence basis; all comments made about the teacher and students were listed and coded. Different categories were developed for the two parties. We begin with teachers' perceptions about their own actions and experiences on a good day.

Of the comments made about the teacher's role on a good day (124 in all), some (29) referred to what the teacher brought to the day, some (69) dealt with the teacher's actions throughout the day, and the rest (36) described the teacher's feelings about such a day. The main idea conveyed in the first category—what the teacher brought to the day—was that the teacher *begins* feeling well. The day starts with a motivated teacher who is in a "good humor," "feels good," "is rested and well." The responses were comparatively homogeneous; the teacher begins in the right frame of mind for teaching.

More distinctions were made when respondents discussed the teacher's actions during the day. The largest number of comments (26) stressed effectiveness in permeating student awareness: they referred to "stimulating students," "being enthusiastic," "getting across," "reaching." Other statements concentrated on the handling of time constraints; some (almost all elementary teachers) stressed that on a good day they finished their work plans. Other respondents used general language indicating higher teacher performance (13); they said "the teacher performs well," "the teacher gets and sees results," and "the teacher reaches his goals." Some commented (8) that preparations proved effective, and others (5) said that the teacher worked hard on a good day. From what we have seen in earlier chapters, it should come as no surprise that the feelings teachers associate with such a good day—the third category of responses—are positive. Some (15) talked about the sense of accomplishment they felt—they feel vindicated as teachers. Others (11) contrasted it with other days, stating that they did not feel aggravated or tired at the end of the day.

To sum up the teacher's role on a good day, then, we can say this. The teacher starts off ready for work, feeling good and having high energy. The day is marked by getting through to the students, finishing one's plans, and effective teaching; plans prove viable and one works hard. At the end of the day, the teacher feels worthy. He has earned his way.

How do respondents define the students' contributions to a good day? The emphasis here is somewhat different; students contribute by responding and cooperating (62), behaving themselves (29), and demonstrating positive feelings (11). They are excellent followers of the teacher's leadership. They participate actively, show interest, and give their full attention. They work hard. They behave themselves by conforming to the teacher's rules. They show positive affect by "wanting to learn," "being in a good mood," and "enjoying the classes."

The outcomes for students are instructional; forty-five of the statements dealt with student learning and accomplishment. The teachers said things like "the students learn," "they get it," and "they grasp the lesson." The benefits reaped by students and teachers are different but complementary; student learning is matched to the teacher's sense of accomplishment.

Most of the themes disclosed in these observations have been discussed earlier. We note that the teacher is reaching the students; instructional goals are met. We also note that relational complexities are mastered and assessment worries allayed; the students' enthusiasm affirms the teacher's leadership skill and reduces anxiety about effectiveness. One theme is somewhat novel; teachers believe that the teacher is the essential catalyst for student achievement. Teacher leadership stands at the center of this benign and desirable activity; it is portrayed as the sine qua non of student learning. The role of the teacher approaches the heroic.

The themes of distraction and attention also emerged in comments which were not coded in the scheme we have just reviewed. Teachers described unlikely times for good days; they mentioned Mondays and Fridays, days before and after major holidays, and days immediately before major school events—particularly in high schools—such as dances or important games. In such instances the teacher finds it difficult to claim and hold student attention; the underlying belief is that when outside influences are at their highest point the teacher's is at its lowest. A zero-sum conceptualization appears to be at work; the belief that student attention belongs to other activities *or* to the teacher is probably connected with the wish to separate classroom activities from the rest of the world.

The events of a good day reaffirm earlier analyses. They occur behind boundaries in the cathected classroom setting; they yield treasured rewards and reassure teachers. We see the fusion of achievement and satisfaction and the belief that teachers are the essential catalysts of student learning. There are times when difficulties in teaching are overcome and when sought-after goals and relationships are attained. One wonders, then, can teachers ensure the occurrence of such days? We turn next to the issue which underlies teacher answers to that question. What do they believe causes a good day?

Uncertainty Reiterated: Subtleties of Mood

The advantages of a question which uses indirection to provoke spontaneity are offset, unfortunately, by disadvantages; one sometimes wishes more specific probes had been used. In trying to ascertain the "theories" held by respondents, it is difficult to be sure when causation is implied. Did those teachers who stressed boundedness intend to say that boundedness "caused" the good day? Or were they merely mentioning a necessary but not sufficient cause? In deciding to check on this, I identified all instances in which respondents made clear-cut statements on the cause of a good day. To my surprise, most of those statements (33 of 44) dealt not with boundedness but with psychological states of teachers and students.[5] Obviously one must treat such counts with caution; but it is useful to note that a proportion of Five Towns teachers feel that a good day requires more than boundedness.

The preoccupation with psychological states, and the attributions of cause and effect, revolved around what we can call factors of "mood." Some respondents (13) explained the good day in terms of the mood of both teacher and students; it arose only when both were in the appropriate frame of mind. Sometimes mood itself depended on external events like health or environmental conditions (e.g., the time of year, the weather). But other respondents located mood origins in the interaction between teacher and students; their talk reminds one of the processes discussed by students of collective behavior (Blumer 1957). Thus a good day evolves as students and teacher positively reinforce one another—there is an emphasis on rapport. (Some made comments such as "there's sort of a two-way radio between the children and me" or "the children and teacher seem to be in tune all day.") This suggests that further research might inquire into two discrete kinds of theories among teachers to account for points of high productivity and satisfaction. In one individuals react primarily to external influences, and in the other the emphasis is on a cycle of mutual sensitivity and positive reinforcement.

Some respondents, however, select either the teacher's or students' moods as controlling. A teacher who feels bad may infect students with the same attitude. For example:

If you didn't get enough sleep the night before . . . the children won't be as interested . . . more discipline problems.

Like when my husband was sick . . . that reacted on the children.

A few teachers said that a good day depended on the mood of students. "Students may tune you out," for example, or "many are going to come in and are not going to learn anything no matter what you do." Another teacher talked about "bad actors" and remarked, "Sometimes a good day is when those students stay home." Student moods are frequently depicted as volatile; one teacher said snow falling outside on a December morning means "that is the end of it, they have been distracted." Student moods are seen as will-o'-the-wisps; they are unpredictable, quixotic, and ultimately mysterious.

The fact that some teachers explain good days (and the attendant results and satisfactions) in terms of subtle, changeful moods is provocative. The explanatory theories they are relying upon do not, in such instances, emphasize rational choice. Strategy counts for less than chance when mood is king. Such a view underlines the transitory, uncertain course of teaching; it also magnifies psychological processes which are usually thought to be beyond intentional control. One suspects that most people think of mood as something that happens to them, not as something they select. To link teaching effectiveness and rewards to mood is to make them contingent rather than manipulable—it connotes caprice rather than craft. Those who hold to such a view telegraph uncertainty rather than sure control; good days—and their benefits—are not something one orders up at will.

Summary: High Points

The teachers in our samples are preoccupied with classroom matters; they attach secondary importance to organizational affairs. Five Towns teachers talk largely about efforts to get and hold student attention and their attempts to permeate student awareness. The testimony in this chapter reaffirms the central importance of psychic rewards, instructional goals, and evocative relationships. Respondents evidently resent incursions on their teaching time; whatever distracts teachers or students, assuming that the interaction is essential to learning, is counterproductive. Respondents obviously have difficulty in warding off such incursions; their status does not provide them with the power to do so. Yet it is not clear that they believe boundedness is enough to ensure high results; some respondents emphasize the importance of subtle, difficult-to-control flows of mood. They seem to believe that short-term productivity and key rewards have an element of caprice.

What these teachers want matches their preoccupations and their beliefs—they want to teach. Since they also believe that the teacher is the essential catalyst in the learning process, they feel their impulses are legitimate. Whatever impedes their efforts impedes student progress. They want to concentrate their efforts on the core tasks of teaching, not on distractive organizational duties. One senses their yearning for uninterrupted, productive engagements with students.

The Anatomy of Discontent

Teacher complaint is almost ritualized in quality—its major components have been heard many times. In order to keep the same base for analysis, I shall present the responses to questions about dissatisfactions asked in the Five Towns interviews. There is an additional advantage to using those data, since they were open-ended and it was possible to analyze details which are usually omitted in questionnaire studies. Table 8.1 presents the results to two

Table 8.1 Complaints of Five Towns Teachers

Area of Complaint	Question 46 Mentions	%	Question 48 Mentions	%	Total Mentions
Tasks and Time Use					
Clerical duties	29	34	16	19	45
Interruptions, time pressures	16	19	29	35	45
Duties outside class	13	15	7	8	20
Large classes, schools	7	8	—	—	7
Grading papers, etc.	7	8	—	—	7
Fringe subjects	3	4	—	—	3
Interpersonal relationships					
Troublesome students	19	22	25	30	44
Administrative superordinates	20	24	9	11	29
Parents	14	17	6	7	20
Fellow teachers	7	8	13	16	20
Other					
Income and prestige of occupation	5	6	—	—	5
Facilities and supplies	—	—	5	6	5
Miscellaneous	10	—	11	—	21

questions using conventional survey coding; in the text, we will discuss an additional analysis of the same data.

Respondents talked about two major sources of difficulty in their work. The first deals with their tasks and their use of time; the second refers to relationships with students, co-workers, and parents. We will discuss tasks and time use first and then briefly discuss interpersonal difficulties; the latter will receive considerably more attention in the next chapter. We are again faced with the scientific benefit but aesthetic problem of repetition. As we shall see, the difficulties teachers discuss are the other side, in large part, of what we have learned about their wants. I shall try to be concise, therefore, in reviewing the data.

Tasks and Time Use

Since teachers assign priority to classroom work with students, we can better understand their specific complaints if we make a simple distinction between two kinds of teacher time. The first can be called "potentially productive time." It refers to occasions when the teacher is engaged in either direct instruction of students or activities closely related to it (e.g., preparation, counseling). The second kind of time is "inert time"; this refers to occasions when the potential for learning is absent or very low because the teacher's activities are not instructional. The classification builds on *teacher* perceptions; teachers link students' learning to teachers' activities and, of course, to their psychic rewards. To them, potentially productive time can be salutary for students and personally rewarding; inert time is neither.

The content of Table 8.1 makes sense when we bear that distinction in mind. The three most frequently mentioned problems and irritants (clerical duties, interruptions and time pressures, and extra duties) all involve inert time. Clerical duties usually originate in organizational needs for reports, forms, and so on; extra duties refer to supervising areas outside one's own domain, such as playgrounds, corridors, study halls, and lunchrooms. Interruptions occur when the flow of teaching is broken by the principal's making an announcement over the public address system, a parent's making an unscheduled call, or a fellow teacher's "visiting too long." Time pressures refer to sudden requests (usually from administrators) or short deadlines which require that planned activities be put aside. In each instance time is lost.

The time dimension to the other complaints listed in Table 8.1 may be less immediately apparent. Large classes increase the proportion of inert time by requiring more clerical work, greater attention to managerial issues, and more disciplinary activity. Large schools increase the administration's managerial load; the result is probably an increase in administrative requests of staff members. Grading papers is notoriously time-consuming; some teachers, moreover, do not consider it instructionally productive. They resist evaluating students comparatively, possibly on philosophical grounds and possibly because it increases the social distance between them and their students. References to fringe subjects were made by elementary teachers who would prefer to spend the time required for art and music on "basic" subjects like arithmetic and reading; interestingly, they often support their objections by disclaiming any talent in the arts.

Teachers' objections to inert time are understandable, but one or two points are worth making. First, we can think of time as the single most important, general resource teachers possess in their quest for productivity and psychic reward; ineffective allocations of time are costly. Second, from one perspective teaching processes are ultimately interminable; one can never strictly say that one has "finished" teaching students. At what point has one taught every student everything he might possibly learn about the curriculum? More broadly, when can one feel that one has taught everything any particular student should learn? The theme of concern about incompleteness ran throughout the interviews; unfortunately, it occurred in various places, making systematic collation next to impossible. Presumably teachers develop defenses against overexpectation for themselves; yet these defenses do not always seem to work. If one is inwardly pressed by a feeling of not having finished one's work, inert time must be particularly galling.

Interpersonal Relationships

Table 8.1 identifies four categories of people who stimulate teacher complaints. Students can disrupt the teacher's plans and day, and one child who acts out can create considerable difficulty for a teacher.[6] Overall, however, adults are mentioned more often than students; how do administrators, parents, and fellow teachers pose problems for the classroom teacher?

There is a common theme in the complaints respondents registered about administrators, parents, and fellow teachers; time and again they said that they failed to give them sufficient "support" in their work. The specifics of support apparently differ with each category. With administrators, complaints centered on sudden, interruptive demands and the principals' failure to protect teachers against parental intrusions and harassments. Respondents criticized parents for either interfering in the teacher's classroom work or for not backing him up at home. Colleagues were berated for avoiding their fair share of what Hughes (1958) calls "dirty work"; fellow teachers who fail to participate equally in unpopular tasks of hall duty, lunch-room supervision, and so forth increase the others' load. "Support" seems to mean that those who work in conjunction with the teacher should contribute to rather than detract from favorable work conditions; they should forward the teacher's strivings for boundaries, time control, and effective relationships with students.

The responses listed in Table 8.1 were analyzed in another fashion. In all instances where teachers complained about interpersonal relationships, the responses were coded in terms of this question: What grounds does the respondent supply for his complaint? The results bring us back, strikingly, to concerns with time usage; sixty-two of the ninety-eight reasons given for complaint dealt with time erosion or the disruption of work flow. Some quotations reveal how those who intruded on the teacher's potentially productive time evoked annoyance:

I think last-minute interruptions more than anything else. To go along with the class-room interruption business we have a P.A. system. It is overused. Instead of sending a notice around at the beginning and end of the day, and telling us what he has in mind for a particular thing... if you were in the middle of an arithmetic lesson, you'd just be ham-mering a point across and the loudspeaker would come on and the principal would talk for two or three minutes. By then, they are gone. Some kiddo will come in wanting to bor-row our paper. The milk collection boy or the attendance book coming through the room ... these things irritate me very much. I hate like the devil to be in the middle of a lesson and have this happen. You are in the middle of a lesson and a youngster will walk up to the wastebasket to deposit a piece of paper.... This burns me to no end. They learn it early in my class that this I don't go for. I think interruptions more than anything else bother me.

I do think that sometimes too much of our actual school day has to be taken up with collecting things or making our reports and so forth. It isn't that I object to doing them, but I do object to the time it takes away from my class. The only practical thing is, I guess, for the teacher to do it, but it does take away from—the children should be here—the town's paying to have them educated—not to have you collect milk money and I mean there are so many little things like that. I suppose maybe that's what is dissatisfying to teachers.

I don't know that they bother but I think we have so much secretarial work, so many other things to do besides teach. Sometimes it seems to me that teaching comes last instead of first. And so I think that would be the part of our teaching for which all the sec-retarial work would be the parts for which we have the least training really, and yet more and more and more we have to do that... fill out insurance papers and take care of all the P.T.A. notices, collect money for this and for that, and all these other odd jobs that we have to do that are so time-consuming. By the time that we do all that there's not too much time left to teach.

Interruptions. Interruptions during class time. Additional duties that are actually not assigned that you just pick up along the way. In other words, you may have something planned, you may have a free period, and you may plan on doing some work, and you get a call saying, well, cover a class, or cover study hall. Changing of programming at times by them in other words, you're on a schedule, you're on a routine perhaps if you want to call it that, and you have things planned because you have to plan ahead, and all of a sudden, the P.A. system says, well, there'll be no first period today, or today's first will be tomorrow's third or sixth or something like that. This aggravates me. Or that some event will take precedence over the classroom time. For instance, a football rally or something like that.

The reader will see that there is a note of hurt, of dignity offended, in this talk about disruption and managing time. Intrusions on teaching carry a symbolic meaning—they depreciate the importance of those tasks the teacher considers central. The principal who interrupts the class with an announcement about a football rally can be thought to feel that teaching is less important than boosting athletic contests. Accounts must balance, but when administrators stress receipts for milk sales, they are not signaling grave concern for instruction. There is an undercurrent in these responses, then, of more than annoyance at work disrupted and time lost. Those who intrude on the teacher's scarce time are doing more than inhibiting work processes; they are manifesting a lack of respect for what teachers consider their core functions. The frustration of the teacher is doubled. Potentially productive time, already limited, is reduced, and the teacher's craft is depreciated. Such lack of "support" is the opposite of the reassurance teachers apparently need to offset the uncertainties of their work.

The second major set of grounds for complaint about other persons centered on issues of status—on instances where others offended the teacher's dignity. (It is obvious that the distinction between the two sets of grounds is subtle; perhaps we cannot get an accurate count where meanings become entwined as they do in this instance.) The following quotations illustrate such instances (27) and the third, smaller category (9) illustrates cases where colleagues irritated respondents by failing to do their share of the dirty work:

I don't like the caste system in school today. It seems, you know the old joke, the teacher's afraid of the supervisor; the supervisor's afraid of the principal, and the principal's afraid of the superintendent, the superintendent's afraid of the school committee, the school committee's afraid of the parents, the parents are afraid of the kids, and the kids aren't afraid of anything. The teachers are at the bottom of the ladder. Everybody counts but the teacher.

The hiring of so-called specialists who don't work directly with the teacher, that rather talk with the principal who knows little or nothing about work problems and then once the decision has been made, the teacher is the last to be consulted.

I think the thing that aggravates them most is that no one else takes their job, considers their job as seriously as do teachers. I think teachers consider their job most seriously and expend themselves no end in it and I think it bothers them because people are not aware how they feel, how important this particular job is and I think it annoys them no end.

The trend in recent years has been to pacify the parent and do what the parents want. In any situation involved with disputes with parents, in my opinion, all too often the supervisory people back down and give in. My own instance several years ago I was keeping a boy back and my own principal had gone over the records and decided it was the best thing for him. The parents complained and the principal just automatically let him go. Things along that nature.

Well, there's no question that it's having another teacher question your authority. That is—in my way of thinking, that's the worst of all, you know, for example, say a kiddo is late leaving the gymnasium and you write him a note and send him to another class and the teacher won't accept the note. Well, that really burns you.

I probably do more corridor duty than the average teacher but I am quite conscious of the need of it. I think that I don't overlook the discipline in the corridors and I know it, it annoys me when other people don't do their work. I think that is one thing that does bother me, the fact that other teachers aren't cooperating and doing their job.

Waller discussed the special sensitivity of teachers to issues of prestige and dignity; my data suggest that his observations are not outdated (1961, p. 388). But the reasons which underlie that sensitivity may rest in the imperatives of teaching and their misalignment with teacher status. It is one thing for teachers to prefer boundedness, to want autonomy and more potentially productive time; it is another thing to get them. Teachers cannot take such matters for granted—their complaints reveal that others complicate their work by witholding the support they consider their due. Thus teachers cannot act as if they were fully independent workers. Since they cannot "command" the assistance of others, they must hope that these will be voluntarily forthcoming. They are thus *dependent* on the readiness of administrators, fellow teachers, and parents to grant them the work conditions they desire.

There is a dilemma built into the situation of the classroom teacher—a tension between his sentiments and his status realities. He cannot prevent others from eroding his potentially productive time, and so he has limited control over the flow of psychic rewards. (This is in addition to the inherent uncertainties he faces.) Were his position more powerful, he might move away from other people, counting primarily on his personal capacities in teaching students. But his status proscribes this withdrawal, at least as the sole strategy; he must temper his self-isolation by seeking the support of others whom he needs in order, ironically, to make autonomy work. A kind of ambivalence is inherent in his role; we shall have occasion later to note the significance of this ambivalence for his interpersonal relationships with adults.

The Changes Teachers Want

Information on what changes teachers would like to see in their work arrangements can test the arguments I have advanced. If the orientations described previously are significant, teachers should reveal them in their proposals for change—their suggestions should be conservative rather than radical, individualistic rather than collectivist, and present- rather than future-oriented. They should be closer to tinkering than revolution, in short, and consist of minor adjustments rather than demanding reforms. If they reflect the sentiments I have described in this chapter and immediately preceding chapters, suggested changes should reflect tensions between task imperatives (as seen by teachers) and status constraints.

My data on changes desired by teachers are taken from the Five Towns interviews and consist of responses to two questions. The first asked respondents what changes would help them to be more effective in meeting their teaching goals; the second asked what changes would augment their satisfaction with teaching. It will surprise no one by now that the responses were largely similar; the fusion of work achievement and satisfaction was again manifest. The responses to both questions are displayed in Table 8.2.

More than half the proposals which respondents linked with work effectiveness dealt with time use. Most have already been discussed in the preceding section. The novel ones are "fewer

Table 8.2 Proposals for Change: Five Towns Teachers (Number of Times Mentioned)

Area	Effectiveness (Question 35)	Satisfaction (Question 45)
Time Use		
Smaller classes	18	15
Less clerical, extra duty	17	18
Fewer interruptions	13	–
More time for basic subjects	9	8
Fewer sections	8	4
Longer school schedules	7	–
Miscellaneous time factors	8	5
Subtotal	80	50
Better Facilities	25	10
Curricular Improvements	14	4
Better Students	11	5
Improved Administration	7	6
Better Parents	7	6
More Money, Promotion	–	21
Better Profession	–	7
More Autonomy	3	4
Changes in Self	7	3
All Other	4	4
Subtotal	74	70
Total	154	120

sections" and "longer school schedules"; in the first instance, some junior high school teachers wanted to have more time with fewer students by rearranging the schedule. Those advocating longer school schedules did so with comments about "not telling my colleagues," joking that they feared retribution if their views were known. It is a point worth making here that the concern respondents showed about potentially productive time took place *within* their allocations of life space discussed in chapter 4. Few were ready to advocate longer school days or years; the vast majority wanted to reapportion inert and potentially productive time within their existing commitments. But again we witness the overriding preoccupation with time and the preference for teaching versus other tasks.

Comments about facilities centered primarily on books (respondents wanted more, better, and more up-to-date books), more audiovisual equipment, and, in some instances, more or better-designed space. (Physical facilities seem to matter more to teachers in physical education, science, and home economics, where equipment plays a major part in instruction.) Teachers criticize complicated curricula, preferring those which increase student options, include recent developments, and feature good articulation. Wistful comments were made about students; some teachers wished aloud for ways of ridding themselves of those who are troublesome, and other teachers, particularly in the high schools, wished they would be assigned brighter students. Improved administration referred primarily to remarks about "better-educated" administrators and superordinates who would lay less emphasis on organizational rules. Parents would be "better" if they interfered less and helped more—at home. A very small number called for greater autonomy for teachers. A handful responded by referring to self-improvement; these were elementary teachers who lamented their teachers college training or yearned for opportunities to observe colleagues at work, saying they thought such observation would help them improve their own performance. It is clear, however, that the vast majority, when asked what changes would improve their performance, thought in terms of structural change or change in the behavior of others.

Responses to the question on increasing satisfaction were similar (Table 8.2). There are suggestive differences, however. Respondents linked money and promotion to satisfaction, but not to effectiveness; that distinction raises a question about the allegations of union and teacher association leaders that more monetary rewards will yield greater productivity. These teachers, at least, do not link them. A few respondents said their satisfaction would increase if colleagues were better ("better profession") but did not link this preference to effectiveness. Perhaps they see the occupation's reputation in terms of reward rather than performance; such respondents, who complained about other teachers, possibly find inadequate colleagues frustrating but do not consider them serious obstacles to their personal work goals.

How do these responses fit with the orientations we mentioned above and with previous observations on teacher sentiments? They appear consistent with conservatism, individualism, and presentism in several respects. The structural proposals, for example, are hardly radical; they are familiar themes heard for many years and do not question the basic assumptions of the schooling system. They call for modifications in practice which are consistent with established ways of acting and thinking; they are "a little more" or "a little less" kinds of suggestions. The hopes that others will behave differently may be somewhat Utopian, but they cannot be called radical; the norms they apply to others (e.g., better behavior by students, more democratic administration, helpful parents) are consistent with accepted social definitions. Nor do we find departure from individualistic or presentist orientations. There is no call for notable changes in collegial relationships or protracted programs of action directed toward a different tomorrow.

Some information is added, however, to our understanding of teacher sentiments; the proposals for change emphasize the importance teachers attribute to more and better resources besides time. Greater concentration of time on potentially productive activities is of course reiterated, but we also see that teachers desire better facilities and more flexible, workable curricula. They also express views on students, but they seem unsure about how such preferences might be fulfilled. There is an underlying possibility which is rarely permitted to surface in the talk of these teachers; perhaps they want greater personal control over resources as well as more ample supplies. Such a wish, of course, edges toward open conflict wich the school hierarchy; it raises the issue of managerial discretion. In Five Towns few apparently wanted to make that issue explicit; they did not seem to propose striking new departures in the allocative mechanisms of school systems.

Teachers have been criticized for advocating programs which are "more of the same"; those who think present educational circumstances are critical view such proposals as seriously inadequate (Fantini 1972). One can argue whether the criticism is justified or moot; one can understand how teachers might feel they have not been given the chance to show what they can do. But the "more of the same" description seems largely accurate; the foregoing proposals, for example, do not represent a major shift from the pedagogical strategies of the past. The beliefs and preferences expressed suggest individualistic teachers who wane more elbow room to practice their craft. But the state of the craft does not come under review. Respondents voiced little concern about teachers' limitations in ensuring predictable results; doubts expressed in other parts of the interview did not come into play here. The underlying critique is directed toward the organization of teacher effort and the behavior of adult coparticipants. There is no discernible preoccupation with deficiencies in the technical culture of the teaching occupation.

Summary: The Roots of Ambivalence

The sentiments of teachers mirror their daily tasks and the realities of classroom life. The world of those teachers who have shared their feelings with us is more complex than it looks at first glance. The key rewards are hard to come by, and the daily demands are not easily met. The complexities draw teachers more deeply into their involvement with classroom events; they foster preoccupation with influencing students and with conditions which seem to increase that influence. Our informants seem harassed by a lack of time; protracted institutional contact with students seems scarce. Nor do they feel sufficiently well-supplied with physical materials. They worry about how others treat them. Others intrude and disrupt their teaching rather than help them reach the students. They wonder if their central purposes are understood and appreciated.

Teachers in Five Towns see boundaries around the classroom as useful; principally, they ward off the constant threat to task completion and the ever-present sense of time eroded. They believe that the teacher is the essential catalyst of student effort and learning and fret when their energies are used up in tasks they consider trivial. Yet they do not seem certain that a bounded classroom is quite enough to ensure high results; some believe that high points require a lucky conjunction of moods. When our teachers think about improving things, their thoughts turn to concentrating time and effort to more teaching. If only others would let them, they seem to say, they could do much more. They picture themselves as constrained, undersupplied, and underappreciated; their aims and their context do not jibe.

What teachers want seems to revolve around their preoccupations and their beliefs. The teachers we interviewed want to pinpoint their effort; the time and energies they have for teaching ought not, they feel, be splayed over a range of organizational tasks. They want to focus on instruction; they wish others would understand that and respect their wish by helping them fulfill it. They clearly feel that obstacles are placed in their way—and they cannot order them removed. Some reveal a certain prickliness, a sense of dignity offended: instead of reassurance and support, they sense denigration. They want to do their jobs as they see them and get the rewards that (sometimes) result.

These feelings are easier to understand, I think, if we recall the imperatives we linked to getting and sustaining attention, managing work groups, and coping with subtle individual differences. Teachers seem to want conditions which favor more control over student involvement, more discretion to make decisions, and greater trust from principals and parents. Yet one senses a reluctance to press the case to its logical extreme; it is as if these teachers half accept and half reject the limitations imposed by their status. Their status clearly does not grant them control over the conditions they believe are important and necessary; they are not permitted to arrange instruction in a driving, aggressive way. They would like abler or more compliant students, but have no concrete suggestions on how to get them. They cannot order superordinates, parents, and peers to support their efforts. Yet they hold back from asking for full autonomy and official independence. There are, of course, informal norms which permit some degree of teacher autonomy in the classroom, but such norms remain informal, fragile (particularly when trouble arises), and limited. These respondents do not suggest that teacher independence be formalized or that they be granted official discretion and control over resources. They do not challenge the basic order. They accept the fact that students, space, supplies, and schedules are "owned and controlled" by others and do not assert that they should control the means of production. They want more favorable dispositions within the prevailing system; but they apparently accept the terms imposed by the organization. For at the base of teacher status is the indisputable constraint that without access to a position in the schools the teacher cannot practice his craft.

There is a certain ambivalence, then, in the teacher's sentiments. He yearns for more independence, greater resources, and, just possibly, more control over key resources. But he accepts the hegemony of the school system on which he is economically and functionally dependent. He cannot ensure that the imperatives of teaching, as he defines them, will be honored, but he chafes when they are not. He is poised between the impulse to control his work life and the necessity to accept its vagaries; perhaps he holds back partly because he is at heart uncertain that he can produce predictable results. In any event, the feelings I have discerned among Five Towns teachers are internally contradictory and reflect dilemmas in the role. In the pages which follow we will see how relationships with others represent attempts to balance the tensions between independence and dependence, autonomy and participation, control and subordination.

Notes

1. It is ironic that high school teachers would opt for more time counseling students—about 24 percent, compared with 15 percent for elementary teachers. Counseling is more institutionalized as a specialized role in high schools, and this points to conflict between teachers and counselors on these tasks.
2. Question 13 and 14, App. B-2, dealt with this issue, the responses presented here are to question 14.
3 Shirley Stokes found that elementary teachers in Ontario, Canada, placed loyalty to students and peers considerably ahead of loyalty to administrators.
4. In Five Towns, one teacher went on at great length about an incident where her recommendation on the promotion of a child was overruled by the principal. It was obviously a seriously disturbing event for her.
5. The coding here was done in a highly conservative fashion. Only those cases where definite cause and effect language was used were included.
6. I am well acquainted with one teacher who decided to leave teaching after a year in which one disturbed child constantly disrupted classroom work. The child was later placed under psychiatric care, but that one year alienated a teacher who had ranked first in her graduating class and had received high commendation for her earlier teaching.

References

Blumer, H. (1957). Collective behavior. pp. 167–222 in A.M. Lee (ed.) *Principles of sociology*. New York: Barnes and Noble.

Hughes, B.C. (1958). *Men and their work*. Glencoe, Ill.: Free Press.

Lindesmith, A.R. (1947). *Opiate addiction*. Bloomington, Ind.: Principia Press.

Stokes, S. (N.d.) The shortest shadow. Multilithed. Toronto: Federation of Women Teachers' Associations of Ontario.

Waller, W. (1961). *The sociology of teaching*. New York: Russell and Russell.

9

The Tracking Wars

Jeannie Oakes

Much has changed over the past twenty years, but much remains the same. Academic standards and test-based accountability, ideas only germinating in 1985, now dominate American schooling. Market mechanisms for improving schools—choice and competition, relief from regulations, a focus on bottom-line outcomes, and straightforward privatization—that were pretty marginal in 1985 now sit at the center of the school reform stage. Equity remains a prominent value, but its framing has shifted dramatically. Desegregation has been supplanted for the most part by a high-stakes, "no excuses" agenda composed of reforms that push all schools, however segregated by race or social class, to have all students moot challenging academic standards, with "no child left behind."

These new directions in American schooling seem profoundly incompatible with practices that sort students into classrooms where they experience strikingly different and unequal resources, opportunities and expectations. Nevertheless, tracking remains firmly entrenched in American schools. That tracking persists is not the result of inattention; neither is it for a lack of effective alternatives . . .

. . . Here, I describe the push by those seeking to end tracking and the push back by those determined to keep it. I also address, with research evidence, issues that have been debated on the overlapping battlegrounds of research, school practice, and reform. Although the detracking movement has not supplanted tracking as the norm, many schools did detrack, and many continue to do so. The experiences of these schools demonstrate the potential that detracking has to remove huge obstacles standing in the way of success for students (particularly students of color from low-income families) across the country. They also offer sobering lessons about Americans' profound ambivalence about what they want from their schools.

The Push to End Tracking

By the end of the 1980s, concerns about tracking had entered the popular discourse and influenced public policy goals. Harsh judgments about tracking's effects were reported in the popular media, including such articles as "Is Your Child Being Tracked for Failure?" *(Better*

Homes and Gardens), "The Label That Sticks" *(U.S. News and World Report)*, and "Tracked to Fail" *(Psychology Today)*.[1] Leading policy groups made recommendations for eliminating or at least curtailing tracking practices, and many school reformers took action.

The National Governors' Association, for example, proposed eliminating tracking as a strategy for meeting the ambitious national education goals they had set in 1989. The governors saw tracking as a major impediment to their goal of educating all students to demonstrate mastery of challenging subject matter, so that the United States would be first in the world in science and mathematics achievement on tests taken at the completion of grades four, eight, and twelve.[2] The NAACP Legal Defense Fund, the ACLU, and the Children's Defense Fund all raised tracking as a second-generation segregation issue. And the U.S. Department of Education's Civil Rights Division targeted tracking as critical in determining racially mixed schools' compliance with Title VI regulations. Educator groups also adopted antitracking policy positions . . . Some state education agencies, including those in California and Massachusetts, declared that tracking should be eliminated, at least prior to senior high school.[3] These policy proclamations reflected some actions already being undertaken around the country, and they triggered others. Many have been remarkably successful. In 1987, for example, the Southern Regional Education Board, led by Gene Bottoms, joined with a group of state partners to launch *High Schools That Work (HSTW)*. *HSTW* sought to diminish tracking by eliminating the general track and combining challenging academic courses and modern vocational studies . . . *HSTW* tried to improve the high school curriculum for everyone, including the highest achievers.

In 1990, the Carnegie Corporation, acting on the recommendations in the Council for Adolescent Development's widely distributed report, *Turning Points,* identified detracking as central to reforming middle grades education. Creating heterogeneous classrooms (read, detracking) was one of seven key recommendations meant to create school environments that are caring, healthy, and democratic as well as academic. Throughout the 1990s, Carnegie made major investments in states and schools as they restructured their junior high schools and middle schools, including moving away from tracking to small, heterogeneous teams as the schools' central organizing feature. *Turning Points* prompted hundreds of middle schools to change the way students were grouped for instruction, both between and within classrooms. Most created inclusive, mixed-ability teams of students who were taught by an interdisciplinary team of teachers.[4]

The Coalition of Essential Schools (CES), a major high school reform network, declared in 1992 that high schools must abandon tracking for both academic and social reasons. The *CES* director, Ted Sizer, argued, "If we want citizens who take an active and thoughtful part in our democracy, they must get trained for this in school—working together on equally challenging problems, and using every possible talent toward their solutions."[5] Detracking should proceed, *CES* argued, through structural changes, such as breaking large schools into smaller heterogeneous "houses" and teaming teachers; organizing curriculum around themes or projects; and practicing more personalized relationships between adults and children.

Even the College Board, long thought to be concerned only with the college preparation of high-track high school students, criticized tracking for posing barriers to minorities' access to college. In 1989 the College Board launched its *Equity 2000* project aimed at replacing lower-level math classes with college preparatory math in two hundred racially diverse high schools in partner districts. Teachers received assistance in working with mixed-ability classes, creating backup classes, and increasing parental support. Students were supported with Saturday and summer academies on college campuses for entire families.[6]

At the same time these policy initiatives were beginning, courts began to take a more intense look at tracking. In Rockford, Illinois; San Jose, California; New Castle County (Wilmington), Delaware; Woodland Hills, Pennsylvania; and Augusta, Arkansas, plaintiffs in school desegregation cases charged that the districts' tracking undermined desegregation because it resegregated minority and white students within schools. In 1994, the federal magistrate and judge in Rockford found, based in large part on analyses of its tracking practices, that the district engaged in racial discrimination. The same year, the federal judge in Arkansas ordered that the district cease its use of ability grouping by class.

In 1992, Woodland Hills schools, and in 1994, San Jose schools accepted consent decrees and the continued jurisdiction of their federal courts, partly because of evidence that the tracking system in each district was segregating students and restricting African American and Latino students' access to the schools' best educational opportunities. In contrast, the plaintiffs were unsuccessful in the Wilmington, Delaware desegregation case, where the judge virtually ignored the tracking evidence, and no detracking order was ever issued.[7] In 1995 the four Delaware county school systems involved were released from further court supervision with their tracking systems intact.

Other detracking efforts were very much homegrown. For example an innovative San Diego high school English teacher, Mary Catherine Swanson, noticed that when her mostly white school became more diverse owing to an attendance boundary change, the school's tracking system relegated most of the newcomers to low-track classes. Outraged, Swanson created AVID (Advancement via Individual Determination), a scheme that placed supposedly unqualified students into college-track classes and provided them with a support course in which they learned study skills and received academic tutoring. AVID has now expanded to schools across the nation . . .

. . . Responses to the new awareness of tracking were often deeply personal. In my own experience speaking about *Keeping Track* to researchers, educators, and policymakers, nearly everyone recognized him- or herself in the tracking scheme. Conversations often began with uncharacteristically personal reflections and revelations: "My daughter was in the honors class, but she moved to her new school and . . ."; "I never knew I wasn't taking college prep classes . . ."; "my child already knows how to read, but he's stuck in a class where kids don't know the alphabet . . ."; "I was the only Latina taking calculus"; and so on.

Often, discussions of tracking also produced instant tension. After all, the data were saying some very unappealing things about American schools and the willingness of Americans to participate in the unequal treatment of children. These data could not be dismissed out of hand, since they were consistent with what most people could observe or experience in one form or another. To suddenly hold tracking as problematic in public discussions or in print could and did open a Pandora's box of challenges and controversies. On the one hand, many equity-minded reformers were quick to embrace the data, not only because tracking per se was an obstacle to equal treatment, but because it might bolster their broader, preexisting equity agenda. On the other hand, detractors were incensed that what they had long considered the best, perhaps only, way to ensure (and protect) pockets of academic excellence in otherwise less-than-excellent schools was now being cast in so glaring and negative a light. Educators were often frustrated as they recognized inequality but felt there was no reasonable alternative.

I was optimistic, or at least hopeful, that the data from the twenty-five schools discussed in *Keeping Track,* which showed more positive conditions in heterogeneous classes, could assuage fears and point everyone in a helpful direction, even though these data were not conclusive. After all, not one of the heterogeneous classes in the *Keeping Track* schools was formed because of a detracking policy. It was hard to know how they might differ from classes that reform-minded schools might create. However, the data made me comfortable about repeating to educators and parents what I'd recommended in the book: Schools should get out of the business of sorting and find alternatives that provide all students with challenging learning opportunities. I also shared with these groups what I knew from the research about the extraordinary promise of cooperative, small-group learning. It wasn't much, but many educators seemed encouraged to try.

The Push Back

Objections to detracking were immediate and loud, often undermining the potential for reasoned dialogue about legitimate concerns that detracking would compromise the education received by the most academically able students. Such concerns could not be addressed in environments in which detracking was instantly assumed to be an assault on opportunities for high achievers. It wasn't so much that anybody questioned the findings of inequality (at least at first); rather the implications of heterogeneity were so totally unacceptable that thoughtful discussion was often derailed with caricatures and scenarios of doom ... The loudest and most highly organized objections came from educators who specialized in "gifted and talented" education. Separate programs were the cornerstone of their practice and theory, and they feared, probably correctly, that calls for detracking placed those programs at risk. Supported by powerful parent advocacy groups, the gifted-education community soon came out swinging.

The arguments ran the gamut, asserting that gifted students were as far from the norm and as "needy" of separate learning environments as low-IQ students; ridiculing the idea of mixed-ability classrooms by comparing them to a varsity football team that accepts everyone who wants to play, regardless of skills; warning that detracking would place "our nation's most precious resource" (gifted students) at risk; and suggesting that average and below-average students feel better if they are not confronted each day by the intellectual superiority of their gifted peers. These arguments were bolstered by "research reviews" purporting to show that students, particularly gifted students, should be kept in separate, homogeneous classes.[8] Most shrewdly, opponents of detracking quickly defined tracking out of existence. As long as there was a theoretical possibility that a student's track might change, they contended, assignment to low or high classes was simply an educational determination more properly called ability grouping. Conceding that the narrower, rigid tracking may well be bad, they distanced those critiques from "ability-grouped classes." High-ability groups, they concluded, are not discriminatory, even though minority students may be underrepresented in them. "Flexible grouping," particularly as applied to elementary classrooms, became the key definitional defense.

Notably, these new arguments and research reviews were not, as a rule, published in mainstream research or peer-reviewed journals. Rather, they appeared in professional journals for teachers and administrators, such as *Education Leadership,* in specialized publications for professionals, advocates, and parents of gifted students, and in the popular media.[9] Although these reviews were mostly produced in the early 1990s, they continue circulating in the advocacy literature today.

Another set of objections emerged in the school desegregation cases. In most of these cases, the defending school districts' experts lauded the district's tracking practices. For example, Christine Rossell, a political scientist and defense expert in the San Jose, Rockford, New Castle County, and Woodland Hills cases, argued that racial bias played no role in tracking and that racially identifiable classes were a consequence of racially neutral meritocratic assignments based on students' achievement.

Most recently, resistance to detracking policy and court orders has come from some conservative education policy analysts and advocates who argue that detracking is part of a liberal school reform agenda seeking to impose governmental regulations on schools. Conflating rnajoritarian preferences and local control, they minimize policy and legal rationales for protecting some groups of students from the misapplication of those preferences. They argue that any necessary redress is available to all through the ballot box (electing a new school board, for example) or through the educational marketplace, where parents can choose their children's schools.[10] The central theme in this argument is that schools should be held accountable only for outcomes and that regulations—even those intended to ensure equity—are illegitimate impositions on community preferences. Such supposed regulation hamstrings local efforts to accomplish the real business of schools increasing student achievement. Prominent among this group is Tom Loveless, whose paper for the Fordham Foundation, "The Tracking and Ability Grouping Debate" (1998), and book *The Tracking Wars* (1999) argue that research fails to support the indictment of tracking, so local communities should be free to decide whether or not to detrack their schools.

Battlegrounds and Evidence

From my perspective, the tracking wars have taken place on three overlapping battlegrounds. The first is the battleground of research. Tracking's defenders charge repeatedly that the research on tracking is inconclusive and that detracking advocates either misread or, worse, deliberately distort the evidence. Their claim is that we don't really have solid evidence that tracking creates unequal opportunity, or that it discriminates against low-income students or students of color, or that it affects students' outcomes negatively. The second is the battleground of school practice. Here, tracking's defenders assert that tracking has changed so fundamentally in the past twenty years that whatever problems might have characterized it previously are no longer present. (A related argument is that, given these changes, findings from earlier research on tracking are no longer relevant.) A third battleground is that of the direction of reform. Here, tracking advocates have adopted a "mend it but don't end it" stance, asserting that, because detracking would bring more harm than good, whatever flaws actually remain can be fixed within the context of tracking. For example, if low-track classes are found lacking, they can be improved. If placement practices work against low-income and minority students, they can be made fairer. In fact, a very recent concession is that, ironically, the detracking movement itself has made tracking more equitable.

The Research Battleground: Scientific Uncertainty or Solid Evidence?

In sum, defenders of tracking dismiss the claim that solid evidence shows tracking's serious constraints on educational opportunities, its unfairness to any particular group of students, or its negative effects on students' schooling outcomes.

Some of the most visible tracking advocates have attacked reformers' motives as well as researchers' findings. The professor of gifted education John Feldhusen charged in 1991 that "some school reformers have arrogated unto themselves a political-social agenda" and that "research is cited and twisted." James Kulik, the author of a widely circulated and widely critiqued research review favoring ability grouping, wrote, "Our children will be the losers if reviewers continue to twist research findings to fit their personal and political philosophies." Other critics are less overtly combative and affect evenhandedness, preferring to charge opponents of tracking with obtuseness and poor scholarship rather than with purposefully endangering children and democracy. Loveless, for example, argues that the research is simply too inconclusive to warrant any recommendations for change. Asserting this point repeatedly in *The Tracking Wars,* he claims that "the best evidence and the most informed, fair-minded experts were so evenly divided when the move toward detracking began]" that the "empirical research has failed to resolve the most important questions about tracking." He continues, "Information is sparse on the curriculum and instruction employed by different tracks" and claims "the suspicion that schools unfairly assign poor or minority students to low-track classes has been refuted." He writes further that "few, if any of the questions about tracking's effects are settled, and research is ambiguous on the policy direction schools should pursue."[11]

I do not believe the research is ambiguous. Backers of tracking have produced no credible challenge either to the core findings of *Keeping Track* or to the increasing body of evidence from other research: tracking students is a common practice; tracking supports and creates systems of unequal education; tracking is not necessary (or even helpful) for achieving the nation's educational goals. Certainly, the research on tracking, like that in any area of social science investigation, has not been perfectly consistent in its findings.[12] Neither has the serious research community been unanimous in its agreement about what the findings mean or what they imply for practice. However, the weight of evidence makes clear that tracking has created unequal schooling, and that in turn has had a disproportionate limiting effect on the schooling of African Americans, Latinos, and low-income students. And virtually all researchers agree that practices that label some students "low achievers" and give them dumbed-down schooling—whether called ability grouping, tracking, or something else—do neither the students nor the nation any good. In the following section, I offer the conclusions I've reached on three important questions: Does tracking create unequal opportunity? Does tracking discriminate? Does tracking matter for students' outcomes?

Soon after the publication of *Keeping Track,* I began to examine whether the findings in the twenty-five schools would hold up across a broader range of schools and classrooms. Whether tracking creates unequal opportunity and whether those inequalities were most detrimental to low-income students and students of color lay at the heart of the analyses in *Keeping Track.* Those findings have been replicated over and over throughout the ensuing years. Extensive research has also added to our knowledge of the discriminatory effects of tracking and its detrimental effects on our system's most vulnerable groups of students.

In a nutshell, more recent research confirms the critique offered in *Keeping Track.* The central rationale for tracking is that differences in curriculum and teaching are essential to address the differences in students' abilities and that addressing these differences benefits both high- and low-tracked students. However, no serious reader of the tracking research disputes that tracking brings with it very different expectations for achievement, access to subject matter and critical learning opportunities, instructional strategies, and resources (including teachers). These disparate expectations, access, and resources have predictable effect on student learning: low-track students fall further behind. Similarly, there is broad agreement that the differences among various tracks are typically not reasonable accommodations to student differences.

This evidence of disparities in opportunity, on its own, should spark serious educational and policy concern. But the disparities per se are compounded. The advantages and disadvantages associated with tracking are not distributed fairly (if such fair allocation of opportunities were even possible), and they result in racial inequalities. African Americans and Latinos bear a disproportionate burden of disadvantage because of their overrepresentation in lower classes. Again, this compounded and unfair assignment of disparities should redouble concern to the level of outrage. But there's more.

In practice, placing students into tracks is accomplished by a variety of mechanisms that have enormous potential for discrimination. More recent research reveals that these mechanisms include subjective assessments of ability, parental influence, irrelevant or narrow evaluations, counseling and advice, and so forth. Further, even when Latino and African American students meet the school's or district's own stated criteria for admission into higher-level classes, it is no guarantee that they will be placed in those classes: yes, those students who overcome the disparate impact of unequal opportunities and evaluations are still, often, placed in lower-level classes. Finally, the following sections demonstrate that fixing the practices that tracking engenders or requires (improving testing and counseling; resisting parental pressure for favored positions, etc.) cannot make tracking an educative or equitable school practice.

Does Tracking Create Unequal Opportunity? Working with a team of research colleagues at RAND and with the support of the National Science Foundation, I examined the relationship of race, social class, and tracking to students' opportunities to learn science and mathematics in a national sample of six thousand classrooms in twelve hundred schools. Survey data from school principals and from mathematics and science teachers allowed us to examine differences between schools and within schools.[13] The results, which we ended up calling *Multiplying Inequalities,* were striking. Differences in opportunities to learn science and mathematics resulted from the combined effects of disparities between tracks within schools and differences among schools' tracking practices. Consistent with the data reported in *Keeping Track,* high-track classes consistently offered richer learning opportunities and more resources, including more highly qualified teachers, than low-track classes.

At the grossest level, we found that senior high school tracking shapes the number and type of academic courses students take. Low-track students are seldom required to take as many math and science classes; as high-track students, and they rarely do. Additionally, those not preparing for college take advanced classes only rarely. In every aspect of what makes for a quality education, kids in lower-track classes typically get less than those in higher tracks and gifted programs.

At all levels of schooling, low-track math and science courses offered less demanding topics and skills, while high-track classes typically included more complex material and more thinking and problem-solving tasks. Teachers of low-ability classes also placed considerably less emphasis than teachers of high-track classes on more general learning goals, such as having students become interested in science and mathematics, acquire basic concepts and principles, and develop an inquiry approach to science and a problem-solving orientation to mathematics. The ability to meet such goals does not depend on students' prior achievement or skill levels. Researchers and educators increasingly see reaching these goals as possible for all but seriously impaired students, and policymakers increasingly describe them as essential for all students. Nevertheless, those teaching low-tracked classes typically reported these goals as less important for their students. Additional research is consistent with these findings of clear track-related differences in students' access to knowledge.[14]

Multiplying Inequalities reaffirmed that low-track teachers of mathematics and science consistently spend more time on routines, seatwork, and worksheet activities. They introduce technology, such as computers, in conjunction with low-level tasks, such as computation . . .

. . . Teacher quality also differed among tracks. Although some schools rotate the teaching of low- and high-ability classes, one outcome of tracking is that classes at different track levels are not equally desirable to teachers. Teachers may jockey among themselves for high-track assignments, or principals may use assignments as rewards and sanctions . . .

. . . These troublesome assignments are most evident in schools with large minority and low-income populations because these schools have fewer well-qualified teachers to begin with. In such schools, low-track students are frequently taught math and science by teachers who are not certified to teach those subjects, if they are certified at all. Here, too, our findings are consistent with other national studies.[15]

Students of all abilities benefit from these sorts of high-group advantages. Further, there is not so much as a hint in the research literature that supports the construction of meritocratic school norms in which "high-ability" students are more deserving of these advantages than other students.

Does Tracking Create Racial Disparities in Educational Opportunity? What the above discussion confirms is that American schools do not serve high-track and low-track students equally. Likewise, no one disputes that low-income African American and Latino students are enrolled disproportionately in low-track classes. *Multiplying Inequalities* revealed that the racial disparities associated with tracking are national patterns that appear in three contexts. First, many schools that serve predominantly poor and minority populations offer a lower percentage of high-track classes when compared to affluent schools serving white and Asian students. Second, in racially mixed schools minorities are typically underrepresented in high-ability classes. In senior highs, low-income, African American, and Latino students are underrepresented in college preparatory programs, and they are more frequently enrolled in those vocational programs that train for the lowest-level occupations. A third context of racial disparity related to tracking is in classes that are purportedly at the same track level but turn out to be quite different in the quality of their resources and opportunities at schools serving more- and less-advantaged students. For example, a class called Algebra 2 at a school serving poor students is likely to be less rigorous and be taught by a less-qualified teacher than a class with the same title at a school serving advantaged students. These racial patterns have been documented repeatedly by researchers over the past two decades.[16]

Is Tracking Discriminatory? Are the racial patterns fair? We certainly can argue that they are not fair, given that the differences in the quality of what students experience constrain rather than expand the opportunities of students in low-track classes and that African Americans and Latinos suffer these constraints more often than other students. But many critics argue that disproportionate placements are based on race-neutral data and informed judgments that tailor course offerings and course placements to students' achievement levels. Further, what if it is the students themselves who choose their own classes?

Christine Rossell, who has not studied tracking in research outside of her role as an expert witness, has defended the racially skewed track placements in San Jose, Rockford, Wilmington, and Woodland Hills. Her testimony represented the school districts' view that the racially identifiable classes created by tracking followed the meritocratic assignment of students based on students' achievement levels. In fact, she argued that more racial minorities were placed in high-track classes than actually merited such placement.[17] The segregation within schools that comes with tracking, she argued, is a legitimate consequence of the lower achievement of African American and Latino students, as compared to whites and Asians.

Throughout the 1990s, my colleagues and I examined whether Rossell and other tracking defenders are correct in denying racial bias in track placements. Researchers tend to agree that students' socio-economic status is associated with track placements, with more advantaged students more likely to be placed in higher tracks than less advantaged students,[18] but the question of racial bias has been much more contentious.

My conclusion is that race in itself does indeed influence track placements, Latinos and African Americans being more likely than whites and Asian students to be placed in low-track classes. Although the lower average of achievement of Latinos and African Americans certainly "explains" (in a statistical sense) much of the disproportionate assignment of these students to lower-track classes, we also find significant and disturbing evidence of racial bias.

I found evidence of how race affects track placements in a second RAND study of tracking—*Educational Matchmaking*.[19] My colleagues and I looked closely at the placement practices in three high schools located in neighboring communities. The schools were preparing students for the same or similar postsecondary opportunities and local labor market; they had similar state resources and were bound by the same state policies. Coolidge High had a very diverse student body, since it was the only high school in its diverse community. Washington High's affluent community location made its student body almost entirely middle- and upper-middle class, white, and Asian. McKinley High's student body mirrored its low-income, African American, and Latino community.

We spent lots of time observing, studying school documents, talking with educators and students, and analyzing students' transcripts and test scores. What we found shed new light on the dynamics of tracking and racial stratification. All three schools offered a wide array of academic courses, from remedial to Advanced Placement. Each school also offered a range of vocational courses; some gave credit for work experience or school service programs, and others offered highly technical and occupationally specific training. Notably, following national patterns, the predominantly white and wealthy school had far more high-track courses, and the high-track classes at this school were far richer in curriculum and instructional resources than the high-track classes at the other two schools.

Each school sought to be fair and accurate as it matched students with courses. They took into account achievement test scores, course-taking histories, grades, teachers' recommendations, and students' aspirations. Nevertheless, our transcript analyses revealed familiar patterns of racial differences. Although most students took *some* vocational education, low-income African American and Latino students took more if than others—particularly more occupationally oriented vocational courses. African American and Latino students also took low-track academic courses more often than white and Asian students. At Coolidge and Washington, for example, nearly 75 percent of the Asian students took college-track math, compared with about 33 percent of the whites, only 25 percent of the African Americans, and fewer than 10 percent of the Latinos. Differences in English were not as dramatic, but, at Coolidge, both Asians and whites participated at much higher rates than African Americans and Latinos. At McKinley, African Americans and Latinos took college-track math at about the same rates, but the African Americans were about 15 percent more likely to be in college-track English.

Certainly, these patterns reflected very real differences in minority and white students' previous learning opportunities and their effects on academic preparation. Yet these associations with students' prior achievement do not demonstrate that the schools in our study made fair and racially neutral assignments. In fact, students' race or ethnicity was often important in *determining* the probability of participating in college preparatory math and English, over and above their measured achievement. For example, at diverse Coolidge High Asian students scoring at the 80th percentile nationally in math were more than twice as likely to be in college preparatory math as were Latinos at the 80th percentile. Asian students scoring at the 50th percentile were ten times more likely to be enrolled in college preparatory math *than comparably scoring* Latinos, and four times more likely than African Americans *with the same scores.* At affluent Washington, Asians scoring at the 80th percentile were enrolled in college preparatory at more than twice the rate of Latinos. Whites, too, were advantaged in college preparatory placement over their comparably achieving Latino peers. In the only departure from the pattern of white and Asian advantage, high-scoring African Americans at Coolidge took college preparatory math at slightly higher rates than white students.

Further, because the competition for slots in high-track classes was greater at schools with affluent and white students, minority students had a much better chance of being in the college track if they attended all-minority McKinley. Some students with achievement scores that qualified them for the high track at McKinley would not have qualified at more diverse Coolidge.[20] Latino students with math achievement in the 80th percentile nationally had an 84 percent probability of participating in college preparatory math at McKinley, but less than a 40 percent probability of being in college track at Coolidge. Thus, minority and low-income student found themselves *either* in schools with fewer and less challenging high-level classes or in schools where their own competitive position might not gain them access to resource- and opportunity-rich high-track classes.

In the 1990s, my UCLA research group began a series of studies that, for more than a decade, examined tracking and detracking in four medium-sized, diverse cities where tracking had become part of their desegregation lawsuits: San Jose, Rockford, Wilmington, and Woodland Hills. Notably, each of the cities had maintained majority white populations, even as their federal school desegregation cases proceeded. In San Jose, Rockford, and Wilmington, the plaintiffs' litigation teams had asked me to examine district, school, teacher and student records and report to the court about whether tracking segregated students by race, whether the schools' tracking practices were discriminatory, and whether tracking deprived students of color of equal educational opportunities. In Woodland Hills, I was asked by the judge—with the superintendent's agreement—to study the impact of the district's desegregation effort.

In San Jose, Rockford, and Wilmington, we conducted qualitative analyses of documents such as curriculum guides, course catalogs, course descriptions, district compliance reports, school plans, assessments by court-appointed monitors, and depositions taken of school district employees in the course of the litigation discovery process. We also did extensive statistical analyses of several years of computerized student enrollment and achievement data. These analyses allowed us to answer a comprehensive set of questions: What were the tracking systems like in these districts? Was tracking an integral structure with other practices (testing, counseling, etc.) that combined to create racially imbalanced classrooms? Could any racial pattern be explained or justified by reasonable educational considerations? What were the consequences for students' educational opportunities? What were the effects on students' achievement and other schooling outcomes? Would it be feasible to dismantle tracking in these districts? Did the districts have the support and capacity necessary to create high-quality, heterogeneously grouped classrooms?

As in my earlier studies, patterns of unequal opportunity and racial stratification were clear. Lower-track classes in all three systems provided far fewer learning opportunities than high-track classes. Teachers expected less of these students and gave them less exposure to curriculum and instruction in essential knowledge and skills. Patterns of racial stratification were also clear. This meant that tracked systems provided African American and Latino students with disproportionately less access to a whole range of resources and opportunities, including highly qualified teachers, classroom environments conducive to learning, opportunities to earn extra "grade points" that would bolster their grade point averages, and courses that would qualify them for college entrance and, in turn, to high-status adult careers.

Moreover, the statistical analyses of students' transcripts and test scores yielded disturbing findings about the accuracy and fairness of track placements. Classes designated for students at a particular level actually enrolled students who spanned a broad range of measured achievement. In other words, the tracked classes produced considerable *racial* homogeneity, but little "ability" homogeneity as determined by the districts' stated criteria.

In all three school systems, African American and Latino students were more likely than their white and Asian peers *with the same test scores* to be placed in low-track classes. For example, in San Jose, white and Asian students with average scores on standardized tests were more than twice as likely to be in "accelerated" classes as Latinos with the same scores. Further, while only 56 percent of very high-scoring Latinos were in accelerated classes, 93 percent of whites and 97 percent of Asians *with comparable test scores* were enrolled in these classes. The table below shows the patterns in Rockford, Illinois. Here, we find discrimination *at both high and low levels of achievement.* Even very high scoring minority students were less likely than their majority peers to be in high-track classes.[21]

Consider the results in Decile 10 in Table 9.1—the very highest-scoring students. Only 63 percent of the 92 minority students in this top decile were in advanced classes, compared to 85 percent of the 1,853 majority students. In Decile 6, a majority student had roughly a 33 percent greater likelihood of being in an advanced class than a comparably scoring minority student. And so on, up and down the range of achievement. It was not surprising, given these findings, that both San Jose and Rockford undertook detracking as part of their desegregation remedies. As noted above, however, similar findings in Wilmington, Delaware were insufficient to prompt court intervention.

Why, given these findings, is there contentiousness over whether or not tracking includes racial bias? In part, the debate continues because the impact of discriminatory placements is often masked when researchers analyze large-scale survey data that aggregate data across

Table 9.1 Placement of Majority and Minority High School Students with Comparable Achievement in Regular and Advanced Classes—1998–99, Rockford, Illinois

Math/Reading Achievement— (NCEs)*	Majority Students	Minority Students
Decile 1	775	962
	Percent Advanced: 3%	Percent Advanced: 2%
Decile 2	973	1,056
	Percent Advanced: 6%	Percent Advanced: 4%,
Decile 3	1,199	959
	Percent Advanced: 10%	Percent Advanced: 6%
Decile 4	1,371	895
	Percent Advanced: 16%	Percent Advanced: 13%
Decile 5	1,482	689
	Percent Advanced: 21%	Percent Advanced: 19%
Decile 6	1,787	583
	Percent Advanced: 34%	Percent Advanced: 23 %
Decile 7	1,810	444
	Percent Advanced: 46%	Percent Advanced: 43%
Decde 8	1,925	305
	Percent Advanced: 58%	PercentAdvanced: 45%
Decile 9	2,350	207
	Percent Advanced: 72%	Percent Advanced: 59%
Decile 10	1,853	92
	Percent Advanced: 85%	Percent Advanced: 63%

*NCE: Normal Curve Equivalent

school systems. Such analyses obscure differences in track assignments resulting from the student composition of schools as well as the nature of their tracking systems. Moreover, the measures in these surveys are usually too gross to detect differential placement practices within schools. In other words, students are tracked in particular schools with unique student body compositions, and that is where they experience disadvantage and unequal access. This is plain enough to see when one looks at a school or school district. However, when aggregating across school systems, distinct contextual differences are blurred, making racial bias in placements.

Virtually all senior high schools—low-income, high minority, and white and wealthy suburban—are going to have high-track classes. Because tracking tends to be highly normative, relatively high-scoring students, not necessarily students with high scores, will be in the top track. Aggregate across districts, states, or the nation, then average the scores and you might find (as is the case) that some students of color with poorer scores than whites and Asians are admitted to high tracks. Consequently, when data about two such communities are aggregated, we may find a pattern of track placement that appears to give a slight advantage to black students (after controlling for ability) of being assigned to academic tracks. This aggregation can hide considerable discrimination and underrepresentation of minority students in wealthier, racially diverse communities.[22]

Analyses of the relationship among race, ability, and placements within particular schools and school systems yield a very different understanding. As illustrated in the *Matchmaking* study and the studies of the three desegregating school systems and in similar studies by other researchers, differences in average levels of achievement mask clear evidence of discriminatory placements, with whites and Asians being considerably (and statistically significantly) more likely to be placed in academic classes than comparably achieving African American and Latino students. Substantial discrimination against even high-scoring minorities skewed the racial composition of classes beyond what would have been the case had track placements been made by an unfailingly strict adherence to achievement as the criterion.[23] Notably, researchers who have reconsidered the relationship between race and track placement in large databases, using multilevel methods that control for these between school differences, have sometimes been able to untangle these school and track placement effects. They, too, find that the supposed "black advantage" found in high-track placement nationally does not exist once the model accounts for the racial composition of the school that a student attends.[24]

Does Tracking Affect Students' Schooling Outcomes? The best new evidence from the past twenty years adds to *Keepings Track*'s claim that tracking fails to foster the outcomes schools value—academic excellence and educational equity. Tracking is particularly inconsistent with today's national goals of having all students meet high academic standards and leaving no child behind. There is little disagreement that grouping affects students' schooling outcomes with exactly the opposite effect. Nobody today makes evidence-based claims that students in low-track classes benefit from tracking.[25] Incontrovertibly, tracking widens the inequality among students in what they learn in school; students in high-track classes learn more than students in low-track classes. In today's rhetoric, tracking systematically leaves children not in the high track behind. The widening gap is associated with obvious and measurable advantages that allow high-track students to reach their "potential" and disadvantages that depress the achievement of low-track students.

However, the research on the relationship between tracking and students' schooling outcomes is complicated. Researchers' answer to the question of whether tracking affects outcomes depends on their definition of tracking, the outcomes they are interested in, the specific formulation of their research questions, and their research methods. Since achievement test scores are the most frequently studied outcome, let's begin there: the research on tracking and ability grouping consistently finds that the achievement gap between students in high- and low-classes groups grows over time.[26]

My colleagues and I found this differential effect of tracking on students' measured achievement in the *Matchmaking* studies of three comprehensive high schools as well as in our studies of tracking in San Jose, Rockford, Wilmington, and Woodland Hills. In all of these schools, high-track placement led to achievement gains, and low trade placement had negative effects. Students in lower-level courses consistently demonstrated lesser gains in achievement than their comparably scoring peers in high-level courses. These results were consistent across achievement levels: whether students began with relatively high or relatively low achievement, those placed in lower-level courses showed smaller gains (or greater losses) over time than similarly situated students placed in higher-level courses . . .

. . . We are not the only researchers to note that achievement benefits from high-track placement accrue to students at all levels of prior achievement.[27] These tracking effects appear to result, at least in part, from differences in learning opportunities, rather than homogeneity (which, after all, exists as much in the low- as in the high-track classes).[28] Even staunch advocates of ability grouping concede that research counters the claim that high-ability students benefit simply from separate classes.[29] Separate classes for high-achieving students benefit participants *only* when schools provide those students with an enriched curriculum that differs from that provided to lower-group students. What seems to make a difference for high achievers, then, is not the grouping itself, but the special resources, opportunities, and support that usually exist in high-level classes.[30] But the most significant finding is that track-level differences in teaching and learning cannot typically be defended as educationally appropriate adaptations to individual differences in learning aptitudes, or prior achievement. After all, in the four desegregating cities and in the *Matchmaking* study, the beneficial high-track classes were actually quite heterogeneous. And students at all achievement levels benefited academically from being in the high track.

The most significant "tailoring" of curriculum and instruction was to skew the distribution of high-quality opportunities and expectations toward the high track and away from the low-track classes. Considerable research demonstrates that ability-grouped classes negatively affect low-group students in comparison to their low-ability counterparts in nongrouped classes.[31] Some studies also show that high-ability students often learn less in these classes,[32] at the same time that others show that high-achieving students do equally well in both grouped and nongrouped schools, particularly when the curriculum and instruction are similar.[33]

In addition to tracking's effects on students' measured achievement, tracking influences students' school attainment and life chances. Track placements are quite stable, partly because early assignments shape students' later school experiences. By high school, track location has a far-reaching influence—with college track students(relative to their otherwise comparable non-college-track peers) enjoying better prospects for high school completion; college attendance, grades, and graduation; and, indirectly, high-status occupations.[34] Moreover, students in low-ability classes have far lower aspirations and take fewer (subsequent) college preparatory classes than do students in higher groups, even when the students are similar in their socioeconomic status, middle school grades, achievement test scores, and post-high school plans.[35] These results are explained, in part, by the fact that college preparatory students receive more information and assistance in developing four-year high school plans and long-term educational and career plans than general education students.[36] The cumulative effects on college matriculation of taking rigorous middle and high school math and science courses are particularly strong for low-income students. Low-income students who take algebra and geometry are almost three times as likely to attend college as those who do not.[37] . . .

The Reform Battleground: Mend It or End It?

A third battleground in the tracking wars, the terrain of reform, has been especially contentious and confusing. It hinges on whether the harms associated with tracking are inherent in the structure of tracking or whether they stem from an ill-advised implementation of an otherwise neutral schooling structure.[38] I subtitled *Keeping Track* with the words *How Schools Structure Inequality*. By emphasizing the structural nature of tracking, I hoped to make clear that tracking exists not because it is a commonsense way of organizing schooling, but because it is embedded in a society that expects schools to sort, stratify, and treat students unequally.

Tracking is the structural manifestation of a complex web of norms (beliefs and assumptions) and power (politics) that makes it anything but neutral.

Defenders of tracking claim that the rough edges of tracking *practices* have been or can be mended in spite of those obstacles. Loveless, for example, argues that research is so equivocal that local communities should decide whether to detrack or maintain tracked schools. He cautions against detracking, however, asserting that it risks both student achievement and community support. That said, he also advises schools to monitor their low-track classes to be sure that low-track students are being pushed to excel.

To say that tracking's structure systematically perpetuates inequality does not mean that tracked classes can't be improved. Some researchers who have documented and acknowledged tracking's many problems have suggested a menu of fixes to mitigate harms caused by tracking; for example, improve the quality of low-track classes, make the course placement processes fairer, and provide students with heterogeneous and equitable opportunities outside the classroom. These researchers may see eliminating tracking in U.S. schools as far too politically ambitious, or they may worry that implementing high-quality untracked classes is too difficult. However, the fact that equitable tracking has only rarely been documented is sobering evidence of just how politically and professionally challenging (or impossible) ending equality within the structure of tracking would be.

Can Tracking Be Fixed Within the Context of a Tracked System? The sociologist Maureen Hallinan acknowledges the evidence of tracking inequalities and notes that schools' responses to calls for detracking have been mixed. She cautions that many educators favor detracking, but detracking may not be feasible because so many parents, politicians, and other educators resist. She also suggests that teaching in a detracked school is far more difficult than in a tracked school, and that detracking requires reallocating teachers and administrators, modifying the curriculum, and providing professional training that may be prohibitive. Detracking, she asserts, is also problematic because parents of high-ability students tend to prefer rigorous, homogeneous classes, and parents of other students remain unconvinced about the benefits of heterogeneous classes. In the end, she concludes that schools should fix the problems in their tracking systems rather than dismantle tracking altogether.[39]

Hallinan has herself provided evidence of some problems resulting from tracking.[40] But her view is that the well-documented negative effects of tracking result from educators' failure to enact tracking theory faithfully (that is, in ways that benefit students in all tracks). Tracking's unintended consequences, she argues, are what impede its intended goal of enabling students at all levels to learn more than they would in mixed-ability classes. Some of these unintended consequences, she explains, are inherent to tracking, while others represent an implementation failure. For example, tracking's race and social class segregation may be inevitable, given the unfortunate coincidence of "low ability" with low-income and minority status, but the diminished outcomes are not, since they result from a flawed enactment of tracking's theory.

Hallinan advocates a tempered response that calls upon schools to improve their tracking practices and tracking's inherently negative features with more positive practices beyond the classroom, such as extracurricular activities in which diverse groups of students participate together. Further, she argues that educators could make tracks more homogeneous by basing students' placements on the most "objective" measures of ability and achievement and by frequently reassessing and reassigning students. The educational discrepancies among tracks could be remedied with a beefed-up low-track curriculum. In addition, the lamentable impact of students' social status, motivation, and effort could be circumvented if schools altered their reward structures; in ways that extend higher status to low-track students. Tracking's segregative effects could be counterbalanced by mixing students by race and social class in their untracked classes and by creating a non-racist school atmosphere.[41]

Similarly, the sociologist Adam Gamoran, whose work has illuminated how tracking widens achievement inequality between high- and low-track students, has sought ways to fix tracking so that the low-track disadvantage can be eliminated while the high-track advantages are preserved. He was prompted to pursue this goal when he found that some tracking systems are better than others. That is, schools with tracking systems that permit greater mobility among tracks and that allow more students to take high-track classes seem to produce higher overall achievement and create smaller achievement gaps among tracks. Gamoran recommends that schools reduce tracking and that they make the tracking they retain more effective. Like Hallinan, he advocates that tracked schools must improve instruction in low groups. He also recommends that schools regularly reassess students' capabilities and take new information into account when making assignment decisions, so that students are not locked into their track assignments. He argues that schools should offer tutorials during the school year or the summer so that students can make up curricular material they may have missed by being in a low-track class. That way, they can learn what they need and would not be prevented from moving up in the tracking system by lack of curriculum coverage.[42]

What's wrong with these suggestions for improving tracking? Frankly, nothing. If schools could actually do the things that Hallinan and Gamoran suggest, tracking wouldn't be the problem it has been and remains today. But it wouldn't be tracking either. Hallinan and Gamoran are, in fact, recommending a massive redistribution of resources; yet tracking is a structure designed not on educative principles but rather on the exact distributional principles that Hallinan and Gamoran disdain.

Nearly all educators are well aware that low-track students consistently have lower-quality opportunities to learn than their peers in higher tracks. They also acknowledge that persistent inequalities in access to knowledge, instructional resources, and well-qualified teachers combine to create a nearly insurmountable obstacle to sustained improvement of curriculum and instruction for low-track classes. Many educators have spent their careers trying to beef up the low-track curriculum, to adopt a more positive disposition toward the capacities of low-track students, and to alter the reward systems that work against these students. Gamoran himself acknowledges that high-quality low-track classes are rare and very difficult to create. In his study, he found only two low-track classes from among all classes in twenty-five middle and high schools in which low-track students made progress at rates similar to their higher-track counterparts, and both were at Catholic schools.[43]

Why is creating good tracking so difficult? The answer lies in the deep connections between schooling and the larger social structure. Tracking is certainly a schooling technology often implemented with good intentions, but it may entail messy human decision making and unintended negative consequences. My research over the past two decades has persuaded me that tracking also reflects deep cultural and political tensions in American society. It manifests a web of cultural, assumptions about what is true—what is "normal"—and cultural values about what constitutes appropriate action given particular "truths."[44] For example, tracking embodies the largely unquestioned assumption that students' individual needs and capacities differ enormously and in ways over which schools have little influence. It also reflects an extensive list of American biases around race, language, and poverty to cast doubt on the learning capacities of African Americans and of Latino immigrants. Tracking's opportunity inequalities both reflect and perpetuate these assumptions. Its "improvers" seldom acknowledge the deep, entrenched passions these cultural dimensions embody, hoping instead that incremental progress can lessen the salience of schooling inequalities around race, language, and poverty.

Tracking also reflects racial and social class stratification outside of school. Its inequalities perpetuate that stratification by facilitating (and helping to rationalize) the intergenerational transfer of social, economic, and political status and constraining social and economic mobility. The tracking debate is almost always argued in terms of its effectiveness as related to academic achievement. Certainly, this is a concern. Unspoken is tracking's clear connection to sorting, preparing, and certifying students for very different roles in society. Advantaged families are well aware of this function of tracking, so students' track placements become part and parcel of their quest for comparative advantage in the distribution of school resources, opportunities, and credentials that have exchange value in the larger society.

In sum, tracking is far more than a neutral curriculum structure that can be adjusted to eliminate the inequalities it creates. I am not suggesting that educators are engaged in a conscious conspiracy to make poor, minority students ignorant or to keep them at the bottom of the social and economic structure. However, I do remain persuaded that the results of tracked schooling—widening inequalities in achievement and aspirations—make for a compelling logic in a society marked by huge inequalities by race in economic and social power . . .

. . . The response of schools to calls for fair track placements—as a fix for unfair tracking—tends to be closely examined by parents. Not surprisingly, some of those parents (wealthier and in the main white and with more formal education) respond with speed and power. Savvy, high socioeconomic status (SES) parents use their political capital on behalf of their own children, and educators should be neither surprised nor disappointed by this. However, educators should be aware that lower-SES and minority students, whose ascribed characteristics already work against them in their initial track placements, tend to have families who are precluded from such political maneuvering by their timidity or unfamiliarity with how to manipulate the school's response to their own children. A placement system that facilitates greater inequities, grounded in the social and political capital of each student's parents, is inconsistent with broader American ideals of fairness and opportunity.[45]

By way of analogy, we might look to our national initiative to correct the ill effects of smoking cigarettes. We can demand warning labels, prohibit smoking in public places, mount media campaigns to educate, apply filter tips, bring litigation against those who make false claims, and so on. And indeed, these are all worthwhile steps in a comprehensive approach that will likely reduce overall smoking damage and affect the culture. Perhaps, after generations, many fewer people will smoke. Yet smoking today remains a widespread, damaging practice, and we recognize that mitigating some of the most egregious effects is still not adequate to protect the most impressionable and vulnerable among us: children. All states prohibit selling cigarettes to children because, in spite of various "improvements," there is no way to make smoking "safe enough."

Similarly, tracking can be improved, but it remains tracking. The harm to children is revisited each new school day and will continue as long as we wait for the practice to wither away. Suggestions to improve tracking simply beg the question. We are asked to believe that the inequities of tracking are somehow different from tracking itself. In fact, schools can no more remove those inequities from tracking than corporations can remove carcinogens from cigarettes.

Would Detracking Do More Harm Than Good? If improving tracking seems to be untenable, and detracking mobilizes powerful normative and political tensions and combativeness, what course might reformers, researchers, policymakers, educators, and communities take? In my view, this struggle must continue on many fronts, but an important place to start is to disarm the fears and misinformation held by powerful groups who see detracking as necessarily diminishing their children's advantages. Although tracking's most vociferous defenders warn of irremediable harms, there is no evidence to support claims that detracking puts students at risk—high achievers or low. On the contrary, over the past two decades, we've learned a great deal more about how to create high-quality, heterogeneous classrooms. We've also gained insights about the benefits that accrue from increasing students' access to the advantages of high-track classes.

Warnings about the likely harms of detracking emerged in the early 1990s, as advocates of separate programs for gifted students argued that heterogeneous grouping would be devastating for gifted students. They worried that students would be bored by the slow pace of instruction; that they would be exploited by teachers asking them, in the name of cooperative learning, to spend their time teaching lower achievers instead of challenging themselves; and that their achievement would fall dramatically. In the spring 1993 newsletter of the National Center for Gifted and Talented Education, for example, James Kulik warned,

> American education would be harmed by the wholesale elimination of programs that group learners for instruction by ability.... Bright, average, and slow students would suffer academically from elimination of such programs. The damage would be greatest, however, if schools, in the name of de-tracking, eliminated enriched and accelerated classes for their brightest learners. The achievement level of such students falls dramatically when they are required to do routine work at a routine pace. No one can be certain that there would be a way to repair the harm that would be done if schools eliminated all programs of enrichment and acceleration.

More recently, Loveless voiced concerns that detracking would both undermine achievement and drive advantaged parents away:

> Detracking is a gamble.... [T]he risks of the gamble are being assumed disproportionately by urban schools, low-socioeconomic-status schools and schools with low achievement. This should cause great concern. Some of society's most disadvantaged children are now part of an educational experiment with the outcome completely unknown.... High-achieving minority students in low- income urban schools are most at risk of suffering from the abolition of tracking.... Educators should also assess the political costs of detracking ... Researchers have described schools where parents threaten to transfer their children if tracking is abolished.

Cautioning that detracking should wait until studies have documented its likely impact, the researcher Laura Argys told an *Education Week* reporter, "Somebody's going to pay for the choice to go to de-tracking, and it's either the low-skilled or the high-skilled students. That's a decision society is going to have to make."[46]

What Is the Evidence for These Claims? Tracking advocates generally rely on analyses of large national databases that use self-reporting (by principals or teachers) to distinguish types of classrooms. Using such databases, a researcher may compare learning outcomes in classes described as composed of either (1) a wide range of student ability or (2) homogeneous groups at different ability levels. These analyses have typically found that low achievers do better in the mixed-ability classes than in the low track. But they have usually also found that high achievers do worse than in high-track classes. The researchers may therefore conclude that although detracking is likely to boost the test scores of students in the bottom tracks, it will hurt average and high-achieving students.[47] . . .

. . . Whatever the merits of these warnings about detracking, many well-meaning educators and parents have been cautious about detracking out of concern that there are no well-specified, proven alternatives to tracked schools. Some even doubt the *possibility* of curriculum and instruction in heterogeneous classes that won't leave slower students behind or force quicker ones to wait—a concern rooted in norms that essentialize the idea of faster and slower students who can be accommodated only by faster and slower versions of the curriculum.

It is true, as detracking critics charge, that there have been no experimental or statistically controlled studies comparing tracked and detracked schools. However, over the past two decades, the evidence has been accumulating about the efficacy of mixed-ability classes when educators use strategies that presume classroom heterogeneity and provide "multi-ability" instruction. This evidence should allay the fears of those who assume that detracking reform will necessarily harm high-achieving students, even as it benefits low achievers. I provide just a sampling of the evidence in what follows.

Some of the detracking policy initiatives described at the outset of this chapter have increased students' outcomes. For example, the *High Schools That Work* intervention has proven to be a promising approach to making the essential concepts from the college preparatory curriculum accessible to all students. Independent evaluations of the impact of the SREB reforms, using an exam developed by the Educational Testing Service to match the National Assessment of Educational Progress, compared the achievement of students at schools with "high implementation" of the reform to those where the levels of implementation were low. The schools that had implemented the reforms had significantly higher student achievement in reading, mathematics, and science as compared to students at low-implementation schools, and the gaps between African American and white students were smaller at high-implementation schools than at low-implementation schools.[48]

The College Board reports significant gains from its *Equity 2000* project. Their internal monitoring of the data about project students' course taking, grades, and other college preparation behaviors found that, by 1996, all six pilot sites dramatically increased student enrollment in Algebra I by the ninth grade; in three pilot districts all ninth graders took Algebra I. The percentage of students passing algebra did not decline significantly; and in some cases rose, as more students from the discontinued lower tracks enrolled in algebra classes. Moreover, participation in PSAT, SAT, ACT, and AP programs increased significantly; the percentage of students indicating that they plan to attend college after graduation from high school was substantially higher; and significantly greater numbers of students enrolled in higher mathematics such as second-year algebra, trigonometry, precalculus, and calculus than the national enrollments. These positive outcomes led the College Board to integrate the *Equity 2000* strategy into its core work with high schools across the nation, including working with schools to eliminate tracking and provide supplementary educational experiences for students beyond their regular academic courses.[49]

A longitudinal study of Mary Catherine Swanson's AVID program by the sociologist Hugh Mehan and his colleagues found that the four-year college attendance rates of AVID graduates outpaced both San Diego and national averages (50, 37, and 39 percent, respectively). Particularly impressive, AVID minority graduates' rates far exceed those of their African American and Hispanic peers (44 percent of the AVID Hispanic group, compared with 25 percent across San Diego, and 29 percent nationally; 50 percent of the AVID African American group, compared with 35 percent in San Diego, and 33 percent nationally). Mehan and his colleagues documented additional social benefits accruing to AVID participants. In particular, Hispanic and African American participants developed what Mehan terms a "reflective system of beliefs, a critical consciousness . . . about the limits and possibilities of the actions they take and the limitations and constraints they face in life." That is, AVID taught students they could achieve if they were motivated and studied hard. Even so, AVID students did not adopt a belief that their hard work would automatically bring success. Neither did they abandon their cultural identities. Rather, they maintained "dual identities" and adopted the view that, even though they would continue to face considerable discrimination and inequality, they could succeed if they developed "certain cultural practices, notably achieving academically, that are acceptable to the mainstream."[50]

Other new evidence comes from research studies showing the positive impact of mixed-ability classrooms. For example, the Stanford professor Jo Boaler studied British schools, examining the impact of traditional instruction (whole-class, textbook-based, with frequent tests) in a highly-tracked school and of multidimensional instruction (open-ended projects and a variety of teaching strategies) in an untracked school. Boaler followed three hundred students over three years, amassing a comprehensive database from observations, interviews, questionnaires, and assessments that show the ways students' beliefs and mathematical understandings were shaped by the various approaches to mathematics teaching. Three times as many students in the school with heterogeneous, multidimensional instruction as those in the tracked groups in the textbook school attained the highest possible grade. They also developed a different type of mathematical knowledge that allowed them to adapt what they had learned to fit new and demanding problems.[51]

In a follow-up study in three U.S. high schools, Boaler monitored approximately seven hundred students over four years. She reports the incredible success of one of the schools, Railside High. Classes at Rail-side were heterogeneous. Teachers worked collaboratively to design the curriculum, drawing from different "reform" curricula. Mathematics was organized into the traditional sequence of algebra, geometry, advanced algebra, and so on, but the students worked in groups on longer, nontraditional problems. At the end of four years, Railside's diverse population of lower socioeconomic status students achieved more, enjoyed mathematics more, and stayed with mathematics to higher levels than at the more traditional schools she studied. Moreover, the achievement differences that were in place between students of different ethnic groups at the beginning of high school were reduced in all cases and disappeared in some. Studies of other detracked schools have yielded equally encouraging findings.[52]

Similar results were obtained in a researcher-designed heterogeneous classroom intervention called QUASAR (Quantitative Understanding Amplifying Student Achievement and

Reasoning), which was designed to raise low levels of student participation and performance in mathematics. Based in urban middle schools, this demonstration project of the University of Pittsburgh's Learning Research and Development Center sought to help all students acquire a deeper, more meaningful understanding of math ideas and to demonstrate their proficiency in mathematical reasoning and complex problem solving. Schools in the project eliminated most forms of academic tracking and implemented programs to develop deeper student understanding and high-level thinking and reasoning skills. All project sites received extensive professional development and teacher support. Evaluation data show that students in the program performed as well as others on basic and traditional items from 1992 NAEP math assessment and outperformed others on less-traditional middle school math content.[53]

Also notable is the mounting evidence in the past twenty years of the positive effects of certain kinds of cooperative, small-group learning. Perhaps the most sophisticated and most rigorously studied form or cooperative learning is complex instruction, a strategy developed and rigorously tested by the sociologist Elizabeth Cohen. The theoretical and empirical knowledge base of complex instruction is the result of many years of programmatic research in heterogeneous classrooms at the elementary and middle school levels. In complex instruction, teachers use cooperative group work to teach at a high academic level in diverse classrooms. They also use multi-ability curriculum materials, assign open-ended, interdependent group tasks, and organize the classroom to maximize student interaction around major ideas and concepts. Explicit teacher interventions aim at reducing the status differences that exacerbate disparities in students' academic expectations for themselves and each other. In one careful study of the implementation of complex instruction, middle-grade teachers proved to be enormously skillful in adapting old curriculum materials to the new strategies. Moreover, students displayed sophisticated intellectual competencies in these classrooms.[54] Not one of these program evaluations and studies suggests that the highest-achieving students were harmed by these interventions.

Over time, some researchers specializing in the education of gifted students have endorsed strategies very similar to those employed in these detracking interventions. In doing so, they parted company with those warning of the damage that would be done to high-achieving students in mixed-ability classes.[55] In part, the discourse about gifted students requiring separate classes has softened with a growing consensus that mainstream classrooms with accommodations probably provide the best settings for most students with special needs. In part, as IQ has become discredited as a single criterion for identification of giftedness, and as a wider range of more relevant criteria are included, "gifted" students themselves are becoming a more heterogeneous group both racially and in the type and range of their skills. In part, however, the research and discussion on detracking have resonated with those researchers of gifted education who have looked carefully at the evidence about the harms of tracking and the potential benefits of mixed classrooms.

Joseph Renzulli, director of the National Center for Gifted and Talented Education, argues that gifted students can be served in regular classrooms containing students of varying ability so long as classroom teachers have special training in teaching gifted students or access to specialists who can come into the classroom to provide assistance. Under Renzulli's directorship, the center focuses its research on ways to provide "high-end learning" opportunities for all of America's students—opportunities that challenge the highest levels of learning and creativity. The center promotes high expectations, rigorous standards, and greater engagement with subject matter for all students, not simply those currently identified as gifted. Carol Tomlinson, a noted researcher of gifted education, has written a number of books and articles showing that the heterogeneous classroom can meet the needs of gifted learners, and she provides teachers with strategies for differentiating instruction within classrooms to challenge advanced learners.[56]

Finally, my most recent study of tracking and detracking has added evidence about the positive effects that are possible. My UCLA colleagues and I have worked over the past seven years with a group of thirty young people, who as ninth graders were not placed in the college preparatory track at their diverse comprehensive high school.[57] Although the school had a stellar record in preparing many white and Asian students for elite universities, it historically had sent very few students of color to four-year colleges. Partnering with the superintendent, the principal, and a handful of teachers, we designed and tested an intervention aimed at interrupting the schooling trajectories that were firmly in place for these thirty African American and Latino students. The students enrolled in courses that would prepare them for four-year colleges and universities, including some honors and advanced placement classes for some, and we provided them with a program that combined academic and social support (typical of college access programs like AVID) with opportunities for the students themselves to become researchers of the sociology of schooling. Our hypothesis was that this combination could help the students learn to navigate their high school successfully, develop a college-going identity, and move on to four-year colleges.

These high school students became research collaborators, rather than simply subjects, in our study. As members of a new sort of research community—high school students, teachers, and university researchers—they investigated schooling, social stratification, and educational equity. In their social studies class and in summer seminars at UCLA, these students (called the Futures students) produced original research examining such topics as tracking, schools' relationships with families, student resistance, and inequalities between schools in affluent and low-income communities. The classes, supports, and summer seminars were sustained from grades nine through twelve, during which time the students presented their research to a broad array of critical audiences: school and community groups, civil rights attorneys, graduate students and faculty at several universities, and directors of college access and university outreach programs. Initially, the Futures students associated their courses, their status at school, and their treatment by teachers with their track placements, and they had taken this status to be a natural and inevitable outcome of their social and personal worth. This changed as they studied these phenomena and drew connections between their personal experiences and the structures, practices, beliefs, and politics that sustain or disrupt patterns of inequality in the schools.

In spring 2000, all but one of the Futures students graduated from high school. Twenty-five had college acceptances in hand. In 2001, sixteen enrolled in four-year schools, and eight others went to two-year colleges. They far outpaced the high school graduation and four-year college-going rates of a matched comparison group of African American and Latino students who began ninth grade with the Futures students, but who did not participate in Futures. Although most students from both groups went on to college, the percentages attending selective four-year schools and less selective two-year schools differed significantly—53 percent and 26 percent, respectively, for the Futures, compared with 15 and 67 percent for the comparison group. Moreover, only 14 percent of the Futures students attend college part-time compared to 48 percent of their non-Futures peers. They all had a strong sense of themselves as young intellectuals who both belonged in college and hoped to return ready to contribute to their home communities.

As of this writing, the Futures participants are three years beyond high school graduation. Using their experience as members of a powerful research and action network in high school, many are now building similar networks in their colleges as they continue to draw upon their fellow Futures students for academic, political, and spiritual support. Their college persistence rate is laudable. As of spring 2004, 89 percent of those who started at any institution of higher education are still in school. Of the eight students who entered community college in fall 2001, three will transfer to four-year universities in fall 2004. These figures compare favorably to national averages showing that 59 percent of African Americans and 68 percent of Hispanics who enrolled in an institution of higher education (four-year, two-year, or a vocational education program) in 1995–96 either attained their degree goal or persisted three years beyond initial enrollment.[58] Like many students, however, few will earn a bachelor's degree within four years. Moreover, like other low-income, first-generation college students, they continue to struggle. Nevertheless, they have defied those who judged them as ninth graders to be unsuited for four-year college preparation.

What Happens When Schools *Begin* to Detrack?

The Futures project was not a naturally occurring school-based event, but what we termed a design experiment to generate ideas and test hypotheses. Although we gained important insights about tracking, it was not, principally, a detracking study. Over the past two decades, however, I have studied reforms expressly designed to detrack. I wanted to understand better why tracking persists in the face of the evidence against it. What happens when local policy-makers and educators seek to reduce or eliminate tracking in diverse schools? What lessons might we derive from their experiences? In brief, my research and that of others demonstrates that, although equity reforms are technically difficult, the most powerful forces maintaining the status quo of unequal schooling and most threatening equity reforms, are the deeply entrenched beliefs about low-income students and students of color and the competition among parents to make sure their children get the "best" education (and the life chances that follow).

Notes

1. "Is Your Child Being Tracked for Failure?" *Better Homes and Gardens,* October 1988, 34–36; J. Rachlin, "The Label That Sticks," *U.S. News and World Report,* July 3, 1989, 51–52; S. Tobias, "Tracked to Fail," *Psychology Today,* September 1989, 54–60.
2. National Governor's Association, *Ability Grouping and Tracking: Current Issues and Concerns* (Washington: author, 1993).
3. See, for example, "Ability Grouping in Social Studies," Prepared by the Ad Hoc Committee on Ability Grouping Approved by NCSS Board of Directors, 1992 (*http://www.socialstudies.org/position/ability,* last visited September 21, 2004); National Council of Teachers of English Position Statement on Tracking (Seattle: author, 1991) (*http://www.ncte.org/about/over/positions/category/profcon/107542.htm,* last visited October 23, 2004); National Council of Teachers of Mathematics, *Curriculum and Evaluation Standards for School Mathematics* (Reston, Vir.: author,

1989); California State Department of Education, *Caught in the Middle* (Sacramento: author, 1989); Massachusetts Department of Education, State Plan to Eliminate the General Track (Maiden, Mass.: author, 1996).

4. The Carnegie Council for Adolescent Development, *Turning Points: Preparing American Youth for the 21st Century* (New York: Carnegie Corporation of New York, 1989). See also A. Jackson and G. Davis, *Turning Points 2000: Educating Adolescents in the 21st Century* (New York: Teachers College Press, 2000); J. Oakes, K.H. Quartz, S. Ryan, and M. Lipton, *Becoming Good American Schools: The Struggle for Civic Virtue in Education Reform* (San Francisco: Jossey-Bass, 2000).

5. *Horace*, May 1992, 8 (*http://www.essentialschools.org/cs/resources/view/ces-res/9*, last visited September 22, 2004).

6. The College Board, *Equity 2000* (New York: author, 1989).

7. For an analysis of the evidence offered to the Wilmington court and the way this evidence was understood (and misunderstood) by the court, see K.G. Welner and H. Kupermintz, "Rethinking Expert Testimony in Education Rights Litigation," *Educational Evaluation and Policy Analysis,* 2004, 26(2), 127–42.

8. See, for example, C-L.C. Kulik and J.A. Kulik, "Ability Grouping and Gifted Students," in *Handbook of Gifted Education,* edited by N. Colangelo and G.A. Davis, pp. 178–96 (Boston: Allyn and Bacon, 1991); J.A. Kulik and C-L.C. Kulik, "Synthesis of Research on Effects of Accelerated Instruction," *Educational Leadership,* 1984, 42(2), 84–89; J. F. Feldhusen, "Synthesis of Research on Gifted Youth," *Educational Leadership,* March 1989, 46, 6–11; Susan Demirsky Allan, "Ability Grouping Research Reviews: What Do They Say about Grouping and the Gifted?" *Educational Leadership,* March 1991, 48, 60–65.

9. The following policy position, approved in 1991, still appears on the website of the National Association for Gifted Children: "The practice of grouping, enabling students with advanced abilities and/or performance to be grouped together to receive appropriately challenging instruction, has recently come under attack. NAGC wishes to reaffirm the importance of grouping for instruction of gifted students. . . . Strong research evidence supports the effectiveness of ability grouping for gifted students in accelerated classes, enrichment programs, advanced placement programs, etc. Ability and performance grouping has been used extensively in programs for musically and artistically gifted students, and for athletically talented students with little argument. Grouping is a necessary component of every graduate and professional preparation program, such as law, medicine, and the sciences. It is an accepted practice that is used extensively in the education programs in almost every country in the Western world. NAGC does not endorse a tracking system that sorts all children into fixed layers in the school system with little attention to particular content, student motivation, past accomplishment, or present potential. To abandon the proven instructional strategy of grouping students for instruction at a time of educational crisis in the U.S. will further damage our already poor competitive position with the rest of the world, and will renege on our promise to provide an appropriate education for all children. (Approved 11/91) (*http://www.nagc.org/Policy/abilgroup.htm,* last accessed September 23, 2004).

10. T. Loveless, "The Tracking and Ability Grouping Debate" (Fordham Foundation, unpublished paper, 1998); Loveless, *The Tracking Wars.*

11. J.F. Feldhusen, "Susan Allan Sets the Record Straight: Response to Allan," *Educational Leadership,* March 1991. J.A. Kulik, "Findings on Grouping are Often Distorted, Response to Allen," *Educational Leadership,* March 1991. For critiques of Kulik's own reviews see R.E. Slavin, "Ability Grouping and Student Achievement in Elementary Schools: A Best-Evidence Synthesis," *Review of Educational Research,* 1987, 57, 293–336. Loveless, *The Tracking Wars,* pp. 3, 12, 17, 16, 15.

12. Some research finds that, in comparison with the practices in most public schools, Catholic high school students enrolled in nonacademic tracks typically take more academic courses and fewer

electives than their counterparts in public schools. See, for example, V.E. Lee and A.S. Bryk, "Curriculum Tracking as Mediating the Social Distribution of High School Achievement," *Sociology of Education,* 1988, 61, 78–94. Other researchers have found, in contrast to the national trends in public schools, that particular low-ability classes do have adequate facilities, a solid curriculum, and qualified teachers. Here, too, most of the examples are from Catholic schools. See, for example, L. Valli, "A Curriculum of Effort: Tracking Students in a Catholic High School," in *Curriculum Differentiation: Interpretive Studies in U.S. Secondary Schools,* R. Page and L.Valli, pp. 45–65 (Albany: SUNY Press, 1990).

13. The study examined science and mathematics curriculum, teachers, facilities, equipment, and learning activities at the school and within school (track) level using data from the National Science Foundation's 1985–86 National Survey of Science and Mathematics Education. Crosstabulations, correlational analyses, and analysis of variance documented the distribution of these features of science and mathematics programs. Multivariate analyses sorted out the effects of school and classroom characteristics, and separate track-level analyses were performed on groups of similar schools. This juxtaposition enabled a policy analytic interpretation of whether and how the distribution of specific features of schools and classrooms is likely to affect the learning opportunities of various groups, and it permitted me to draw implications for changes in policy and practice. J. Oakes (with T. Ormseth, R. Bell, and P. Camp), *Multiplying Inequalities: The Effects of Race, Social Class, and Tracking on Opportunities to Learn Mathematics and Science* (Santa Monica: RAND, 1990); J. Oakes, "Can Tracking Research Inform Practice?" *Educational Researcher,* 1992, 21(4), 12–22.

14. Raudenbush, Rowan, and Cheong found that variation in teachers' emphasis on teaching higher-order thinking in four subjects (and most strongly in mathematics and science) was a function of hierarchical conceptions of teaching and learning related to perceived ability group (track). That is, teachers placed much greater emphasis on higher-order thinking and problem solving in high-track classes than in others. See S.W. Raudenbush, B. Rowan, and Y.F. Cheong, "Higher Order Instructional Goals in Secondary Schools: Class, Teacher, and School Influences," *American Educational Research Journal,* 1992, 30, 523–53. Gamoran and Nystrand found high-track students more often experienced "authentic" assignments and higher-order cognitive tasks. By authentic, Gamoran and Nystrand mean questions and assignments request information that is new to the teacher, rather than requiring a prespecified answer. A. Gamoran and M. Nystrand, "Background and Instructional Effects on Achievement in Eighth-Grade English and Social Studies," *Journal on Research in Adolescence,* 1991, 1(3), 277–300. Reba Page's ethnographic account of differentiated English and social studies classes shows that lower-track classes were characterized by what Page called a "skeletal curriculum," in which academic topics from regular classes were covered in less depth; a basic skills curriculum, in which academic subjects such as history and literature were reduced to reading, largely to decoding; and a "therapeutic curriculum," in which practical or "relevant" topics such as drug or law education replaced traditional academics. R. Page, *Lower-Track Classrooms: A Curricular and Cultural Perspective* (New York Teachers College Press, 1991).

15. See, for example, J.E. Talbert and M. Ennis, "Teacher Tracking: Exacerbating Inequalities in the High School" (Stanford: Center for Research on the Context of Teaching, 1990, *www.stanford.edu/group/CRC/publications.htm*); R.M. Ingersoll, "The Problem of Underqualified Teachers in American Secondary Schools," *Educational Researcher,* 1999, 28, 26–37.

16. See, for example, R.J. Coley, R. Ekstrom, J. Gant, A.M. Villegas, R. Mitchell, and S.M. Watts, *On the Right Track* (Princeton: Educational Testing Service, 1992); K.J. Meier, J. Stuart, and R.E. England, *Race, Class and Education: The Politics of Second Generation Discrimination* (Madison: University of Wisconsin Press, 1989). J.H. Braddock, "Ability Grouping, Aspirations and Attainments: Evidence from the National Educational Longitudinal Study of 1988," *Journal of*

Negro Education, 1993, 62(3); C. Adleman, *Answers in the Tool Box* (Washington: U.S. Department of Education, 1999); R. Atanda, *Do Gatekeeper Courses Expand Education Options?* (Washington: National Center for Education Statistics, 1999); L. Horn, A. Nunez, L. Bobbitt, *Mapping the Road to College: First Generation Students' Math Track, Planning Strategies, and Context of Support* (Washington: U.S. Department of Education, National Center for Education Statistics [NCES], 2000) p. 153; X. Ma and J.D. Willms, "Dropping Out of Advanced Mathematics: How Much Do Students and Schools Contribute to the Problem?' *Educational Evaluation and Policy Analysis,* 1999, 21(4), 365–83.

17. For a comprehensive discussion of Rossell's testimony and its methodological problems, see Welner and Kupermintz, "Rethinking Expert Testimony in Education Rights Litigation."

18. In contrast, other research has found that socioeconomic status (SES) has important effects on track placement above and beyond students' academic performance, with higher SES students more likely to be placed in higher tracks when compared to lower SES students with similar academic records (see, for example, A. Gamoran and R.D. Mare, "Secondary School Tracking and Educational Equality: Compensation, Reinforcement, or Neutrality," *American Journal of Sociology,* 1989, 94, 1146–83). Additionally, controlling for academic achievement, family income, and family structure, a study using the NELS 88/94 data by Horn, Nunez, and Bobbitt, *Mapping the Road to College,* found the "first-generation" students from immigrant families were less likely to participate in college-preparatory programs.

19. J. Oakes and G. Guiton, "Matchmaking: The Dynamics of High School Tracking Decisions," *American Educational Research Journal,* 1995, 32(1), 3–33; see also M. Selvin, J. Oakes, S. Hare, K. Ramsey, and D. Schoeff, *Who Gets What and Why? Curriculum Decision-Making at Three Comprehensive High Schools* (Santa Monica: RAND Corporation, 1989).

20. Other researchers have found that differences among schools—such as the size of various tracks, entry criteria for particular tracks, and scheduling practices—affect the likelihood of a student with particular characteristics being placed in particular classes. See, for example, A.B. Sorensen, "The Organizational Differentiation of Students in Schools as an Opportunity Structure," in *The Social Organization of Schools: New Conceptualizations of the Learning Process,* edited by M.T. Hallinan, pp. 103–29 (New York: Plenum Press, 1987); M. Garet and B. DeLany, "Students, Courses, and Stratification," *Sociology of Education,* 1988, 61, 61–77.

21. The results of these studies were reported in expert analyses presented to the court in conjunction with the school desegregation cases. In addition, however, these studies are reported in J. Oakes, "Two Cities: Tracking and Within-School Segregation," *Teachers' College Record,* 1995, 96, 681–90; and, most comprehensively, in K.G. Welner, *Legal Rights, Local Wrongs: When Community Control Collides with Educational Equity* (Albany: SUNY Press, 2001).

22. See, for example, S. Lucas, *Tracking Inequality: Stratification and Mobility in American High Schools* (New York: Teacher College Press, 1999); B.E. Vanfossen, J.D. Jones, and J.Z. Spade, "Curriculum Tracking and Status Maintenance," *Sociology of Education,* 1987, 60, 104–22.

23. For similar findings, see A. Gamoran, "Access to Excellence: Assignment to Honors English Classes in the Transition from Middle to High School," *Educational Evaluation and Policy Analysis,* 1992, 14, 185–204; R.A. Mickelson, "Subverting Swann, First- and Second-Generation Segregation in the Charlotte-Mecklenburg Schools," *American Educational Research Journal,* 2001, 38, 215–52; Sean P. Kelly, "The Black-White Gap in Mathematics Course Taking," University of Wisconsin-Madison, unpublished paper, 2003.

24. S.R. Lucas and A. Gamoran, "Race and Track Assignment: A Re-consideration with Course-Based Indicators of Track Locations" (University of Wisconsin Working Paper, 1993).

25. One exception is a recent paper from the National Bureau of Economic Research that concludes there is no evidence that separating students into tracks harms disadvantaged students. The report

also suggests that tracking can support diversity, in that separate gifted programs are likely to attract and keep students from higher-income families. D. Page and M. Figlio, "School Choice and the Distributional Effects of Ability Tracking: Does Separation Increase Equality?" (Washington: National Bureau of Economic Research, Working Paper no. W8055, 2000).

26. See, for example, R.S. Weinstein. "Reading Group Membership in First Grade: Teacher Behaviors and Pupil Experience Over Time," *Journal of Educational Psychology,* 1976, 68(1), 103–16; R.Barr and R. Dreeben, *How Schools Work* (Chicago: University of Chicago Press, 1983); A. Gamoran and M. Berends, "The Effects of Stratification in Secondary Schools: Synthesis of Survey and Ethnographic Research," *Review of Educational Research,* 1987, 57, 415–36; R.E. Slavin, "Ability Grouping and Student Achievement in Elementary Schools: A Best-Evidence Synthesis," *Review of Educational Research,* 1987, 57(3), 293–336; R.E. Slavin, "Achievement Effects of Ability Grouping in Secondary Schools: A Best Evidence Synthesis," *Review of Educational Research,* 1990, 60(3), 471–500; R.E. Slavin, "Ability Grouping in the Middle Grades: Achievement Effects and Alternatives," *Elementary School Journal,* 1993, 93(5), 535–52.

27. See, for example, P. White, A. Gamoran, A.C. Porter, and J. Smithson, "Upgrading the High School Math Curriculum: Math Course-Taking Patterns in Seven High Schools in California and New York," *Educational Evaluation and Policy Analysis,* 1996, 18, 285–307; T. Madigan, *Science Proficiency and Course Taking in High School* (Washington: U.S. Department of Education, National Center for Education Statistics [NCES], 1997), pp. 97–838; M.T. Hallinan and W.N. Kubitschek, "Curriculum Differentiation and High School Achievement," *Social Psychology of Education,* 1999, 3, 41–62.

28. See, for example, A. Gamoran, "The Variable Effects of High School Tracking," *American Sociological Review,* December 1992, 812–28.

29. See, for example, J. Kulik, *An Analysis of the Research on Ability Grouping: Historical and Contemporary Perspectives* (Storrs, Conn.: National Research Center on the Gifted and Talented, 1992).

30. Resource differences among tracks may also include the resources that students bring (prior knowledge, enthusiasm for learning, an ethic of trying hard, etc.) as well as the resources that schools provide.

31. See, for example, V.E. Lee and A.S. Bryk, "A Multilevel Model of the Social Distribution of Achievement," *Sociology of Education,* 1989, 62(3), 623–45.

32. See, for example, L.M. Argys, D.I. Rees, and D.J. Brewer, "Detracking America's Schools: Equity at Zero Cost?" *Journal of Policy Analysis and Management,* 1996, 15 (4), 623–45.

33. See, for example, R.E. Slavin, "Achievement Effects of Ability Grouping in Secondary Schools: A Best Evidence Synthesis," *Review of Educational Research,* 1990, 60(3), 471–500; R.E. Slavin, "Ability Grouping in the Middle Grades: Achievement Effects and Alternatives," *Elementary School Journal,* 1992, 93 (5), 535–52; see also Figlio and Page, 2000; F. Mosteller, R.J. Light, and J.A. Sachs, "Sustained Inquiry in Education: Lessons from Skill Grouping and Class Size," *Harvard, Educational Review, 1996,* 66, 797–843.

34. A. Gamoran and R.D. Mare, "Secondary School Tracking and Educational Inequality; Compensation, Reinforcement, or Neutrality?" *American Journal of Sociology,* 1989, 94(5), 1146–83; Vanfossen, Jones, and Spade, "Curriculum Tracking and Status Maintenance"; F. Paul, "Academic Programs in a Democratic Society: Structured Choices and Their Consequences," *Advances in Educational Policy,* 2 (Philadelphia: Falmer Press, 1995).

35. See J. Braddock and M.P. Dawkins, "Ability Grouping, Aspirations, and Attainments: Evidence from the National Educational Longitudinal Study of 1988," *Journal of Negro Education,* 1993, 62 (3), 1–13; S. Dornbush, "Off the Track" (Paper presented as the 1994 Presidential Address to the Society for Research on Adolescence, San Diego).

36. P. McDonough, *Choosing Colleges* (Albany: SUNY Press, 1997); F. Paul, "Academic Programs in a Democratic Society."

37. Atanda, *Do Gatekeeper Courses Expand Education Options?* Horn, Nunez, and Bobbitt, *Mapping the Road to College.*

38. Later in this chapter I'll have more to say about the cultural and political tensions that make it impossible to address tracking as a strictly technical issue or to find credibility in suggestions that tracking is all about doing a good job of educating children.

39. Maureen Hallinan, "The Detracting Movement," *Education Next,* Fall 2004.

40. Hallinan wrote in 2004, "In studies published in 1986 and 1999, my colleagues and I found that students assigned to low-ability groups score lower on standardized tests than if they had been placed in mixed-ability or high-ability groups." Ibid.

41. Maureen T. Hallinan, "Tracking: From Theory to Practice," *Sociology of Education,* 1994, 67, 79–84.

42. Gamoran's 1987 analyses of nationally representative survey data documented that the gains bright students in higher-level tracks make in homogeneous groups are canceled out by the losses weaker students suffer by being placed in low-level tracks. A. Gamoran, "The Stratification of High School Learning Opportunities," *Sociology of Education,* 1987, 60: 135–55. A. Gamoran, "Alternative Uses of Ability Grouping in Secondary Schools: Can We Bring High-Quality Instruction to Low-Ability Classrooms?" *American Journal of Education,* 1993, 102(1), 1–22.

43. A. Gamoran, Public Lecture: "Standards, Inequality and Ability Grouping," April 9, 2002 (*http://www.ed.ac.uk/ces/conferences/Gamoran-Lecture.htm*).

44. The term *norm* is defined broadly here, going beyond a common but narrower definition of norms as formal or informal standards that prescribe acceptable action in a setting.

45. Oakes et al., *Good American Schools.*

46. J. A. Kulik, "An Analysis of the Research on Ability Grouping" (National Center for Research on Gifted and Talented Education, Newsletter, Spring, 1993) (*http://www.gifted.uconn.edu./nrcgt/newsletter/spring93/ sprng935.html,* last visited September 27, 2004) Loveless, *The Tracking Wars,* p. 155; Figlio and Page, "School Choice and the Distributional Effects of Ability Tracking." Argys, Brewer, and Rees, "Detracting America's Schools."

47. See, for example, Gamoran, "The Stratification of High School Learning Opportunities."

48. P. Frome, *High Schools That Work: Findings from the 1996 and 1998 Assessments.* Prepared by the Research Triangle Institute for the Planning and Evaluation Service, U.S. Department of Education, Washington, 2001; P. Kaufman, D. Bradby, and P. Teitelbaum, *High Schools That Work and Whole School Reform: Raising Academic Achievement of Vocational Completers Through the Reform of School Practice* (Berkeley: University of California at Berkeley, National Center for Research in Vocational Education, 2000).

49. The College Board, "Equity 2000: A Systemic Education Reform Model" (*http://www.college-board.com/about/association/equity.html*). Note, however, Gamoran's caution: "In 1991 in this system, 31% of these kids were in algebra and therefore nearly 70% in watered down general math—moving up to 99% in 1997. So much greater uptake of academic programmes, but failure rates got worse, so 25% of kids were failing in 1991, 55% were failing in 1997. So it is very difficult to implement a programme like this successfully. Great progress, but still many failures." A. Gamoran, Public Lecture: "Standards, Inequality and Ability Grouping," April 9, 2002 (*http://www.ed.ac.uk/ces/conferences/Gamoran'Lecture.htm*).

50. Hugh Mehan, L. Hubbard, and I. Villanueva, *Constructing School Success: The Consequences of "Untracking" Low Achieving Students* (London: Cambridge University Press, 1994), pp. 100, 105.

51. J. Boaler, *Experiencing School Mathematics* (London; Lea, 2002).

52. J. Boaler, "Promoting Equity in Mathematics Classrooms—Important Teaching Practices and Their Impact on Student Learning," *Proceedings of the International Congress on Mathematics*

Education (Copenhagen, 2004). See, for example, C.C. Burris, J.P. Heubert, H.M. Levin, "Accelerating Mathematics Achievement Using Heterogeneous Grouping," forthcoming.

53. U.S. Department of Education, "Mathematics Equals Opportunity," *White Paper Presented for U.S. Secretary of Education Richard W. Riley* (Washington: author, 1997).

54. E.G. Cohen and R.A. Lotan, "Equity in Heterogeneous Classroom," in *Handbook of Research on Multicultural Education,* edited by J. Banks and C. Banks, 2nd ed. (New York: Teachers College Press, 2003). D.K. Cohen, M.W. McLaughlin, and J.E. Talbert, eds., *Teaching for Understanding: Challenges for Policy and Practice* (San Francisco: Jossey-Bass, 1992). See also Elizabeth Cohen and Rachel Lotan, *Working for Equity in Heterogeneous Classrooms* (New York: Teachers College Press, 1977).

55. Continued resistance to heterogeneous grouping can be found in *The Roeper Review.* Rather than a research journal, Roeper identifies itself as follows: "Published by The Roeper School in Michigan, the Roeper Review applies the highest standards of peer review journalism to cover a broad range of issues—for professionals who work with teachers and psychologists, and for professionals who work directly with gifted and talented children and their families." For example, K. Rogers, "Grouping the Gifted and Talented," *Roeper Review,* 2002, 24(4), 103–7; C. Shields, "A Comparison Study of Student Attitudes and Perceptions in Homogeneous and Heterogeneous Classrooms," *Roeper Review,* 2002, 24(3), 115–19. The Roeper School is a day school for gifted and talented children located fn Bloomfield Hills, Michigan, a suburb of Detroit.

56. The center's mission and work are detailed on its website: *http://www.gifted.uconn.edu/nrcgt.html,* last visited September 27, 2004. C.Tomlinson, *How to Differentiate Instruction for Mixed-Ability Classrooms* (Alexandria, VA.: Association for Supervision and Curriculum Development, 1995); C. Tomlinson, "Differentiated Instruction in the Regular Classroom: What Does It Mean? How Does It Look?" *Understanding Our Gifted,* 2001, 14(1), 3–6. Tomlinson also argues that most schools will need to provide a variety of services and learning options for the full range of learners, in addition to differentiated heterogeneous classrooms.

57. A. Collatos and E. Morrell, "Apprenticing Urban Youth as Critical Researchers: Implications for School Reform," in *Critical Voices in School Reform: Students Living Through Change,* edited by B. Rubin and E. Silva (New York: RoutledgeFalmer, 2002); J. Oakes, K. Rogers, M. Lipton, and E. Morrell, "The Social Construction of College Access: Confronting the Technical, Cultural, and Political Barriers to Low-Income Students of Color," in *Extending Our Reach: Strategies for Increasing Access to College,* edited by W.G. Tierney and L.S. Haggedorn (New York: SUNY Press, 2002); E. Morrell and A. Collatos, "Toward a Critical Teacher Education Pedagogy: Using Student Sociologists as Teacher Educators," *Social Justice,* 2003, 29(4), 60–71; A. Collatos, E. Morrell, A. Nuno, and R. Lara, "Critical Sociology in K-16 Early Intervention: Constructing Latino Pathways to Higher Education," *Journal of Hispanic Higher Education,* 2004, 3(2), 164–79; E. Morrell, *Becoming Critical Researchers: Literacy and Empowerment for Urban Youth* (New York: Peter Lang, 2004). The students as ninth graders happened to be taking the same ninth-grade humanities class.

58. L. Berkner, L. Horn, and N. Clune, *Descriptive Summary of 1995–96 Beginning Postsecondary Students: Three Years Later (NCES 2000–154).* U.S. Department of Education, National Center for Education Statistics. Washington: U.S. Government Printing Office, 2000.

Part IV
The Philosophy of Education

10

Experience and Education

John Dewey

The great educational theorist's most concise statement of his ideas about the needs, the problems, and the possibilities of education—written after his experience with the progressive schools and in the light of the criticisms his theories received.

Traditional vs. Progressive Education

Mankind likes to think in terms of extreme opposites. It is given to formulating its beliefs in terms of *Either-Ors*, between which it recognizes no intermediate possibilities. When forced to recognize that the extremes cannot be acted upon, it is still inclined to hold that they are all right in theory but that when it comes to practical matters circumstances compel us to compromise. Educational philosophy is no exception. The history of educational theory is marked by opposition between the idea that education is development from within and that it is formation from without; that it is based upon natural endowments and that education is a process of overcoming natural inclination and substituting in its place habits acquired under external pressure.

At present, the opposition, so far as practical affairs of the school are concerned, tends to take the form of contrast between traditional and progressive education. If the underlying ideas of the former are formulated broadly, without the qualifications required for accurate statement, they are found to be about as follows: The subject-matter of education consists of bodies of information and of skills that have been worked out in the past; therefore, the chief business of the school is to transmit them to the new generation. In the past, there have also been developed standards and rules of conduct; moral training consists in forming habits of action in conformity with these rules and standards. Finally, the general pattern of school organization (by which I mean the relations of pupils to one another and to the teachers) constitutes the school a kind of institution sharply marked off from other social institutions. Call up in imagination the ordinary schoolroom, its time-schedules, schemes of classification, of examination and promotion, of rules of order, and I think you will grasp what is meant by "pattern of organization." If then you contrast this scene with what goes on in the family, for example, you will appreciate what is meant by the school being a kind of institution sharply marked off from any other form of social organization.

The three characteristics just mentioned fix the aims and methods of instruction and discipline. The main purpose or objective is to prepare the young for future responsibilities and for success in life, by means of acquisition of the organized bodies of information and prepared forms of skill which comprehend the material of instruction. Since the subject-matter as well as standards of proper conduct are handed down from the past, the attitude of pupils must, upon the whole, be one of docility, receptivity, and obedience. Books, especially textbooks, are the chief representatives of the lore and wisdom of the past, while teachers are the organs through which pupils are brought into effective connection with the material. Teachers are the agents through which knowledge and skills are communicated and rules of conduct enforced.

I have not made this brief summary for the purpose of criticizing the underlying philosophy. The rise of what is called new education and progressive schools is of itself a product of discontent with traditional education. In effect it is a criticism of the latter. When the implied criticism is made explicit it reads somewhat as follows: The traditional scheme is, in essence, one of imposition from above and from outside. It imposes adult standards, subject-matter, and methods upon those who are only growing slowly toward maturity. The gap is so great that the required subject-matter, the methods of learning and of behaving are foreign to the existing capacities of the young. They are beyond the reach of the experience the young learners already possess. Consequently, they must be imposed; even though good teachers will use devices of art to cover up the imposition so as to relieve it of obviously brutal features.

But the gulf between the mature or adult products and the experience and abilities of the young is so wide that the very situation forbids much active participation by pupils in the development of what is taught. Theirs is to do—and learn, as it was the part of the six hundred to do and die. Learning here means acquisition of what already is incorporated in books and in the heads of the elders. Moreover, that which is taught is thought of as essentially static. It is taught as a finished product, with little regard either to the ways in which it was originally built up or to changes that will surely occur in the future. It is to a large extent the cultural product of societies that assumed the future would be much like the past, and yet it is used as educational food in a society where change is the rule, not the exception.

If one attempts to formulate the philosophy of education implicit in the practices of the new education, we may, I think, discover certain common principles amid the variety of progressive schools now existing. To imposition from above is opposed expression and cultivation of individuality; to external discipline is opposed free activity; to learning from texts and teachers, learning through experience; to acquisition of isolated skills and techniques by drill, is opposed acquisition of them as means of attaining ends which make direct vital appeal; to preparation for a more or less remote future is opposed making the most of the opportunities of present life; to static aims and materials is opposed acquaintance with a changing world.

Now, all principles by themselves are abstract. They become concrete only in the consequences which result from their application. Just because the principles set forth are so fundamental and far-reaching, everything depends upon the interpretation given them as they are put into practice in the school and the home. It is at this point that the reference made earlier to *Either-Or* philosophies becomes peculiarly pertinent. The general philosophy of the new education may be sound, and yet the difference in abstract principles will not decide the way in which the moral and intellectual preference involved shall be worked out in practice. There is always the danger in a new movement that in rejecting the aims and methods of that which it would supplant, it may develop its principles negatively rather than positively and constructively. Then it takes its clew in practice from that which is rejected instead of from the constructive development of its own philosophy.

I take it that the fundamental unity of the newer philosophy is found in the idea that there is an intimate and necessary relation between the processes of actual experience and education. If this be true, then a positive and constructive development of its own basic idea depends upon having a correct idea of experience. Take, for example, the question of organized subject-matter—which will be discussed in some detail later. The problem for progressive education is: What is the place and meaning of subject-matter and of organization *within* experience? How does subject-matter function? Is there anything inherent in experience which tends towards progressive organization of its contents? What results follow when the materials of experience are not progressively organized? A philosophy which proceeds on the basis of rejection, of sheer opposition, will neglect these questions. It will tend to suppose that because the old education was based on ready-made organization, therefore it suffices to reject the principle of organization *in toto*, instead of striving to discover what it means and how it is to be attained on the basis of experience. We might go through all the points of difference between the new and the old education and reach similar conclusions. When external control is rejected, the problem becomes that of finding the factors of control that are inherent within experience. When external authority is rejected, it does not follow that all authority should be rejected, but rather that there is need to search for a more effective source of authority. Because the older education imposed the knowledge, methods, and the rules of conduct of the mature person upon the young, it does not follow, except upon the basis of the extreme *Either-Or* philosophy, that the knowledge and skill of the mature person has no directive value for the experience of the immature. On the contrary, basing education upon personal experience may mean more multiplied and more intimate contacts between the mature and the immature than ever existed in the traditional school, and consequently more, rather than less, guidance by others. The problem, then, is: how these contacts can be established without violating the principle of learning through personal experience. The solution of this problem requires a well thought-out philosophy of the social factors that operate in the constitution of individual experience.

What is indicated in the foregoing remarks is that the general principles of the new education do not of themselves solve any of the problems of the actual or practical conduct and management of progressive schools. Rather, they set new problems which have to be worked out on the basis of a new philosophy of experience. The problems are not even recognized, to say nothing of being solved, when it is assumed that it suffices to reject the ideas and practices of the old education and then go to the opposite extreme. Yet I am sure that you will appreciate what is meant when I say that many of the newer schools tend to make little or nothing of organized subject-matter of study; to proceed as if any form of direction and guidance by adults were an invasion of individual freedom, and as if the idea that education should be concerned with the present and future meant that acquaintance with the past has little or no role to play in education. Without pressing these defects to the point of exaggeration, they at least illustrate what is meant by a theory and practice of education which proceeds negatively or by reaction against what has been current in education rather than by a positive and constructive development of purposes, methods, and subject-matter on the foundation of a theory of experience and its educational potentialities.

It is not too much to say that an educational philosophy which professes to be based on the idea of freedom may become as dogmatic as ever was the traditional education which is reacted against. For any theory and set of practices is dogmatic which is not based upon critical examination of its own underlying principles. Let us say that the new education emphasizes the freedom of the learner. Very well. A problem is now set. What does freedom mean and what are the conditions under which it is capable of realization? Let us say that the kind of external imposition which was so common in the traditional school limited rather than promoted the intellectual and moral development of the young. Again, very well. Recognition of this serious defect sets a problem. Just what is the role of the teacher and of books in promoting the educational development of the immature? Admit that traditional education employed as the subject-matter for study facts and ideas so bound up with the past as to give little help in dealing with the issues of the present and future. Very well. Now we have the problem of discovering the connection which actually exists *within* experience between the achievements of the past and the issues of the present. We have the problem of ascertaining how acquaintance with the past may be translated into a potent instrumentality for dealing effectively with the future. We may reject knowledge of the past as the *end* of education and thereby only emphasize its importance as a *means*. When we do that we have a problem that is new in the story of education: How shall the young become acquainted with the past in such a way that the acquaintance is a potent agent in appreciation of the living present?

Experience—The Means and Goal of Education

In what I have said I have taken for granted the soundness of the principle that education in order to accomplish its ends both for the individual learner and for society must be based upon experience—which is always the actual life-experience of some individual. I have not argued for the acceptance of this principle nor attempted to justify it. Conservatives as well as radicals in education are profoundly discontented with the present educational situation taken as a whole. There is at least this much agreement among intelligent persons of both schools of educational thought. The educational system must move one way or another, either backward to the intellectual and moral standards of a pre-scientific age or forward to ever greater utilization of scientific method in the development of the possibilities of growing, expanding experience. I have but endeavored to point out some of the conditions which must be satisfactorily fulfilled if education takes the latter course.

For I am so confident of the potentialities of education when it is treated as intelligently directed development of the possibilities inherent in ordinary experience that I do not feel it necessary to criticize here the other route nor to advance arguments in favor of taking the route of experience. The only ground for anticipating failure in taking this path resides to my mind in the danger that experience and the experimental method will not be adequately conceived. There is no discipline in the world so severe as the discipline of experience subjected to the tests of intelligent development and direction. Hence the only ground I can see for even a temporary reaction against the standards, aims, and methods of the newer education is the failure of educators who professedly adopt them to be faithful to them in practice. As I have emphasized more than once, the road of the new education is not an easier one to follow than the old road but a more strenuous and difficult one. It will remain so until it has attained its majority and that attainment will require many years of serious co-operative work on the part of its adherents. The greatest danger that attends its future is, I believe, the idea that it is an easy way to follow, so easy that its course may be improvised, if not in an impromptu fashion, at least almost from day to day or from week to week. It is for this reason that instead of extolling its principles, I have confined myself to showing certain conditions which must be fulfilled if it is to have the successful career which by right belongs to it.

I have used frequently in what precedes the words "progressive" and "new" education. I do not wish to close, however, without recording my firm belief that the fundamental issue is not of new versus old education nor of progressive against traditional education but a question of what anything whatever must be to be worthy of the name *education*. I am not, I hope and believe, in favor of any ends or any methods simply because the name progressive may be applied to them. The basic question concerns the nature of education with no qualifying adjectives prefixed. What we want and need is education pure and simple, and we shall make surer and faster progress when we devote ourselves to finding out just what education is and what conditions have to be satisfied in order that education may be a reality and not a name or a slogan. It is for this reason alone that I have emphasized the need for a sound philosophy of experience.

11
Wide-Awakeness and the Moral Life

Maxine Greene

"Moral reform," wrote Henry David Thoreau, "is the effort to throw off sleep." He went on:

> Why is it that men give so poor an account of their day if they have not been slumbering?
> They are not such poor calculators. If they had not been overcome with drowsiness they
> would have performed something. The millions are awake enough for physical labor; but
> only one in a million is awake enough for effective intellectual exertion, only one in a
> hundred million to a poetic or divine life. To be awake is to be alive. I have never yet met
> a man who was quite awake. How could I have looked him in the face? We must learn to
> reawaken and keep ourselves awake, not by mechanical aids, but by an infinite expecta-
> tion of the dawn, which does not forsake us in our soundest sleep. I know of no more
> encouraging fact than the unquestionable ability of man to elevate his life by a conscious
> endeavor.[1]

It is of great interest to me to find out how this notion of wide-awakeness has affected contemporary thought, perhaps particularly the thought of those concerned about moral responsibility and commitment in this difficult modern age. The social philosopher Alfred Schutz has
talked of wide-awakeness as an achievement, a type of awareness, "a plane of consciousness of
highest tension originating in an attitude of full attention to life and its requirements."[2] This
attentiveness, this *interest* in things, is the direct opposite of the attitude of bland convention-
ality and indifference so characteristic of our time.

   We are all familiar with the number of individuals who live their lives immersed, as it were,
in daily life, in the mechanical round of habitual activities. We are all aware how few people ask
themselves what they have done with their own lives, whether or not they have used their freedom or simply acceded to the imposition of patterned behavior and the assignment of roles.
Most people, in fact, are likely to go on in that fashion, unless—or until—"one day the 'why'
arises," as Albert Camus put it, "and everything begins in that weariness tinged with amaze-
ment." Camus had wide-awakeness in mind as well; because the weariness of which he spoke

comes "at the *end* of the acts of a mechanical life, but at the same time it inaugurates the impulse of consciousness."[3]

The "why" may take the form of anxiety, the strange and wordless anxiety that occurs when individuals feel they are not acting on their freedom, not realizing possibility, not (to return to Thoreau) elevating their lives. Or the "why" may accompany a sudden perception of the insufficiencies in ordinary life, of inequities and injustices in the world, of oppression and brutality and control. It may accompany, indeed it may be necessary, for an individual's moral life. The opposite of morality, it has often been said, is indifference—a lack of care, an absence of concern. Lacking wide-awakeness, I want to argue, individuals are likely to drift, to act on impulses of expediency. They are unlikely to identify situations as moral ones or to set themselves to assessing their demands. In such cases, it seems to me, it is meaningless to talk of obligation; it may be futile to speak of consequential choice.

This is an important problem today in many countries of the world. Everywhere, guidelines are deteriorating; fewer and fewer people feel themselves to be answerable to clearly defined norms. In many places, too, because of the proliferation of bureaucracies and corporate structures, individuals find it harder and harder to take initiative. They guide themselves by vaguely perceived expectations; they allow themselves to be programmed by organizations and official schedules or forms. They are like the hero of George Konrad's novel, *The Case Worker*. He is a social worker who works with maltreated children "in the name," as he puts it, "of legal principles and provisions." He does not like the system, but he serves it: "It's law, it works, it's rather like me, its tool. I know its ins and outs. I simplify and complicate it, I slow it down and speed it up. I adapt myself to its needs or adapt it to my needs, but this is as far as I will go."[4] Interestingly enough, he says (and this brings me back to wide-awakeness) that his highest aspiration is to "live with his eyes open" as far as possible; but the main point is that he, like so many other clerks and office workers and middle management men (for all their meaning well), is caught within the system and is not free to choose.

I am suggesting that, for too many individuals in modern society, there is a feeling of being dominated and that feelings of powerlessness are almost inescapable. I am also suggesting that such feelings can to a large degree be overcome through conscious endeavor on the part of individuals to keep themselves awake, to think about their condition in the world, to inquire into the forces that appear to dominate them, to interpret the experiences they are having day by day. Only as they learn to make sense of what is happening, can they feel themselves to be autonomous. Only then can they develop the sense of agency required for living a moral life.

I think it is clear that there always has to be a human consciousness, recognizing the moral issues potentially involved in a situation, if there is to be a moral life. As in such great moral presentations as *Antigone*, *Hamlet*, and *The Plague*, people in everyday life today have to define particular kinds of situations as moral and to identify the possible alternatives. In *Antigone*, Antigone defined the situation that existed after her uncle forbade her to bury her brother as one in which there were alternatives: she could indeed bury her brother, thus offending against the law of the state and being sentenced to death, or (like her sister Ismene) submit to the men in power. In *Hamlet*, the Danish prince defined the situation in Denmark as one in which there were alternatives others could not see: to expose the murderer of his father and take the throne as the true king or to accept the rule of Claudius and his mother and return as a student to Wittenberg. In *The Plague*, most of the citizens of Oran saw no alternative but to resign themselves to a pestilence for which there was no cure; but Dr. Rieux and Tarrou defined the same situation as one in which there were indeed alternatives: to submit—or to form sanitary squads and, by so doing, to refuse to acquiesce in the inhuman, the absurd.

When we look at the everyday reality of home and school and workplace, we can scarcely imagine ourselves taking moral positions like those taken by a Hamlet or a Dr. Rieux. One reason has to do with the overwhelming ordinariness of the lives we live. Another is our tendency to perceive our everyday reality as a given—objectively defined, impervious to change. Taking it for granted, we do not realize that reality, like all others, is an interpreted one. It presents itself to us as it does because we have learned to understand it in standard ways.

In a public school, for instance, we scarcely notice that there is a hierarchy of authority; we are so accustomed to it, we forget that it is man-made. Classroom teachers, assigned a relatively low place in the hierarchy, share a way of seeing and of talking about it. They are used to watching schedules, curricula, and testing programs emanate from "the office." They take for granted the existence of a high place, a seat of power. If required unexpectedly to administer a set of tests, most teachers (fearful, perhaps, irritated or sceptical) will be likely to accede. Their acquiescence may have nothing at all to do with their convictions or with what they have previously read or learned. They simply see no alternatives. The reality they have constructed and take for granted allows for neither autonomy nor disagreement. They do not consider putting their objections to a test. The constructs they have inherited do not include a view of teachers as equal participants. "That," they are prone to say, "is the way it is."

Suppose, however, that a few teachers made a serious effort to understand the reasons for the new directive. Suppose they went out into the community to try to assess the degree of pressure on the part of parents. Suppose that they investigated the kinds of materials dispatched from the city or the state. Pursuing such efforts, they would be keeping themselves awake. They might become increasingly able to define their own values with regard to testing; they might conceivably see a moral issue involved. For some, testing might appear to be dehumanizing; it might lead to irrelevant categorizing; it might result in the branding of certain children. For others, testing might appear to be miseducative, unless it were used to identify disabilities and suggest appropriate remedies. For still others, testing might appear to be a kind of insurance against poor teaching, a necessary reminder of what was left undone. Discussing it from several points of view and within an understood context, the teachers might find themselves in a position to act as moral agents. Like Dr. Rieux and Tarrou, they might see that there are indeed alternatives: to bring the school community into an open discussion, to consider the moral issues in the light of overarching commitments, or to talk about what is actually known and what is merely hypothesized. At the very least, there would be wide-awakeness. The members of the school community would be embarked on a moral life.

Where personal issues are concerned, the approach might be very much the same. Suppose that a young person's peer group is "into" drugs or alcohol or some type of sexual promiscuity. Young persons who are half asleep and who feel no sense of agency might well see no alternative to compliance with the group, when the group decides that certain new experiences should be tried. To such individuals, no moral situation exists. They are young; they are members; whether they want to particularly or not, they can only go along.

Other young persons, just as committed to the group, might be able to realize that there are indeed alternatives when, say, some of their comrades go out to find a supply of cocaine. They might be able to ponder those alternatives, to play them out in their imagination. They can accompany their friends on their search; they might even, if they are successful, get to sniff a little cocaine and have the pleasure such sniffs are supposed to provide. They can, on the other hand, take a moment to recall the feelings they had when they first smoked marijuana—the nervousness at losing touch with themselves, the dread about what might happen later. They can consider the fact that their friends are going to do something illegal, not playful, that they could be arrested, even jailed. They can confront their own reluctance to break the law (or even to break an ordinary rule), imagine what their parents would say, try to anticipate what they would think of themselves. At the same time, if they decide to back away, they know they might lose their friends. If they can remember that they are free, after all, and if they assess their situation as one in which they can indeed choose one course of action over another, they are on the way to becoming moral agents. The more considerations they take into account, the more they consider the welfare of those around, the closer they will come to making a defensible choice.

A crucial issue facing us is the need to find ways of educating young persons to such sensitivity and potency. As important, it seems to me, is the matter of wide-awakeness for their teachers. It is far too easy for teachers, like other people, to play their roles and do their jobs without serious consideration of the good and right. Ironically, it is even possible when they are using classroom manuals for moral education. This is partly due to the impact of a vaguely apprehended relativism, partly to a bland carelessness, a shrugging off (sometimes because of grave self-doubt) of responsibility. I am convinced that, if teachers today are to initiate young people into an ethical existence, they themselves must attend more fully than they normally have to their own lives and its requirements; they have to break with the mechanical life, to overcome their own submergence in the habitual, even in what they conceive to be the virtuous, and ask the "why" with which learning and moral reasoning begin.

"You do not," wrote Martin Buber, "need moral genius for educating character; you do need someone who is wholly alive and able to communicate himself directly to his fellow beings. His aliveness streams out to them and affects them most strongly and purely when he has no thought of affecting them. . . ."[5] This strikes me as true; but I cannot imagine an aliveness streaming out for someone who is half-asleep and out of touch with herself or himself. I am not proposing separate courses in moral education or value clarification to be taught by such a teacher. I am, rather, suggesting that attentiveness to the moral dimensions of existence ought to accompany every effort made to initiate persons into any form of life or academic discipline.

Therefore, I believe it important for teachers, no matter what their specialty, to be clear about how they ground their own values, their own conceptions of the good and of the possible. Do they find their sanctions in some supernatural reality? Are they revealed in holy books or in the utterances of some traditional authority? Do they, rather, depend upon their own private intuitions of what is good and right? Do they decide in each particular situation what will best resolve uncertainty, what works out for the best? Do they simply refer to conventional social morality, to prevailing codes, or to the law? Or do they refer beyond the law—to some domain of principle, of norm? To what extent are they in touch with the actualities of their own experiences, their own biographies, and the ways in which these affect the tone of their encounters with the young? Teachers need to be aware of how they personally confront the unnerving questions present in the lives of every teacher, every parent: What shall we teach them? How can we guide them? What hope can we offer them? How can we tell them what to do?

The risks are great, as are the uncertainties. We are no longer in a situation in which we can provide character-training with the assurance that it will make our children virtuous and just.

We can no longer use systems of rewards and punishments and feel confident they will make youngsters comply. We recognize the futility of teaching rules or preaching pieties or presenting conceptions of the good. We can no longer set ourselves up as founts of wisdom, exemplars of righteousness, and expect to have positive effects. Children are active; children are different at the various stages of their growth. Engaged in transactions with an environment, each one must effect connections within his or her own experience. Using whatever capacities they have available, each one must himself or herself perceive the consequences of the acts he or she performs. Mustering their own resources, each one must embark—"through choice of action," as Dewey put it[6]—upon the formation of a self.

Moral education, it would seem, must be as specifically concerned with self-identification in a community as it is with the judgments persons are equipped to make at different ages. It has as much to do with interest and action in concrete situations as it does with the course of moral reasoning. It has as much to do with consciousness and imagination as it does with principle. Since it cannot take place outside the vital contexts of social life, troubling questions have to be constantly confronted. How can indifference be overcome? How can the influence of the media be contained? How can the young be guided to choose reflectively and compassionately, even as they are set free?

The problem, most will agree, is not to tell them what to do—but to help them attain some kind of clarity about how to choose, how to decide what to do. And this involves teachers directly, immediately—teachers as persons able to present themselves as critical thinkers willing to disclose their own principles and their own reasons as well as authentic persons living in the world, persons who are concerned—who care.

Many teachers, faced with demands like these, find themselves in difficult positions, especially if they are granted little autonomy, or their conceptions of their own projects are at odds with what their schools demand. Today they may be held accountable for teaching predefined competencies and skills or for achieving objectives that are often largely behavioral. At once, they may be expected to represent both the wider culture and the local community, or the international community and the particular community of the individual child. If teachers are not critically conscious, if they are not awake to their own values and commitments (and to the conditions working upon them), if they are not personally engaged with their subject matter and with the world around, I do not see how they can initiate the young into critical questioning or the moral life.

I am preoccupied, I suppose, with what Camus called "the plague"—that terrible distancing and indifference, so at odds with commitment and communion and love. I emphasize this because I want to stress the connection between wide-awakeness, cognitive clarity, and existential concern. I want to highlight the fact that the roots of moral choosing lie at the core of a person's conception of herself or himself and the equally important fact that choosing involves action as well as thought. Moral action, of course, demands choosing between alternatives, usually between two goods, not between good and bad or right and wrong. The problem in teaching is to empower persons to internalize and incarnate the kinds of principles that will enable them to make such choices. Should I do what is thought to be my duty and volunteer for the army, or should I resist what I believe to be an unjust war. Should I steal the medicine to save my mother's life, or should I obey the law and risk letting her die?

These are choices of consequence for the self and others; and they are made, they can only be made in social situations where custom, tradition, official codes, and laws condition and play upon what people think and do. We might think of Huck Finn's decision not to return Jim to his owner or of Anna Karenina's decision to leave her husband. These are only morally significant in relation to a particular fabric of codes and customs and rules. Think of the Danish king's wartime decision to stand with Denmark's Jewish citizens, Daniel Ellsberg's decision to publish the Pentagon Papers, or Pablo Casals' refusal to conduct in fascist Spain. These decisions too were made in a matrix of principles, laws, and ideas of what is considered acceptable, absolutely, or conditionally good and right. To be moral involves taking a position towards that matrix, thinking critically about what is taken for granted. It involves taking a principled position of one's own (*choosing* certain principles by which to live) and speaking clearly about it, so as to set oneself on the right track.

It is equally important to affirm that it is always the individual, acting voluntarily in a particular situation at a particular moment, who does the deciding. I do not mean that individuals are isolated, answerable only to themselves. I do mean that individuals, viewed as participants, as inextricably involved with other people, must be enabled to take responsibility for their own choosing, must not merge themselves or hide themselves in what Soren Kierkegaard called "the crowd."[7] If individuals act automatically or conventionally, if they do only what is expected of them (or because they feel they have no right to speak for themselves), if they do only what they are told to do, they are not living moral lives.

Indeed, I rather doubt that individuals who are cowed or flattened out or depressed or afraid can learn, since learning inevitably involves a free decision to enter into a form of life, to proceed in a certain way, to do something because it is right There are paradigms to be found in many kinds of teaching for those interested in moral education, since teaching is in part a process of moving people to proceed according to a specified set of norms. If individuals are wide-awake and make decisions consciously to interpret a poem properly, to try to understand a period in English history, or to participate in some type of social inquiry, they are choosing to abide by certain standards made available to them. In doing so, they are becoming acquainted with what it means to choose a set of norms. They are not only creating value for themselves, they are creating themselves; they are moving towards more significant, more understandable lives.

Consider, with norms and self-creation in mind, the case of Nora in Ibsen's *The Doll's House.* If she simply ran out of the house in tears at the end, she would not have been engaging in moral action. Granting the fact that she was defying prevailing codes, I would insist that she was making a decision in accord with an internalized norm. It might be called a principle of emancipation, having to do with the right to grow, to become, to be more than a doll in a doll's house. If asked, Nora might have been able to generalize and talk about the right of *all* human beings to develop in their own fashion, to be respected, to be granted integrity.

Principles or norms are general ideas of that kind, arising out of experience and used by individuals in the appraisal of situations they encounter as they live—to help them determine what they ought to do. They are not specific rules, like the rules against stealing and lying and adultery. They are general and comprehensive. They concern justice and equality, respect for the dignity of persons and regard for their points of view. They have much to do with the ways in which diverse individuals choose themselves; they are defined reflectively and imaginatively and against the backgrounds of biography. When they are incarnated in a person's life, they offer him or her the means for analyzing particular situations. They offer perspectives, points of view from which to consider particular acts. The Golden Rule is such a principle, but, as

Dewey says, the Golden Rule does not finally decide matters just by enabling us to tell people to consider the good of others as they would their own. "It suggests," he writes, "the necessity of considering how our acts affect the interests of others as well as our own; it tends to prevent partiality of regard. . . . In short, the Golden Rule does not issue special orders or commands; but it does clarify and illuminate the situations requiring intelligent deliberation."[8] So it was with the principle considered by Ibsen's Nora; so it is with the principle of justice and the principles of care and truth-telling. Our hope in teaching is that persons will appropriate such principles and learn to live by them.

Now it is clear that young people have to pass through the stages of heteronomy in their development towards the degree of autonomy they require for acting on principle in the way described. They must achieve the kind of wide-awakeness I have been talking about, the ability to think about what they are doing, to take responsibility. The teaching problem seems to me to be threefold. It involves equipping young people with the ability to identify alternatives, and to see possibilities in the situations confront. It involves the teaching of principles, possible perspectives by means of which those situations can be assessed and appraised, *as well as* the norms governing historical inquiry, ballet dancing, or cooperative living, norms that must be appropriated by persons desiring to join particular human communities. It also involves enabling students to make decisions of principle, to reflect, to articulate, and to take decisive actions in good faith.

Fundamental to the whole process may be the building up of a sense of moral directedness, of oughtness. An imaginativeness, an awareness, and a sense of possibility are required, along with the sense of autonomy and agency, of being present to the self. There must be attentiveness to others and to the circumstances of everyday life. There must be efforts made to discover ways of living together justly and pursuing common ends. As wide-awake teachers work, making principles available and eliciting moral judgments, they must orient themselves to the concrete, the relevant, and the questionable. They must commit themselves to each person's potentiality for overcoming helplessness and submergence, for looking through his or her own eyes at the shared reality.

I believe this can only be done if teachers can identify themselves as moral beings, concerned with defining their own life purposes in a way that arouses others to do the same. I believe, you see, that the young are most likely to be stirred to learn when they are challenged by teachers who themselves are learning, who are breaking with what they have too easily taken for granted, who are creating their own moral lives. There are no guarantees, but wide-awakeness can play a part in the process of liberating and arousing, in helping people pose questions with regard to what is oppressive, mindless, and wrong. Surely, it can help people—all kinds of people—make the conscious endeavors needed to elevate their lives.

Camus, in an essay called "The Almond Trees," wrote some lines that seem to me to apply to teachers, especially those concerned in this way. He was talking about how endless are our tasks, how impossible it is to overcome the human condition—which, at least, we have come to know better than ever before:

> We must mend what has been torn apart, make justice imaginable again—give happiness a meaning once more. . . . Naturally, it is a superhuman task. But superhuman is the term for tasks men take a long time to accomplish, that's all. Let us know our aims, then, holding fast to the mind. . . . The first thing is not to despair.[9]

Notes

1. Henry David Thoreau, *Walden* (New York: Washington Square Press, 1963), pp. 66–67.
2. Alfred Schutz, ed. Maurice Natanson, *The Problem of Social Reality*, Collected Papers I (The Hague: Martinus Nijhoff, 1967), p. 213.
3. Albert Camus, *The Myth of Sisyphus* (New York: Alfred A. Knopf, 1955), p. 13.
4. George Konrad, *The Case Worker* (New York: Harcourt Brace Jovanovich, 1974), p. 168.
5. Martin Buber, *Between Man and Man* (Boston: Beacon Press, 1957), p. 105.
6. John Dewey, *Democracy and Education* (New York: Macmillan Company, 1916), p. 408.
7. Soren Kierkegaard, "The Individual," in *The Point of View for My Work as an Author* (New York: Harper & Row, 1962), pp. 102–136.
8. Dewey, *Theory of the Moral Life* (New York: Holt, Rinehart and Winston, 1960), p. 142.
9. Camus, "The Almond Trees," in *Lyrical and Critical Essays* (New York: Alfred A. Knopf, 1968), p. 135.

12

The Ideal of the Educated Person

Jane Roland Martin

R.S. Peters calls it an ideal.[1] So do Nash, Kazemias and Perkinson who, in their introduction to a collection of studies in the history of educational thought, say that one cannot go about the business of education without it.[2] Is it the good life? the responsible citizen? personal autonomy? No, it is the educated man.

The educated man! In the early 1960s when I was invited to contribute to a book of essays to be entitled *The Educated Man*, I thought nothing of this phrase. By the early 1970s I felt uncomfortable whenever I came across it, but I told myself it was the thought not the words that counted. It is now the early 1980s. Peters's use of the phrase "educated man" no longer troubles me for I think it fair to say that he intended it in a gender-neutral way.[3] Despite one serious lapse which indicates that on some occasions he was thinking of his educated man as male, I do not doubt that the ideal he set forth was meant for males and females alike.[4] Today my concern is not Peters's language but his conception of the educated man—or person, as I will henceforth say. I will begin by outlining Peters's ideal for you and will then show that it does serious harm to women. From there I will go on to argue that Peters's ideal is inadequate for men as well as women and, furthermore, that its inadequacy for men is intimately connected to the injustice it does women. In conclusion I will explore some of the requirements an adequate ideal must satisfy.

Let me explain at the outset that I have chosen to discuss Peters's ideal of the educated person here because for many years Peters has been perhaps the dominant figure in philosophy of education. Moreover, although Peters's ideal is formulated in philosophically sophisticated terms, it is certainly not idiosyncratic. On the contrary, Peters claims to have captured our concept of the educated person, and he may well have done so. Thus, I think it fair to say that the traits Peters claims one must possess to be a truly educated person and the kind of education he assumes one must have in order to acquire those traits would, with minor variations, be cited by any number of people today if they were to describe their own conception of the ideal. I discuss Peters's ideal, then, because it has significance for the field of philosophy of education as a whole.

I.R.S. Peters's Educated Person

The starting point of Peters's philosophy of education is the concept of the educated person. While granting that we sometimes use the term "education" to refer to any process of rearing, bringing up, instructing, etc., Peters distinguishes this very broad sense of "education" from the narrower one in which he is interested. The concept of the educated person provides the basis for this distinction: whereas "education" in the broad sense refers to any process of rearing, etc., "education" in the narrower, and to him philosophically more important, sense refers to the family of processes which have as their outcome the development of an educated person.[5]

Peters set forth his conception of the educated person in some detail in his book, *Ethics and Education.*[6] Briefly, an educated person is one who does not simply possess knowledge. An educated person has a body of knowledge and some kind of conceptual scheme to raise this knowledge above the level of a collection of disjointed facts which in turn implies some understanding of principles for organizing facts and of the "reason why" of things. Furthermore, the educated person's knowledge is not inert: it characterizes the person's way of looking at things and involves "the kind of commitment that comes from getting on the inside of a form of thought and awareness"; that is to say; the educated person cares about the standards of evidence implicit in science or the canons of proof inherent in mathematics. Finally, the educated person has cognitive perspective. In an essay entitled "Education and the Educated Man" published several years later, Peters added to this portrait that the educated person's pursuits can be practical as well as theoretical so long as the person delights in them for their own sake, and that both sorts of pursuits involve standards to which the person must be sensitive.[7] He also made it clear that knowledge enters into his conception of the educated person in three ways, namely, depth, breadth and knowledge of good.

In their book, *Education and Personal Relationships*, Downie, Loudfoot and Telfer presented a conception of the educated person which is a variant on Peters's.[8] I cite it here not because they too use the phrase "educated man," but to show that alternate philosophical conceptions of the educated person differ from Peters's only in detail. Downie, Loudfoot and Telfer's educated person has knowledge which is wide ranging in scope, extending from history and geography to the natural and social sciences and to current affairs. This knowledge is important, relevant and grounded. The educated person understands what he or she knows, knows how to do such things as history and science, and has the inclination to apply this knowledge, to be critical and to have curiosity in the sense of a thirst for knowledge. Their major departure from Peters's conception—and it is not, in the last analysis, very major—is to be found in their concern with knowledge by acquaintance: the educated person must not merely have knowledge *about* works of art—and, if I understand them correctly, about moral and religious theories—but must know these as individual things.

Consider now the knowledge, the conceptual scheme which raises this knowledge above the level of disjointed facts and the cognitive perspective Peters's educated person must have. It is quite clear that Peters does not intend that these be acquired through the study of cooking and driving. Mathematics, science, history, literature, philosophy—these are the subjects which constitute the curriculum for his educated person. In short, his educated person is one who has had—and profited from—a liberal education of the sort outlined by Paul Hirst in his famous essay, "Liberal Education and the Nature of Knowledge." Hirst describes what is sought in a liberal education as follows:

first, sufficient immersion in the concepts, logic and criteria of the discipline for a person to come to know the distinctive way in which it "works" by pursuing these in particular cases; and then sufficient generalization of these over the whole range of the discipline so that his experience begins to be widely structured in this distinctive manner. It is this coming to look at things in a certain way that is being aimed at, not the ability to work out in minute particulars all the details that can be in fact discerned. It is the ability to recognize empirical assertions or aesthetic judgments for what they are, and to know the kind of consideration on which their validity will depend, that matters.[9]

If Peters's educated person is not in fact Hirst's liberally educated person, he or she is certainly its identical twin.

Liberal education, in Hirst's view, consists in an initiation into what he calls the forms of knowledge. There are, on his count, seven of them. Although he goes to some lengths in his later writings on the topic to deny that these forms are themselves intellectual disciplines, it is safe to conclude that his liberally educated person, and hence Peters's educated person, will acquire the conceptual schemes and cognitive perspectives they are supposed to have through a study of mathematics, physical science, history, the human sciences, literature, fine arts, philosophy. These disciplines will not necessarily be studied separately: an interdisciplinary curriculum is compatible with the Peters-Hirst ideal. But it is nonetheless their subject matter, their conceptual apparatus, their standards of proof and adequate evidence, their way of looking at things that must be acquired if the ideal is to be realized.

II. Initiation into Male Cognitive Perspectives

What is this certain way in which the educated person comes to look at things? What is the distinctive manner in which that person's experience is structured? A body of literature documenting the many respects in which the disciplines of knowledge ignore or misrepresent the experience and lives of women has developed over the last decade. I cannot do justice here to its range of concerns or its sophisticated argumentation. Through the use of examples, however, I will try to give you some sense of the extent to which the intellectual disciplines incorporate a male cognitive perspective, and hence a sense of the extent to which Hirst's liberally educated person and its twin—Peters's educated person—look at things through male eyes.

Let me begin with history. "History is past politics" was the slogan inscribed on the seminar room wall at Johns Hopkins in the days of the first doctoral program.[10] In the late 1960s the historian, Richard Hofstadter, summarized his field by saying: "Memory is the thread of personal identity, history of public identity." History has defined itself as the record of the public and political aspects of the past; in other words, as the record of the productive processes—man's sphere—of society. Small wonder that women are scarcely mentioned in historical narratives! Small wonder that they have been neither the objects nor the subjects of historical enquiry until very recently! The reproductive processes of society which have traditionally been carried on by women are excluded by *definition* from the purview of the discipline.

If women's lives and experiences have been excluded from the subject matter of history, the works women have produced have for the most part been excluded from literature and the fine arts. It has never been denied that there have been women writers and artists, but their works have not often been deemed important or significant enough to be studied by historians and critics. Thus, for example, Catherine R. Stimpson has documented the treatment accorded Gertrude Stein by two journals which exert a powerful influence in helping to decide what literature is and what books matter.[11] Elaine Showalter, pursuing a somewhat different tack, has documented the double standard which was used in the nineteenth century to judge women writers: all the most desirable aesthetic qualities—for example, power, breadth, knowledge of life, humor—were assigned to men; the qualities assigned to women, such as refinement, tact, precise observation, were not considered sufficient for the creation of an excellent novel.[12]

The disciplines are guilty of different kinds of sex bias. Even as literature and the fine arts exclude women's works from their subject matter, they include works which construct women according to the male image of her. One might expect this tendency to construct the female to be limited to the arts, but it is not. Naomi Weisstein has shown that psychology constructs the female personality to fit the preconceptions of its male practitioners, clinicians either accepting theory without evidence or finding in their data what they want to find.[13] And Ruth Hubbard has shown that this tendency extends even to biology where the stereotypical picture of the passive female is projected by the male practitioners of that field onto the animal kingdom.[14]

There are, indeed, two quite different ways in which a discipline can distort the lives, experiences and personalities of women. Even as psychology constructs the female personality out of our cultural stereotype, it holds up standards of development for women to meet which are derived from studies using male subjects.[15] Not surprisingly, long after the source of the standards is forgotten, women are proclaimed to be underdeveloped and inferior to males in relation to these standards. Thus, for example, Carol Gilligan has pointed out that females are classified as being at Stage 3 of Kohlberg's six stage sequence of moral development because important differences in moral development between males and females are ignored.[16]

In the last decade scholars have turned to the study of women. Thus, historical narratives and analyses of some aspects of the reproductive processes of society—of birth control, childbirth, midwifery, for example—have been published.[17] The existence of such scholarship is no guarantee, however, of its integration into the mainstream of the discipline of history itself, yet this latter is required if initiation into history as a form of knowledge is not to constitute initiation into a male cognitive perspective. The title of a 1974 anthology on the history of women, *Clio's Consciousness Raised*, is unduly optimistic.[18] Certainly, the consciousness of some historians has been raised, but there is little reason to believe that the discipline of history has redefined itself so that studies of the reproductive processes of society are not simply tolerated as peripherally relevant, but are considered to be as central to it as political, economic and military narratives are. Just as historians have begun to study women's past, scholars in literature and the fine arts have begun to bring works by women to our attention and to reinterpret the ones we have always known.[19] But there is still the gap between feminist scholarship and the established definitions of literary and artistic significance to be bridged, and until it is, the initiation into these disciplines provided by a liberal education will be an initiation into male perspectives.

In sum, the intellectual disciplines into which a person must be initiated to become an educated person *exclude* women and their works, *construct* the female to the male image of her and *deny* the truly feminine qualities she does possess. The question remains of whether the male cognitive perspective of the disciplines is integral to Peters's ideal of the educated person. The answer to this question is to be found in Hirst's essay, "The Forms of Knowledge Revisited."[20] There he presents the view that at any given time a liberal education consists in an initiation into *existing* forms of knowledge. Hirst acknowledges that new forms can develop and that old ones can disappear. Still, the analysis he gives of the seven distinct forms which he takes to comprise a liberal education today is based, he says on our present conceptual scheme. Thus, Peters's educated person is not one who studies a set of ideal, unbiased forms of knowledge; on the contrary, that person is one who is initiated into whatever forms of knowledge exist in the society at that time. In our time the existing forms embody a male point of view. The initiation into them envisioned by Hirst and Peters is, therefore, one in male cognitive perspectives.

Peters's educated person is expected to have grasped the basic structure of science, history and the like rather than the superficial details of content. Is it possible that the feminist critique of the disciplines therefore leaves his ideal untouched? It would be a grave misreading of the literature to suppose that this critique presents simply a surface challenge to the disciplines. Although the examples I have cited here may have suggested to you that the challenge is directed at content alone, it is in fact many pronged. Its targets include the questions asked by the various fields of inquiry and the answers given them: the aims of those fields and the ways they define their subject matter; the methods they use, their canons of objectivity, and their ruling metaphors. It is difficult to be clear on precisely which aspects of knowledge and inquiry are at issue when Hirst speaks of initiation into a form of knowledge. A male bias has been found on so many levels of the disciplines, however, that I think we can feel quite confident that it is a property also of the education embodied in Peters's ideal.

III. Genderized Traits

The masculinity of Peters's educated person is not solely a function of a curriculum in the intellectual disciplines, however. Consider the traits or characteristics Peters attributes to the educated person. Feelings and emotions only enter into the makeup of the educated person to the extent that being committed to the standards of a theoretical pursuit such as science, or a practical one such as architecture, counts as such. Concern for people and for interpersonal relationships has no role to play: the educated person's sensitivity is to the standards immanent in activities, not to other human beings; an imaginative awareness of emotional atmosphere and interpersonal/relationships need be no part of this person's makeup, nor is the educated person thought to be empathic or supportive or nurturant. Intuition is also neglected. Theoretical knowledge and what Woods and Barrow—two more philosophers who use the phrase "educated man"—call "reasoned understanding" are the educated person's prime characteristics:[21] even this person's practical pursuits are to be informed by some theoretical perspectives; moreover, this theoretical bent is to be leavened neither by imaginative nor intuitive powers, for these are never to be developed.

The educated person as portrayed by Peters, and also by Downie, Loudfoot and Telfer, and by Woods and Barrow, coincides with our cultural stereotype of a male human being. According to that stereotype men are objective, analytic, rational; they are interested in ideas and things; they have no interpersonal orientation; they are neither nurturant nor supportive, empathetic or sensitive. According to the stereotype, nurturance and supportiveness, empathy and sensitivity are female attributes. Intuition is a female attribute too.[22]

This finding is not really surprising. It has been shown that psychologists define moral development, adult development and even human development in male terms and that therapists do the same for mental health.[23] Why suppose that philosophers of education have avoided the androcentric fallacy?[24] Do not misunderstand! Females can acquire the traits and dispositions which constitute Peters's conception of the educated person; he espouses an ideal which, if it can be attained at all, can be by both sexes.[25] But our culture associates the traits and dispositions of Peters's educated person with males. To apply it to females is to impose on them a masculine mold. I realize that as a matter of fact some females fit our male stereotype and that some males do not, but this does not affect the point at issue, which is that Peters has set forth an ideal for education which embodies just those traits and dispositions our culture attributes to the male sex and excludes the traits our culture attributes to the female sex.

Now it might seem that if the mold is a good one, it does not matter that it is masculine; that if the traits which Peters's educated person possesses are desirable, then it makes no difference that in our society they are associated with males. Indeed, some would doubtless argue that in extending to women cognitive virtues which have long been associated with men and which education has historically reserved for men, Peters's theory of education strikes a blow for sex equality. It does matter that the traits Peters assigns the educated person are considered in our culture to be masculine, however. It matters because some traits which males and females can both possess are *genderized*; that is, they are appraised differentially according to sex.[26]

Consider aggressiveness. The authors of a book on assertive training for women report that in the first class meetings of their training courses they ask their students to call out the adjectives which come to mind when we say "aggressive woman" and "aggressive man." Here is the list of adjectives the women used to describe an aggressive man: "masculine," "dominating," "successful," "heroic," "capable," "strong," "forceful," "manly." Need I tell you the list of adjectives they used to describe an aggressive woman?: "harsh," "pushy," "bitchy," "domineering," "obnoxious," "emasculating," "uncaring."[27]

I submit to you that the traits Peters attributes to the educated person are, like the trait of aggressiveness, evaluated differently for males and females. Imagine a woman who is analytical and critical, whose intellectual curiosity is strong, who cares about the canons of science and mathematics. How is she described? "She thinks like a man," it is said. To be sure, this is considered by some to be the highest accolade. Still, a woman who is said to think like a man is being judged to be masculine, and since we take masculinity and femininity to lie at opposite ends of a single continuum, she is thereby being judged to be lacking in femininity.[28] Thus, while it is possible for a woman to possess the traits of Peters's educated person, she will do so at her peril: her possession of them will cause her to be viewed as unfeminine, i.e., as an unnatural or abnormal woman.

IV. A Double Bind

It may have been my concern over Peters's use of the phrase "educated man" which led me to this investigation in the first place, but as you can see, the problem is not one of language. Had Peters consistently used the phrase "educated person" the conclusion that the ideal he holds up for education is masculine would be unaffected. To be sure, Peters's educated person can be male or female, but he or she will have acquired male cognitive perspectives and will have developed traits which in our society are genderized in favor of males.

I have already suggested that Peters's ideal places a burden on women because the traits constituting it are evaluated negatively when possessed by females. The story of Rosalind Franklin, the scientist who contributed to the discovery of the structure of DNA, demonstrates that when a woman displays the kind of critical, autonomous thought which is an attribute of Peters's educated person, she is derided for what are considered to be negative unpleasant characteristics.[29] Rosalind Franklin consciously opted out of "woman's sphere" and entered the laboratory. From an abstract point of view the traits she possessed were quite functional there. Nonetheless she was perceived to be an interloper, an alien who simply could not be taken seriously in relation to the production of new, fundamental ideas no matter what her personal qualities might be.[30]

But experiencing hostility and derision is the least of the suffering caused women by Peters's ideal. His educated person is one who will know nothing about the lives women have led throughout history and little if anything about the works or art and literature women have produced. If his educated person is a woman, she will have been presented with few female role models in her studies whereas her male counterpart will be able to identify with the doers and thinkers and makers of history. Above all, the certain way in which his educated man and woman will come to look at the world will be one in which men are perceived as they perceive themselves and women are perceived as men perceive them.

To achieve Peters's ideal one must acquire cognitive perspectives through which one sex is perceived on its own terms and one sex is perceived as the Other.[31] Can it be doubted that when the works of women are excluded from the subject matter of the fields into which they are being initiated, students will come to believe that males are superior and females are inferior human beings? That when in the course of this initiation the lives and experiences of women are scarcely mentioned, students will come to believe that the way in which women have lived and the things women have done throughout history have no value? Can it be doubted that these beliefs do female students serious damage? The woman whose self-confidence is bolstered by an education which transmits the message that females are inferior human beings is rare. Rarer still is the woman who, having been initiated into alien cognitive perspectives, gains confidence in her own powers without paying the price of self-alienation.

Peters's ideal puts women in a double bind. To be educated they must give up their own way of experiencing and looking at the world, thus alienating themselves from themselves. To be unalienated they must remain uneducated. Furthermore, to be an educated person a female must acquire traits which are appraised negatively when she possesses them. At the same time, the traits which are evaluated positively when possessed by her—for example, being nurturant and empathetic—are excluded from the ideal. Thus a female who has acquired the traits of an educated person will not be evaluated positively for having them, while one who has acquired those traits for which she will be positively evaluated will not have achieved the ideal. Women are placed in this double bind because Peters's ideal incorporates traits genderized in favor of males and excludes traits genderized in favor of females. It thus puts females in a no-win situation. Yes, men and women can both achieve Peters's ideal. However, women suffer, as men do not, for doing so.

Peters's masculine ideal of the educated person harms males as well as females, however. In a chapter of the 1981 NSSE Yearbook I argued at some length that Hirst's account of liberal education is seriously deficient.[32] Since Peters's educated person is to all intents and purposes Hirst's liberally educated person, let me briefly repeat my criticism of Hirst here. The Peters-Hirst educated person will have knowledge about others, but will not have been taught to care about their welfare, let alone to act kindly toward them. That person will have some understanding of society, but will not have been taught to feel its injustices or even to be concerned over its fate. The Peters-Hirst educated person is an ivory tower person: a person who can reason yet has no desire to solve real problems in the real world; a person who understands science but does not worry about the uses to which it is put; a person who can reach flawless moral conclusions but feels no care or concern for others.

Simply put, quite apart from the burden it places on women, Peters's ideal of the educated person is far too narrow to guide the educational enterprise. Because it presupposes a divorce of mind from body, thought from action, and reason from feeling and emotion, it provides at best an ideal of an educated *mind*, not an educated *person*. To the extent that its concerns are strictly cognitive however, even in that guise it leaves much to be desired.

V. Education for Productive Processes

Even if Peters's ideal did not place an unfair burden on women it would need to be rejected for the harm it does men, but its inadequacy as an ideal for men and the injustice it does women are not unconnected. In my Yearbook essay I sketched in the rough outlines of a new paradigm of liberal education, one which would emphasize the development of persons and not simply rational minds; one which would join thought to action, and reason to feeling and emotion. I could just as easily have called it a new conception of the educated person. What I did not realize when I wrote that essay is that the aspects of the Peters-Hirst ideal which I found so objectionable are directly related to the role, traditionally considered to be male, which their educated person is to play in society.

Peters would vehemently deny that he conceives of education as production. Nonetheless, he implicitly attributes to education the task of turning raw material, namely the *un*educated person, into an end product whose specifications he sets forth in his account of the concept of the educated person. Peters would deny even more vehemently that he assigns to education a societal function. Yet an examination of his conception of the educated person reveals that the end product of the education he envisions is designed to fit into a specific place in the social order; that he assigns to education the function of developing the traits and qualities and to some extent the skills of one whose role is to use and produce ideas.[33]

Peters would doubtless say that the production and consumption of ideas is everyone's business and that an education for this is certainly not an education which fits people into a particular place in society. Yet think of the two parts into which the social order has traditionally been divided. Theorists have put different labels on them, some referring to the split between work and home, others to the public and private domains and still others to productive and reproductive processes.[34] Since the public/private distinction has associations for educators which are not germaine to the present discussion while the work/home distinction obscures some important issues, I will speak here of productive and reproductive processes. I do not want to make terminology the issue, however. If you prefer other labels, by all means substitute them for mine. My own is only helpful, I should add, if the term "reproduction" is construed broadly. Thus I use it here to include not simply biological reproduction of the species, but the whole process of reproduction from conception until the individual reaches more or less independence from the family.[35] This process I take to include not simply childcare and rearing, but the related activities of keeping house, running the household and serving the needs and purposes of all the family members. Similarly, I interpret the term "production" broadly to include political, social and cultural activities and processes as well as economic ones.

Now this traditional division drawn within the social order is accompanied by a separation of the sexes. Although males and females do in fact participate in both the reproductive and productive processes of society, the reproductive processes are considered to constitute "woman's sphere" and the productive processes "man's sphere." Although Peters's educated person is ill-equipped for jobs in trades or work on the assembly line, this person is tailor-made for carrying on certain of the productive processes of society, namely those which require work with heads, not hands. Thus his educated person is designed to fill a role in society which has traditionally been considered to be male. Moreover, he or she is not equipped by education to fill roles associated with the reproductive processes of society, i.e., roles traditionally considered to be female.

Once the functionalism of Peters's conception of the educated person is made explicit, the difficulty of including it in the ideal feelings and emotions such as caring and compassion, or skills of cooperation and nurturance, becomes clear. These fall under our culture's female stereotype. They are considered to be appropriate for those who carry on the reproductive processes of society but irrelevant, if not downright dysfunctional, for those who carry on the productive processes of society. It would therefore be irrational to include them in an ideal which is conceived of solely in relation to productive processes.

I realize now, as I did not before, that for the ideal of the educated person to be as broad as it should be, the two kinds of societal processes which Peters divorces from one another must be joined together.[36] An adequate ideal of the educated person must give the reproductive processes of society their due. An ideal which is tied solely to the productive processes of society cannot readily accommodate the important virtues of caring and compassion, sympathy and nurturance, generosity and cooperation which are genderized in favor of females.

To be sure, it would be possible in principle to continue to conceive of the educated person solely in relation to the productive processes of society while rejecting the stereotypes which produce genderized traits. One could include caring and compassion in the ideal of the educated person on the grounds that although they are thought to be female traits whose home is in the reproductive processes of society, they are in fact functional in the production and consumption of ideas. The existence of genderized traits is not the only reason for giving the reproductive processes of society their due in an ideal of the educated person, however. These processes are themselves central to the lives of each of us and to the life of society as a whole. The dispositions, knowledge, skills required to carry them out well are not innate, nor do they simply develop naturally over time. Marriage, childrearing, family life: these involve difficult, complex, learned activities which can be done well or badly. Just as an educated person should be one in whom head, hand and heart are integrated, he or she should be one who is at home carrying on the reproductive processes of society, broadly understood, as well as the productive processes.

Now Peters might grant that the skills, traits, and knowledge necessary for carrying on reproductive processes are learned—in some broad sense of the term, at least—but argue that one does not require an education in them for they are picked up in the course of daily living. Perhaps at one time they were picked up in this way, and perhaps in some societies they are now. But it is far from obvious that, just by living, most adults in our society today acquire the altruistic feelings and emotions, the skills of childrearing, the understanding of what values are important to transmit and which are not, and the ability to put aside one's own projects and enter into those of others which are just a few of the things required for successful participation in the reproductive processes of society.

That education is needed by those who carry on the reproductive processes is not in itself proof that it should be encompassed by a conception of the educated person however, for this conception need not be all-inclusive. It need not be all inclusive but, for Peters, education which is not guided by his ideal of the educated person scarcely deserves attention. Moreover, since a conception of the educated person tends to function as an ideal, one who becomes educated will presumably have achieved something worthwhile. Value is attached to being an educated person: to the things an educated person knows and can do; to the tasks and activities that person is equipped to perform. The exclusion of education for reproductive processes from the ideal of the educated person thus carries with it an unwarranted negative value judgment about the tasks and activities, the traits and dispositions which are associated with them.

VI. Redefining the Ideal

An adequate ideal of the educated person must give the reproductive processes of society their due, but it must do more than this. After all, these processes were acknowledged by Rousseau in Book V of *Emile*.[37] There he set forth two distinct ideals of the educated person, the one for Emile tied to the productive processes of society and the one for Sophie tied to the reproductive processes. I leave open here the question Peters never asks of whether we should adopt one or more ideals of the educated person.[38] One thing is clear, however. We need a conception which does not fall into the trap of assigning males and females to the different processes of society, yet does not make the mistake of ignoring one kind of process altogether. We all participate in both kinds of processes and both are important to all of us. Whether we adopt one or many ideals, a conception of the educated person which is tied only to one kind of process will be incomplete.

An adequate ideal of the educated person must also reflect a realistic understanding of the limitations of existing forms or disciplines of knowledge. In my Yearbook chapter I made a case for granting them much less "curriculum space" than Hirst and Peters do. So long as they embody a male cognitive perspective, however, we must take into account not simply the amount of space they occupy in the curriculum of the educated person, but the hidden messages which are received by those who are initiated into them. An ideal of the educated person cannot itself rid the disciplines of knowledge of their sex bias. But it can advocate measures for counteracting the harmful effects on students of coming to see things solely through male eyes.

The effects of an initiation into male cognitive perspectives constitute a hidden curriculum. Alternative courses of action are open to us when we find a hidden curriculum and there is no reason to suppose that only one is appropriate. Let me say a few words here, however, about a course of action that might serve as at least a partial antidote to the hidden curriculum transmitted by an education in male biased disciplines.[39] When we find a hidden curriculum we can show it to its recipients; we can raise their consciousness, if you will, so that they will know what is happening to them. Raising to consciousness the male cognitive perspective of the disciplines of knowledge in the educated person's curriculum is no guarantee, of course, that educated females will not suffer from a lack of self-confidence and from self-alienation. Yet knowledge can be power. A curriculum which, through critical analysis, exposes the biased view of women embodied in the disciplines and which, by granting ample space to the study of women shows how unjust that view is, is certainly preferable to a curriculum which, by its silence on the subject, gives students the impression that the ways in which the disciplines look at the world are impartial and unbiased.

Now it might seem to be a relatively simple matter both to give the reproductive processes of society their due in an ideal of the educated person and to include in that ideal measures for counteracting the hidden curriculum of an education in the existing disciplines of knowledge. Yet given the way philosophy of education conceives of its subject matter today, it is not. The productive-reproductive dualism is built not simply into Peters's ideal but into our discipline.[40] We do not even have a vocabulary for discussing education in relation to the reproductive processes of society, for the distinction between liberal and vocational education which we use to cover the kinds of education we take to be philosophically important applies within productive processes: liberal and vocational education are both intended to fit people to carry on productive processes, the one for work with heads and the other for work with hands. The aims of education we analyze—critical thinking, rationality, individual autonomy, even creativity—are also associated in our culture with the productive, not the reproductive, processes of society. To give the reproductive processes their due in a conception of the educated person we will have to rethink the domain of philosophy of education.

Given the way we define our subject matter it is no more possible for us to take seriously the hidden curriculum I have set before you than the reproductive processes of society. Education, as we conceive of it, is an intentional activity.[41] Teaching is too.[42] Thus, we do not consider the unintended outcomes of education to be our concern. Moreover, following Peters and his colleagues, we draw a sharp line between logical and contingent relationships and treat the latter as if they were none of our business even when they are the *expected* outcomes of educational processes.[43] In sum, we leave it to the psychologists, sociologists and historians of education to worry about hidden curricula, not because we consider the topic unimportant—although perhaps some of us do—but because we consider it to fall outside our domain.

The redefinition of the subject matter of philosophy of education required by an adequate ideal of the educated person ought not to be feared. On the contrary, there is every reason to believe that it would ultimately enrich our discipline. If the experience and activities which have traditionally been considered to belong to women are included in the educational realm, a host of challenging and important issues and problems will present themselves for study. If the philosophy of education tackles questions about childrearing and the transmission of values, if it develops accounts of gender education to inform its theories of liberal education, if it explores the forms of thinking, feeling and acting associated with childrearing, marriage and the family, if the concepts of coeducation, mothering and nurturance become fair game for philosophical analysis, philosophy of education will be invigorated.

It would also be invigorated by taking seriously contingent as well as logical relationships. In divorcing educational processes from their empirical consequences and the mental structures which are said to be intrinsically related to knowledge from the empirical consequences of having them, we forget that education is a practical endeavor. It is often said that philosophy of education's concerns are purely conceptual, but the conclusion is inescapable that in analyzing such concepts as the educated person and liberal education we make recommendations for action. For these to be justified the contingent relationships which obtain between them and both the good life and the good society must be taken into account. A redefinition of our domain would allow us to provide our educational theorizing with the kind of justification it requires. It would also allow us to investigate the particularly acute and very challenging value questions that arise in relation to hidden curricula of all kinds.

Conclusion

In conclusion I would like to draw for you two morals which seem to me to emerge from my study of Peters's ideal of the educated person. The first is that Plato was wrong when, in Book V of the *Republic,* he said that sex is a difference which makes no difference.[44] I do not mean by this that there are inborn differences which suit males and females for separate and unequal roles in society. Rather, I mean that identical educational treatment of males and females may not yield identical results so long as that treatment contains a male bias. There are sex differences in the way people are perceived and evaluated and there may well be sex differences in the way people think and learn and view the world. A conception of the educated person must take these into account. I mean also that the very nature of the ideal will be skewed. When sex or gender is thought to make no difference, women's lives, experiences, activities are overlooked and an ideal is formulated in terms of men and the roles for which they have traditionally been considered to be suited. Such an ideal is necessarily narrow for it is rooted in stereotypical ways of perceiving males and their place in society.

For some time I assumed that the sole alternative to a sex-biased conception of the educated person such as Peters set forth was a gender-free ideal, that is to say an ideal which did not take sex or gender into account. I now realize that sex or gender has to be taken into account if an ideal of the educated person is not to be biased. To opt at this time for a gender-free ideal is to beg the question. What is needed is a *gender-sensitive* ideal, one which takes sex or gender into account when it makes a difference and ignores it when it does not. Such an ideal would truly be gender-just.

The second moral is that *everyone* suffers when an ideal of the educated person fails to give the reproductive processes of society their due. Ideals which govern education solely in relation to the productive processes of society will necessarily be narrow. In their failure to acknowledge the valuable traits, dispositions, skills, traditionally associated with reproductive processes, they will harm both sexes although not always in the same ways.[45]

Notes

1. R.S. Peters, "Education and the Educated Man," in R.F. Dearden, P.H. Hirst, and R.S. Peters, eds., *A Critique of Current Educational Aims* (London: Routledge & Kegan Paul, 1972), pp. 7, 9.
2. Paul Nash, Andreas M. Kazemias, and Henry J. Perkinson, eds., *The Educated Man: Studies in the History of Educational Thought* (New York: John Wiley & Sons, 1965), p. 25.
3. For a discussion of "man" as a gender neutral term see Janice Moulton, "The Myth of the Neutral 'Man'," in Mary Vetterling-Braggin, Frederick A. Elliston, and Jane English, eds., *Feminism and Philosophy* (Totowa, NJ: Littlefield, Adams, 1977), pp. 124–137. Moulton rejects the view that "man" has a gender-neutral use.
4. Peters, "Education and the Educated Man," p. 11. Peters says in connection with the concept of the educated man: "For there are many who are not likely to go far with theoretical enquiries and who are unlikely to develop much depth or breadth of understanding to underpin and transform their dealings as workers, *husbands* and *fathers*" (emphasis added).
5. Ibid., p. 7.

6. R.S. Peters, *Ethics and Education* (London: George Allen & Unwin, 1966).

7. Peters, "Education and the Educated Man," pp. 9–11.

8. R.S. Downie, Eileen M. Loudfoot, and Elizabeth Telfer, *Education and Personal Relationships* (London: Methuen & Co., 1974), p. 11ff.

9. In Paul Hirst, *Knowledge and the Curriculum* (London: Routledge & Kegan Paul, 1974), p. 47.

10. Nancy Schrom Dye, "Clio's American Daughters," in Julia A. Sherman and Evelyn Torton Beck, eds., *The Prism of Sex* (Madison: University of Wisconsin Press, 1979), p. 9.

11. Catherine R. Stimpson, "The Power to Name," in Sherman and Beck, eds., *Prism*, pp. 55–77.

12. Elaine Showalter, "Women Writers and the Double Standard," in Vivian Gornick and Barbara Moran, eds., *Women in Sexist Society* (New York: Basic Books, 1971), pp. 323–343.

13. Naomi Weisstein, "Psychology Constructs the Female" in Gornick and Moran, eds., *Women in Sexist Society*, pp. 133–146.

14. Ruth Hubbard, "Have Only Men Evolved?" in Ruth Hubbard, Mary Sue Henifin, and Barbara Fried, eds., *Women Look at Biology Looking at Women* (Cambridge: Schenkman Publishing Co., 1979), pp. 7–35.

15. Carol Gilligan, "Women's Place in Man's Life Cycle," *Harvard Educational Review* 49, 4 (1979): 431–446.

16. Carol Gilligan, "In a Different Voice: Women's Conceptions of Self and of Morality," *Harvard Educational Review* 47, 4 (1979): 481–517.

17. See, for example, Linda Gordon, *Woman's Body, Woman's Right: A Social History of Birth Control in America* (New York: Viking, 1976); Richard W. Wertz and Dorothy C. Wertz, *Lying-in* (New York: Free Press, 1977); Jean Donnison, *Midwives and Medical Men: A History of Interprofessional Rivalries and Women's Rights* (New York: Schocken Books, 1977).

18. Mary Hartman and Lois W. Banner, eds., *Clio's Consciousness Raised* (New York: Harper & Row, 1974).

19. See, for example, Carolyn G. Heilbrun, *Toward a Recognition of Androgyny* (New York: Alfred A. Knopf, 1973); Patricia Meyer Spacks, *The Female Imagination* (New York: Avon, 1975); Ellen Moers, *Literary Women* (New York: Anchor Books, 1977): Elaine Showalter, *A Literature of Their Own: British Women Novelists from Bronte to Lessing* (Princeton: Princeton University Press, 1977): Ann Sutherland Harris and Linda Nochlin, *Women Artists: 1550–1950* (New York: Alfred A. Knopf, 1976); Elsa Honig Fine, *Women and Art: A History of Women Painters and Sculptors from the Renaissance to the Twentieth Century* (Montclair and London: Allanheld & Schram/Prior, 1978); and Karen Peterson and J.J. Wilson, *Women Artists: Recognition and Reappraisal from the Early Middle Ages to the Twentieth Century* (New York: New York University Press, 1976).

20. In Paul Hirst, *Knowledge and the Curriculum*, p. 92.

21. R.G. Woods and R.St.C. Barrow, *An Introduction to Philosophy of Education* (Methuen & Co., 1975), Ch. 3.

22. For discussions of our male and female stereotypes see, e.g., Alexandra G. Kaplan and Joan P. Bean, eds., *Beyond Sex-role Stereotypes* (Boston: Little, Brown, 1976); and Alexandra G. Kaplan and Mary Anne Sedney, *Psychology and Sex Roles* (Boston: Little, Brown, 1980).

23. Carol Gilligan, "Women's Place"; I. Broverman, D. Broverman, F. Clarkson, P. Rosencrantz and S. Vogel, "Sex-role Stereotypes and Clinical Judgements of Mental Health," *Journal of Consulting and Clinical Psychology* 34 (1970): 1–7; Alexandra G. Kaplan, "Androgyny as a Model of Mental Health for Women: From Theory to Therapy," in Kaplan and Bean, eds., *Beyond Sex-role Stereotypes*, pp. 353–362.

24. One commits the androcentric fallacy when one argues from the characteristics associated with male human beings to the characteristics of all human beings. In committing it one often commits the naturalistic fallacy because the traits which are said to be natural to males are held up as ideals for the whole species.

25. I say *if* it can be attained by all, because it is not entirely clear that the ideal can be attained by *anyone* insofar as it requires mastery of Hirst's seven forms of knowledge.

26. See Elizabeth Beardsley, "Traits and Genderization," in Vetterling-Braggin, et al., eds., *Feminism and Philosophy*, pp. 117–123. Beardsley uses the term "genderization" to refer to language while I use it here to refer to traits themselves.

27. Lynn Z. Bloom, Karen Coburn, Joan Pearlman, *The New Assertive Woman* (New York: Delacorte Press, 1975), p. 12.

28. For discussion of the assumption that masculinity-femininity is a bipolar dimension see Anne Constantinople, "Masculinity-Femininity: An Exception to a Famous Dictum"; and Sandra L. Bern, "Probing the Promise of Androgyny" in Kaplan and Bean, eds., *Beyond Sex-role Stereotypes.*

29. Anne Sayre, *Rosalind Franklin & DNA* (New York: W.W. Norton & Co., 1975). See also James D. Watson, *The Double Helix* (New York: Atheneum, 1968); and Horace Freeland Judson, *The Eighth Day of Creation* (New York: Simon and Schuster, 1979).

30. It is important to note, however, that some colleagues did take her seriously as a scientist; see Sayre, ibid. Adele Simmons cites historical evidence of the negative effects of having acquired such traits on women who did not opt out of "woman's sphere" in "Education and Ideology in Nineteenth-Century America: The Response of Educational Institutions to the Changing Role of Women," in Berenice A. Carroll, ed., *Liberating Women's History* (Urbana, IL: University of Illinois Press, 1976), p. 123. See also Patricia Meyer Spacks, *The Female Imagination* (New York: Avon Books, 1976), p. 25.

31. See Simone de Beauvoir, *The Second Sex* (New York: Bantam Books, 1961) for an extended discussion of woman as the Other.

32. Jane Roland Martin, "Needed: A Paradigm for Liberal Education," in Jonas F. Soltis, ed., *Philosophy and Education* (Chicago: National Society for the Study of Education, 1981), pp. 37–59.

33. For an account of education as production see Jane Roland Martin, "Sex Equality and Education: A Case Study," in Mary Vetterling-Braggin, ed., *"Femininity," "Masculinity," and "Androgyny"* (Totowa, N.J.: Littlefield, Adams, 1982). It should be noted that an understanding of the societal role for which Peters's educated person is intended illuminates both the sex bias and the class bias his ideal embodies.

34. For an interesting discussion and criticism of the two-sphere analysis of society, see Joan Kelly, 'The Doubled Vision of Feminist Theory: A Postscript to the 'Women and Power' Conference," *Feminist Studies* 5, 1 (1979): 216–227. Kelly argues that a two-sphere analysis distorts reality and that feminist theory should discard it. I use it here as a convenient theoretical device.

35. I am indebted here to Lorenne M.G. Clark, "The Rights of Women: The Theory and Practice of the Ideology of Male Supremacy," in William R. Shea and John King-Farlow, eds., *Contemporary Issues in Political Philosophy* (New York: Science History Publications, 1976), pp. 49–65.

36. In saying that an adequate conception of the educated person must reject a sharp separation of productive and reproductive processes I do not mean that it must be committed to a specific philosophical theory of the relationship of the two. An adequate conception of the educated person should not divorce mind and body, but it does not follow from this that it must be committed to a specific view of the mind-body relationship; indeed, the union of mind and body in a theory of education is quite compatible with a dualistic philosophical account of the relationship between the two. Similarly, a theory of the educated person must not divorce one kind of societal process from the other even if the best account of the relationship of productive to reproductive processes should turn out to be dualistic.

37. Jean-Jacques Rousseau, *Emile* (New York: Basic Books, 1979, Allan Bloom, trans.). See also Lynda Lange, "Rousseau: Women and the General Will," in Lorenne M.G. Cark and Lynda Lange, eds., *The Sexism of Social and Political Theory* (Toronto: University of Toronto Press, 1979), pp. 41–52;

Susan Moller Okin, *Women in Western Political Thought* (Princeton: Princeton University Press, 1979); and Jane Roland Martin, "Sophie and Emile: A Case Study of Sex Bias in the History of Educational Thought," *Harvard Educational Review* 51, 3 (1981): 357–372.

38. I also leave open the question of whether any ideal of the educated person should guide and direct education as a whole.

39. For more on this question see Jane Roland Martin, "What Should We Do with a Hidden Curriculum When We Find One?" *Curriculum Inquiry* 6, 2 (1976): 135–151.

40. On this point see Jane Roland Martin, "Excluding Women from the Educational Realm."

41. See, for example, Peters, *Ethics and Education.*

42. See, for example, Israel Scheffler, *The Language of Education* (Springfield, IL: Charles C. Thomas, 1960), Chs. 4, 5.

43. For a discussion of this point see Jane Roland Martin, "Response to Roemer," in Jerrold R. Coombs, ed., *Philosophy of Education 1979* (Normal, IL: Proceedings of the 35th Annual Meeting of the Philosophy of Education Society, 1980).

44. This point is elaborated on in Jane Roland Martin, "Sex Equality and Education: A Case Study."

45. I wish to thank Ann Diller, Carol Gilligan, Michael Martin and Janet Farrell Smith for helpful comments on earlier versions of this address which was written while I was a Fellow at the Mary Ingraham Bunting Institute of Radcliffe College.

Questions for Further Discussion

1. How does the use of history, sociology, politics, and philosophy inform your knowledge of education in general and schooling in particular?
2. W.E.B. DuBois lays out the groundwork for the debate between Washington, who was viewed by many historians as arguing for vocational education for Blacks and DuBois, who believed in a liberal arts education for Blacks. First, reconstruct the argument. Then, address the question, Should one stream of education exclude the other? Explain, giving examples. How does this debate relate to current discussions of whether the primary role of high schools today is to prepare all students for college?
3. The progressive movement in American education has been defined in myriad ways. How does Cremin view progressive education in his article? Explain and give examples.
4. David Tyack illustrates how the administrative progressives came to be an important, if not dominating group in urban public education, c. 1890–1940. Do you think that their influence is still powerful today? Explain.
5. According to Bowles and Gintis, in retrospect, school reform is a series of "broken promises." How accurate is their assessment? Do you agree with their position? Why/Why not?
6. How does Anyon define "educational policy"? What does she mean by a new paradigm? Do you think it is realistic? Explain.
7. How does Ravitch define the democratic role of schools and why does she think the radical revisionists' critique is unfair?
8. According to Collins, what are the functional and conflict theories of education? How would you apply each to the argument that the achievement gap threatens America's economic position globally?
9. In the years that have passed since Lortie's book first appeared, do you think his description of the teacher still holds? Explain. Do you think current efforts to increase teacher quality and hold teachers accountable for student achievement will change the culture of teaching?
10. After reading Jeannie Oakes, do you think that tracking students makes sense? As a teacher or prospective teacher, would you prefer a homogeneous or heterogeneous classroom? Explain. How would functionalists and conflict theorists differ on the policy of tracking? Finally, what would Bowles and Gintis say?
11. According to Dewey, what is the role of experience in education? Do you agree/disagree

with his notion? Why do you think that he felt it necessary to explain his position once again?

12. What does Greene mean by "wide-awakeness?" In her piece she admonishes teachers to take action against what they know as bad practice. Do you think that this call to action is realistic, given the culture of teaching in today's schools?

13. Demonstrate how Martin first defines the ideal educated person and then, show how she broadens the definition. What is the basis of her argument for revising a traditionally held notion? Why do you think it took so long for someone to argue against traditionally held paradigms?

Permissions

Introduction

The Introduction was adapted and revised with permission from A.R. Sadovnik, P.W. Cookson, Jr. & S.F. Semel, *Exploring Education: An Introduction to the Foundations of Education (Third Edition)*. Needham Heights, MA.: Allyn and Bacon, 2006, pp. 16–21; 25–35; 83–87; 114–117; 163–164.

Chapter 1

DuBois, W.E.B. (2005). Of Mr. Booker T. Washington and Others. In *The Souls of Black Folk* (pp. 35–47). New York: Simon & Schuster, Inc. Copyright © by Simon & Schuster, Inc. Reprinted with permission.

Chapter 2

Cremin, L.A. (1957). The Progressive Movement in American Education: A Perspective. *Harvard Educational Review*, 27(4), 251–270. Copyright © by the President and Fellows of Harvard College. Reprinted with permission.

Chapter 3

Tyack, D.B. (1974). Inside the System: The Character of Urban Schools, 1890–1940. In *The One Best System: A History of American Urban Education* (pp. 177–198). Cambridge: Harvard University Press. Copyright © by the President and Fellows of Harvard College. Reprinted with permission.

Chapter 4

Bowles, S. & Gintis, H. (1976). Broken Promises: School Reform in Retrospect. In *Schooling in Capitalist America* (pp. 18–54). New York: Basic Books. Copyright © by Basic Books, a member of Perseus Books Group.

Chapter 5

Anyon, J. (2005). What "Counts" as Educational Policy? Notes toward a New Paradigm. *Harvard Educational Review*, 75(1), 65–88. Copyright © by the President and Fellows of Harvard College. Reprinted with permission.

Chapter 6

Ravitch, D. (1978). The Democratic-Liberal Tradition Under Attack. In *The Revisionists Revised: A Critique of the Radical Attack on the Schools* (pp. 3–19). New York: Basic Books. Copyright © by Basic Books, a member of Perseus Books Group.

Chapter 7

Collins, R. (1971). Functional and Conflict Theories of Educational Stratification. *American Sociological Review*, 36(6), 1002–1019. Copyright © by American Sociological Review. Reprinted with permission.

Chapter 8

Lortie, D.C. (1975). The Logic of Teacher Sentiments. In *School Teacher: A Sociological Study* (pp. 162–186). Chicago: University of Chicago Press. Copyright © by University of Chicago Press. Reprinted with permission.

Chapter 9

Oakes, J. (2005). The Tracking Wars. In *Keeping Track: How Schools Structure Inequality* (2nd ed.) (pp. 214–260). New York: Yale University Press. Copyright © by Yale University Press. Reprinted with permission.

Chapter 10

Dewey, J. (1938). Experience and Education. In *Experience and Education* (pp. 17–23, 89–91). Indianapolis: Kappa Delta Pi. Copyright © by Kappa Delta Pi. Reprinted with permission.

Chapter 11

Greene, M. (1978). Wide-Awakeness and the Moral Life. In *Landscapes of Learning* (pp. 42–52). New York: Teachers College Press. Copyright © by Teachers College Press, Columbia University. Reprinted with permission.

Chapter 12

Martin, J.L. (1981). The Ideal of the Educated Person. *Educational Theory*, 31(2), 97–109. Copyright by the University of Illinois. Reprinted with permission.

Index